Penguin Education

Power in Economics

Edited by K. W. Rothschild

Penguin Modern Economics Readings

General Editor

B. J. McCormick

Advisory Board

K. J. W. Alexander
R. W. Clower
G. R. Fisher
P. Robson
J. Spraos
H. Townsend

D1552480

Power in Economics

Selected Readings
Edited by K. W. Rothschild

Penguin Books

Penguin Books Ltd, Harmondsworth,
Middlesex, England
Penguin Books Inc., 7110 Ambassador Road,
Baltimore, Md 21207, U.S.A.
Penguin Books Australia Ltd,
Ringwood, Victoria, Australia

First published 1971
This selection copyright © K. W. Rothschild, 1971
Introduction and notes copyright © K. W. Rothschild, 1971

Made and printed in Great Britain by
Richard Clay (The Chaucer Press) Ltd,
Bungay, Suffolk
Set in Monotype Times New Roman

Contents

Introduction

Economics as a separate science is unrealistic, and misleading if
taken as a guide in practice. It is one element – a very important
element, it is true – in a wider study, the science of power.
Bertrand Russell

Economics is a social science. It is concerned with a certain
section of human relationships, and a very important section at
that. Economic activities take up, after all, a large part of the
adult's waking time, and the results of these activities play a
decisive part in determining one's standard of living and social
status. It is almost self-evident that people will be anything but
indifferent to the factors which influence their economic conditions. As in other important social fields we should expect that
individuals and groups will struggle for position; that power will
be used to improve one's chances in the economic 'game'; and
that attempts will be made to derive power and influence from
acquired economic strongholds.

Power should, therefore, be a recurrent theme in economic
studies of a theoretical or applied nature. Yet if we look at the
main run of economic theory over the past hundred years we
find that it is characterized by a strange lack of power considerations. More or less homogenous units – firms and households –
move in more or less given technological and market conditions
and try to improve their economic lot *within the constraints of
these conditions*. This model has been explored in great detail by
modern economic science and very important insights into the
working of the market mechanism have been gained. But that
people will use power to alter the mechanism itself; that uneven
power may greatly influence the outcome of market operations;
that people may strive for economic power as much as for
economic wealth: these facts have been largely neglected.[1]

1. The passionate complaint of the American sociologist, Robert S. Lynd,
raised more than quarter of a century ago, applies today with undiminished
force. In a Foreword to Brady (1943, p. 6), he wrote:
'If the American rank and file – the upwards of four-fifths of the nation

This neglect requires some comment. It is the more necessary since matters have not always been that way. Early classical 'political economy' right up to the days of J. S. Mill was fully aware of the sociological and power background of economic events. The writings of this era abound with remarks and hints at the interplay of market mechanisms and outside intervention. It was only in its later stages that the main strand of traditional economic thinking turned inwards towards 'purely' economic matters, paying increasingly less regard to extra-market and power affairs. Several factors contributed to this development and are still influential.

One of the most important causes was the complete victory of 'perfect competition' as the basic model for economic theorizing. Perfect competition was at no time – even in the days of nineteenth-century small-scale business – an adequate description of economic reality. But for two reasons it provided a great attraction for economists ever since the early days of classical theory.

One reason is a purely scientific one. With the transition from feudal conditions to capitalistic market economies, competition moved rapidly into the foreground as one of the decisive motors of economic adjustment and development. The model of perfect competition could thus be constructed with considerable justification as an abstract picture of reality permitting an intensive study of all the corollaries flowing from the working of *one*, very important economic motive force. The usefulness of this approach has been proved beyond doubt in the progress of economic theory over the past two hundred years.

But there was another reason contributing to the overwhelming

who are working class and small-business folk – are thus illiterate in the language of contemporary power, the case is almost as bad with those experts, the professional social scientists, whom society supports because they profess to know about men's institutions. It is no accident that, as Dr Brady points out, a world of scientists who comb their fields for important problems for research have left the problem of the power organization and politics of big business so largely unexplored. For the most part, contemporary social scientists still exhibit towards the changing business world the encouraging moral optimism of Alfred Marshall. Nor are we helped by the fact that the crucial science of economics derives its data within the assumptions and concepts of a system conceived not in terms of such things as "power" but of blander processes such as the automatic balancing of the market.'

dominance of the perfect competition model. Most of the classical economists wanted an optimal development of the economic forces set free by the industrial revolution and the extension of markets. But this development was everywhere hampered by the intervention of powerful vested interests, in particular by the feudal aristocracy, who acted directly or via the government, and who were aided by entrenched commercial monopolies and similar groups. To set the potential economic energies free it seemed decisive to break down these harmful intrusions of power and influence. Hence came the strong demand for minimizing state interference (which tended to act on behalf of the 'old' interests); hence came also the predilection for a regime of perfect competition, of countless small economic units, none of which would be strong enough to bend circumstances towards its own requirements. On the contrary, each firm or household would have to accept the economic facts and in this way economic forces and development would get a free run.[2]

From the very beginning, therefore, the basic model of perfect competition was both an abstract analysis of a decisive economic force, and the Utopian formulation of a society in which power is so widely and thinly distributed that its influence can be neglected. In this way, the important social phenomenon of power receded into the background as far as the kernel of classical economic theory was concerned.

The question arises why this development was reinforced, rather than weakened in later periods. How is it that additional theoretical constructs, leaving more room for power and its influence, were not created to take the same pride of place as the competition model?[3] This question is the more pertinent, since

2. The classical ideal of a competitive economic universe with widely dispersed power is still strongly upheld as a practical programme by some schools of economists, though most of them realize that it could only be achieved by positive government efforts in this direction. Views of this kind have been particularly stressed by the so-called Chicago school in the United States (e.g. Friedman, Simons) and the Neo-Liberals of the Freiburg school in Germany (Eucken, Müller-Armack).

3. The broad attention given to monopoly and trade union questions is an important exception. But as we shall see later, this approach was also seriously limited by the preponderance of the competition model.

already in the later nineteenth century it became clear that the world was not moving towards the competitive Utopia, characterized by a passive government (in internal and international economic affairs) and the absence of monopolistic groupings and interest lobbies.

Several factors have probably contributed to the continued domination of the competitive set-up in economic thinking and the consequent neglect of power elements. They partly flow from the ways in which knowledge is passed on and developed, partly they have their roots in social and ideological causes.

The great intellectual achievement of Adam Smith, Ricardo and others in creating a closely reasoned systematic framework for analysing and interpreting the economic scene in all its ramifications was such an advance over previous speculations on social and economic matters that it provided a continuous challenge to later generations of economists. To build on this structure, to improve and refine the basic model, to apply it to new problems and situations was often more appealing than attempts to throw light – perhaps with the aid of cruder methods – on neglected, but nonetheless important, other aspects of economic life. This trend has been reinforced by the aesthetic qualities of competitive equilibrium models which ease the path towards 'determinate' solutions of the type achieved by the much envied natural sciences.[4]

Thus a traditional way of economic thinking and theorizing evolved, which rapidly advanced in explaining the mechanics of market adjustment and 'equilibrium' under the impact of competitive forces, but which had little room for such factors as

4. The fear of losing this advantage when the confines of the competition model are left was vividly expressed in a well-known passage by Hicks:
It has to be recognized that a general abandonment of the assumption of perfect competition, a universal adoption of the assumption of monopoly, must have very destructive consequences for economic theory. Under monopoly the stability conditions become indeterminate; and the basis on which economic laws can be constructed is therefore shorn away. . . . It is, I believe, only possible to save anything from this wreck – and it must be remembered that the threatened wreckage is that of the greater part of general equilibrium theory – if we can assume that the markets confronting most of the firms with which we shall be dealing do not differ very greatly from perfectly competitive markets' (1946, pp. 83–4).

power, non-pecuniary motives, group behaviour and the like. Qualms about the neglect of these 'non-economic' factors[5] were increasingly suppressed in view of the rapid specialization of science. Economics could be regarded as being responsible only for the 'purely' economic phenomena while other influences – such as power – should be taken care of by sociologists or political scientists. These are, however, quite often too much occupied with other social spheres; and, at any rate inter-disciplinary cooperation has up till now not been sufficiently developed so as to achieve the necessary combination of eco-nomic and non-economic factors in the interpretation of economic events.

But it would be a mistake to regard the neglect of power elements solely as the result of traditional forces and the inner workings of theoretical expansion. The disregard of power aspects is greatly helped by the fact that concentration on the mechanics of economic and market adjustment within a given framework enables the economist to avoid the detailed occupation with facts which powerful social groups prefer to keep under a cloud of uncertainty. This desire for secrecy is in itself a real and objective difficulty. Nowhere is the analogy of the iceberg more appro-priate than in this sphere: only a tiny fraction of the power play becomes visible (and that in a distorted form). But difficulties arise in other fields too, and they do not necessarily lead to a neglect of the subject.

With power, however, the discovery of the truth is not only difficult, it can also lead to clashes with entrenched interests. Thus the social scientist is faced with difficulties which are unknown to the natural scientist. At its worst, the economist facing this situation turns apologist by covering up existing power relations behind an impressive barrage of 'economic necessities' and 'economic laws'.[6] But one can escape this dilemma without

5. That some of them are called 'non-economic' is already a consequence of the traditional definitions and developments in economic science. One can easily build models of economic reality in which so-called non-economic factors become fundamental parts of the theoretical structure.

6. The sins in this direction were particularly blatant in the second half of the nineteenth century, when many economic theorists saw their main task in defending the ruling circles against the rising wave of socialist

running into trouble by concentrating on those aspects of the economic scene in which power relations are unimportant or can be taken as exogenously given. This possibility of avoiding pressures and conflicts has certainly contributed to the remarkable concentration on competitive market and equilibrium theory and the startling dearth of theoretical and applied reasoning in those fields where power and political influences cannot be disregarded.

In the preceding section we have advanced some reasons why power has been neglected in the main run of economic literature. But the neglect has never been complete. Apart from occasional sidelights on power relations, which continued in the literature even after the early classics, there have always been important exceptions to our main thesis that power questions were not properly integrated into economic analysis.

One far reaching exception arose from the fact that the discrepancy between the competitive Utopia and the realities of big business just could not be overlooked. Thus side by side with the basic competitive model, a model of monopolistic behaviour was developed. And with monopoly the question of power could no longer be shelved. Monopoly power had to be recognized as the essence of the monopoly problem, and the literature on monopoly power in theory and practice is indeed plentiful.

But what is significant in our context is the fact that monopoly power is usually discussed within the narrow boundaries set by the basic competition model. In the competition model, as we saw, the small firm is powerless in the market. It has to accept the market parameters – price, demand etc. – and can only passively adjust to it. Monopoly is usually seen as *the absence of competition* in this sense. One recognizes that larger units exist which can influence the market parameters – prices, sales – through their own isolated actions. This capacity of changing the outcome of the market process is the main content of the traditional

---

demands. Marx and Engels had easy play in disclosing the apologetic nature of some of those theories.

Later these openly apologetic intentions became less frequent. But ideological elements were and are still prevalent in many theoretical structures. See the famous work by Myrdal (1953).

concept of 'monopoly power'. While the importance of this power over prices and demand must be fully acknowledged it is, nevertheless, true to say that this power concept is a very incomplete one. It limits its attention – like competition theory – exclusively to market mechanisms and market adjustments without giving consideration to attempts at changing the conditions under which the the market process – be it competitive or monopolistic – operates.[7]

A line similar to that of monopoly theory was followed in the description of the labour market. Here, too, it was recognized that trade unions and employers' organizations did not tally with the competitive stereotype and that power elements could not be completely cast aside. But here again a large part of the traditional literature concentrated on price-setting power in a given labour market while neglecting other aspects of the power problem.

The other big exception we have to note is the fact that everything we have said so far applies only to the main stream of traditional academic economics. There have always been important schools, side-currents and outsiders who have given full weight to the power problem and to the interplay between economic and power elements. This cannot be the place to give a full account of these various systems of thought. But a few outstanding names should be mentioned in order to show that the importance of power certainly was recognized by some representatives of the economic profession.

First of all we must, of course, mention Marx and his followers. Marx inherited from the classical school not only their 'purely' economic theoretical concepts, but also their less developed attempts to see economic 'laws' in relation to the social and historical background. By laying greater stress on these aspects he formed his grand amalgam of economics and sociology, in which the drives for economic and political position, for economic

7. The restrictive interpretation of monopoly power, inherited from competition theory and limiting it to the play on the price mechanism, explains to a large extent why for a long time economists were so helpless *vis-à-vis* the problems of bilateral monopoly and oligopoly, where quite different forms of power tactics are relevant. See on this the classic new approach by von Neumann and Morgenstern (1944), and Reading 5 in this collection.

and political power are closely interwoven. The Marxist school has never lost sight of the power problem in economics, and in the writings of such Marxist 'classics' as Engels, Hilferding, Kautsky, Rosa Luxemburg or Lenin, one can find innumerable examples of such combined analysis.

Similarly, direct and indirect aspects of power have always obtained some recognition among the so-called 'institutionalist' and 'historical' schools of economic thought. Composed of scholars who were less inclined towards general and predominantly logical analysis and more interested in concrete historical situations these schools were naturally less impressed by the 'competitive Utopia' and more aware of actual power influences. Outstanding early contributors in this sphere were Veblen in the USA and Sombart in Germany, and in both these countries contributions of this type continued to appear in later periods. Some of the writings of Schumpeter belong in this group.

Then we must also mention the miscellaneous writers who came to recognize the importance of power problems in connection with some special field in economics on which their interests centred. Thus some of the students of the labour market came to feel that they would have to pay far more attention to power aspects than current economic theory was prepared to do. Sydney and Beatrice Webb or Tugan-Baranovsky can be cited as outstanding early examples. Others (e.g. Henry George or Oppenheimer) came up against the power question in connection with their studies on the continuing advantages accruing to landed property. Then, of course, writers attracted by the rising phenomenon of economic imperialism could hardly avoid dealing intensively with the problem of power. The name of Hobson readily springs to mind.

It would seem that the last few paragraphs – containing, as they do, a list of 'power-minded' economists and 'schools' – are somehow in contradiction to what has been said earlier about the neglect of power in economic science. The contrary, however, is true. The existence of these 'outsiders' and alternative schools throws into even sharper relief the lack of concern for power relations in the main body of academic economics. The amazing point is how little effect the 'unorthodox' writings had on the formulation of questions and answers in 'traditional' economics.

Quite often no notice at all was taken of the outsiders, in other cases one tried very hard to fence off their influence.[8]

To some extent this cavalier treatment of outsiders could be justified on the ground that quite a number of them paid too little attention to the working of economic mechanisms and to the limits they set to the acquisition and exertion of power. But these shortcomings are not sufficient to explain fully the remarkable immunization of 'traditional' theory against the important problems raised by the 'non-official' literature. To understand this phenomenon one has to take recourse to explanations in terms of traditions, modes of thinking, and social pressures, which were treated in the first section of this introduction.

From what has been said so far it should be clear that a selection of readings to fit the title of this volume faces special problems. Normally, readings on some economic subject have to deal with a well-defined sector of economic theory and reality. The confines of the subject are comparatively easy to discern and the main problem is to pick out relevant excerpts which will give a well-balanced picture of the state of present-day knowledge and its current trends.

With the subject of power the situation is different. There are no clear cut areas which unequivocally belong to this theme. This is above all due to the fact that power elements can pop up to a greater or lesser degree in all sorts of economic situations. The problem is further complicated because 'power' is such a vague concept. In relation to economic affairs it can take on very different forms. Even if we do not bother about niceties of definition[9] and details of form we can easily see that very different things fall under the power-economics complex. Thus we can think of economic power in terms of unequal initial positions in

8. A remarkable classic in this respect is the famous article by Böhm-Bawerk (1914).

9. It may be permitted to quote an old anecdote which is appropriate in this context. It tells of a university professor in the medical faculty who tries to define 'illness' for his students. After having discussed some twenty different definitions, none of which is fully satisfactory, he continues: 'Now look, if a patient comes to me and tells me he is ill, *he* knows what he means, and *I* know what he means, and that, after all, is important.' 'Power' is probably a concept not so very different from 'illness'.

the market which permit some agents to reap special benefits *in and through* the market mechanism. Conversely, one can find situations where the workings of the market are used to derive power which may then be used for economic or non-economic ends or may even be an aim in itself. Again, a relationship arises when power – be it of economic or non-economic origin – is being used to change the institutional framework and the market mechanism itself so that its working yields different results. And, finally, added to all these objective difficulties of delineation and definition is the previously stressed fact that the whole power problem has been badly neglected in economic literature and has never been systematically treated.

In view of these circumstances any choice of readings in this field will by necessity be somewhat haphazard. No rounded picture of a closed subject can be given. The best one can hope is that a perusal of the present selection will provide a certain 'feel' for the lacunae in present-day theory, for the main aspects of the power problem, and for some of the concrete forms in which it appears.

To approach this aim a mixture of general and more special excerpts have been included. The general articles contain both critical remarks about shortcomings of ruling theories as well as positive contributions towards a better understanding of power influences. These general analyses are supplemented by investigations of power emanations in important specific areas. These items should be taken as examples and not as a complete listing of 'power-infested' economic areas.

Two limitations must be mentioned. Firstly, contributions dealing exclusively or primarily with narrowly defined problems of market power have not been included in this selection. As was mentioned earlier, the price-setting powers of monopolies or the higgling of labour market organizations have been taken up early and regularly by the respective chapters of economic theory. They are treated as the main exemptions in the basic competitive model rather than as special examples in the much wider field of power influences. In any case, this type of analysis is well established and can best be studied in its own specific context.[10]

10. Thus, relevant contributions can be found in Penguin Modern Economics series in the volumes edited by Hunter (1969) and by McCormick and Smith (1968).

The second limitation refers to the period covered. All included items have been written in the past thirty years. The exclusion of older works means that some first-rate contributions do not appear. But to go back further and, in particular, to show the ancestry of some of the ideas represented in this book would have increased the number of essential candidates far beyond the possibilities of a single readings volume. Moreover, the concentration on writings of the recent past has the advantage that the illustrations from and references to reality are still more or less significant for the world in which we live.

References

BÖHM-BAWERK, E. (1914), 'Macht oder ökonomisches Gesetz?', *Zeitschrift für Volkswirtschaft, Socialpolitik und Verwaltung*, vol. 23, no. 3–4, pp. 205–71. (Translated into English as 'Control or Economic Law?', *Shorter Classics of Böhm-Bawerk*, Libertarian Press, 1962.)

BRADY, R. A. (1943), *Business as a System of Power*, Columbia University Press.

HICKS, J. R. (1946), *Value and Capital*, Oxford University Press, 2nd edn.

HUNTER, A. (ed.) (1969), *Monopoly and Competition*, Penguin Books.

McCORMICK, B. J., and SMITH, E. O. (eds.) (1968), *The Labour Market*, Penguin Books.

MYRDAL, G. (1953), *The Political Element in the Development of Economic Theory*, Routledge & Kegan Paul.

NEUMANN, J. VON, and MORGENSTERN, O. (1944), *The Theory of Games and Economic Behavior*, Wiley.

Part One
The Neglect of Power in Economic Theory

Traditional economic theory is characterized by a serious neglect of power aspects. This development has been fostered by the increasing concentration on the 'purely' economic elements of the market process in the competition model. Hans Albert's essay shows how this tendency was promoted by a 'purification' of classical theory of some of its roots. He stresses the sociological nature of market processes and maintains that an incorporation of sociological factors into economic reasoning would open the path for a proper recognition of the problem of power.

In the traditional economic models power could be neglected because there is little room for its exercise in a perfectly competitive world where many small firms are fully exposed to the 'automatic' forces of the market mechanisms. To come into closer touch with actual conditions where power has more elbow room one has to relax some of the assumptions of the competitive model. Two important factors to realize are firstly, that economically relevant actions are not restricted to market activity but are also carried on outside the market, and, secondly, that the economic universe is not populated by equally strong (or weak) units but by agents of uneven strength. These two problems – extra-market operations and domination effects – are taken up respectively in the contributions from Walker and Perroux.

The shortcomings of traditional economic theory with respect to the power problem are also dealt with in other items in this collection, particularly in the contributions from Pen (Reading 5) and Ulmer (Reading 13).

1 H. Albert

The Neglect of Sociology in Economic Science

Excerpts from H. Albert, 'The sociological nature of economics: the problems of integration in the social sciences', *Kyklos*, vol. 13, 1960, pp. 1–43. Translated by F. Prager.

The sociological nature of theoretical economics

The conviction appears to be gaining ground among those engaged in social research – the same is happening in other scientific fields – that the traditional boundary lines separating individual disciplines within this realm are becoming increasingly meaningless; and that, in fact, when dealing with problems of demarcation we are really concerned with practical problems affecting the division of labour in scientific work: problems that ought to be decided with a view to feasibility rather than regarded as matters of principle.

Much attention is being paid to so-called marginal problems, to cooperation among exponents from different fields, and attempts at integration and synthesis are becoming popular pastimes; but we cannot help observing that vociferous advocacy of the 'unity of the social sciences' appears perfectly compatible with stubborn last ditch stands for the preservation of traditional fences. The boundary lines are played down, yet they do in fact play the same role in research that ever they did. The fact that to-day they are being justified pragmatically, no longer onthologically, appears to have deprived them of hardly any of their screening function against awkward questions. To this day it is the fashion to oppose sociology and economics, economic sociology and theoretical economics as different specialities; and it is considered useful and profitable to present them as sciences dealing with different aspects or sectors of reality, concerned with differing groups of problems; it is thought wise to pretend that an analysis of their interrelations, that feasibility of cooperation and potential integration must rest on the secure foundation of such essential diversity. It is only when applying oneself to the overall historical complex of the social process that a serious attempt is made to consider full cooperation as a promising possibility.

The distinction between the economic and the sociological approach appears to be paralleled, within the realm of subject matter of the two sciences, by juxtaposing 'economy' and 'society'. Thus a resolution of the problem of integration between the two disciplines appears in some manner connected with an answer to such questions as, how would one have to visualize, in principle and in detail, the relationship of the two fields; was the economy socially determined; might one think in terms of economic determination of social development or was one faced with reciprocal interaction of the two spheres. Economists are still apt to consider sociology as a residual branch of economics: a branch concerned with processing some of the data contained in economic models, or confined to considering extra-economic variables; whilst sociologists incline to regard 'the economy' as a 'complex aspect of social systems', a sub-system which, 'from the point of view of society as a whole' must fulfil certain functions and whose analysis and consistent explanation could be successfully achieved by means of models developed by economic theory (Parsons, 1955, pp. 70 et seq.). But whilst economists increasingly regard the customary delimitations of the economic realm as difficult to maintain, and whilst they feel utterly uncomfortable in the – supposedly – sociologically neutral climate of their theoretical thinking, some practitioners of sociology appear to regard this sort of theorizing with utter admiration, considering it exemplary though, maybe, quite unattainable in their own field in this degree of perfection. For the time being, at any rate, the sensible thing to do would appear to be juxtaposing economics and sociology as comparatively autonomous sciences with their own separate approaches, topics, methods, subject matter and scope; and to concern oneself with their inter-relationships and with the interplay of their respective reality aspects in order to draw conclusions concerning possible co-operation between, and integration of these disciplines.

As for myself, however, I believe that such a view of this whole complex of problems is in no way conducive to the promotion of a comprehensive, unified social science: for its basis – the belief in the existence of autonomous disciplines of the social sciences which are relatively clearly separated and whose subsequent synthesis ought to be considered – blinds us to precisely those characteristics of traditional economic thinking that cause the present state of economic theory to appear so unsatisfactory in the eyes of many of its practitioners. If one wishes to avoid that consequence, one would, in my opinion, have to put aside all glorification of the results of 'model thinking' and would have to concentrate on the question, for what sort of problems economic theories are usually being constructed; what is their relation to sociological problems; and does the attempt at 'purely' economic solutions appear at all auspicious. For, assuming the answer to this latter question were in the affirmative, then the generally prevalent discomfort concerning the autonomy of economics would be hard to understand. For a theory that solves the problems posed does not, on the face of it, appear utterly dependent upon supplementation and cooperation.

Now an examination of the chief works of theoretical economics will convince us that, from the early days of industrial society in its mercantilist phase, this branch of learning concentrated on the market phenomena of that society and especially on the price and income developments within such a social milieu. A logical analysis, however, of the technical language of economics will make it clear that ultimately these questions boil down to problems of the *commercial relationships* between persons and groups, and thus to problems of *interactions* among persons in different roles.

The solution, then, of problems of economic theory amounts to this: that we construct theories which, when applied to social reality, enable us to *explain* human *market behaviour* and its consequences. Market relations – the subject matter of economic thought – are really nothing but a special kind of social relations, of human interactions. Economics accordingly ought to be interpreted as a part of sociology: as the sociology of market relations or of market behaviour (unless, of course, were we to confine ourselves to solving logico-mathematical problems, or problems of politics or of morals).

This interpretation of the subject matter of economics may seem obvious to many. However its explicit formulation may offer a suitable point of departure on an inquiry that takes us deep into the complex subject of integration in the social sciences. And so we must ask ourselves: can there be an autonomous economic theory? If so — how fruitful would its pursuit be? [. . .]

The economic and the sociological perspective

Belief in the feasibility of setting up an autonomous realm of economic problems is not solely the outcome of some economic theorists' institutionalized professionalism, which, after all, merely carries on a certain tradition of economic thought. Critical analysis of this tradition and all its aspects right back to its origins in classical economic theory will disclose that in its development a section of economic thought faithfully adhered to the logic of its original approach. To that extent it is quite intelligible out of the perspective of the classical phase. For the 'vision' of the classicists contains a synthesis of elements belonging, when judged by contemporary methodological standards, to totally heterogenous categories of thought. Their analysis of the contemporaneously unfolding industrial society – arising out of their *metaphysical* background of natural law and utilitarian thinking – fused elements of *market sociology* with rudiments of a *logical* theory of rational action, all being part of an *ideological* concept[1] that tended to let the active interplay of market transactions appear as 'connected in a meaningful way', resulting in a tendency to single out certain social forms as optimal.

The classical perspective (or vision) thus incorporated starting points for widely differing developments, each of which could be taken up by way of purifying the classical perspective. It is most interesting to note that the development of economic doctrine, especially during the neo-classical era of marginal theory, was characterized by the constant recession of the market-sociological

1. For a critique of the metaphysical–ideological components of classical and neo-classical thought see, first, Myrdal (1932), where the normative–explicative ambiguity of economic concepts and language is elaborated. See also my essay (1954) with its application to the problem of the social order.

In his more recent publications Myrdal abandoned the methodological position he had maintained in the above-mentioned work but not the findings of his analysis. In this context, see his book (1958), and my critical reference thereto (1958).

component of classical tradition, and accompanied by the expansion of 'static' economics, partly combining the ideological with the decision-orientated components (especially in welfare economics), partly cultivating the latter unalloyed (especially in the theory of value and price). Empirical illustrations of the resulting alternative–analytical patterns created the impression of an empirical, but nonetheless pure (i.e. non-sociological) economic science.[2]

Elimination of the ideological and sociological components of classical thought leads straightaway to that 'logic of planning' (decision) that, under the label of pure economics, pervades the perspective of the neo-classical theorists, as far as they are prepared to avoid crypto-normative statements and value judgements in their argument. The whole armoury of present-day economic thought rests on this approach, despite all efforts to emphasize its explanatory value. This applies not only to the theory of micro-economic decision making but also and especially to the whole book-keeping system of national accounting (or macro-economics) and its conceptual basis. This is usually presented under the ambiguous designation of a theory of economic flows, but actually contains in essence only registration patterns for a number of facts ('business occurrences'), which are suitable for certain limited purposes.

Marginalism and equilibrium thinking – whose importance I do not wish to minimize – have their proper primary place in the logic of planning, or of decision making. They have little to do with an explanation of social market phenomena, with the sociology of market events. The economic perspective of neo-classical thinking led to a totally different constellation of problems than were to be expected from the sociological point of view. The logic, and not the sociology of price formation and market behaviour, received most of the attention: to that extent the above-mentioned market-sociological interpretation of economic problems represents a return to an earlier approach that had been buried almost completely by neo-classical developments.

2. The paucity of empirical content in neo-classical theories was shown long ago both by Hutchison in his essay (1937) and in his book (1938), and more especially by Akerman (1938; 1939; 1944), without, however, so far achieving much following for his theses.

It is extremely characteristic for the development of the neo-classical economic approach that the Walrasian system can be regarded as a culminating point of pure economics:[3] for the sociologically quite irrelevant problem of general equilibrium under conditions of perfect competition has its roots in an attitude that values the purely economic perspective in its strongest and most undiluted form. The central problem of classical economics, the search for the laws of price determination, is looked upon by Walras – in common with the two other founders of the marginal utility school – as a purely economic problem, i.e. as a value problem to be solved on the basis of a principle of rational action. And so the value perspective of neo-classicism leads not to a sociological theory of price formation but to a logic of economic action, not in danger of being tested empirically. The basic static model of perfect competition, which has practically nothing in common with the actual struggles of the business world, has been found so outstandingly appropriate for an analysis of price formation – and therefore, incidentally, has lost none of its attractions to this day, retaining its popularity, at any rate, as a starting point and for comparative purposes – because it seems to represent economic rationality in a most reliable manner, free from interfering irrational elements, especially the power phenomenon that is always so disturbing to the economic theorist. In this borderline case pure economics seems to be able to neglect completely the sociological element: an illusion that panders to the claim to autonomy encountered in economic thinking to this day.[4]

Furthermore in this case it is very easy to analyse the economy or at any rate its presumptive core, the price mechanism, as a meaningful phenomenon: thus the essentially plan-orientated

3. On this, see Schumpeter (1954). Schumpeter himself always strove – despite his most successful activities in both fields – to keep pure economics and sociology sharply apart. True, he often came very close to recognizing the untenability of the pure theory. All the more surprising, then, his assessment of the Walrasian system.

4. Thus we find the peculiar opinion which holds, as it were, that it depends on the type of market whether price determination may be analysed on a purely economic basis or whether one might feel constrained to draw on sociological findings too; the latter course being conceded as proper when dealing with problems of oligopoly.

rationality approach may be applied to the economy as a whole, and the competition model ideologically utilized, just as was done in the classical period. [. . .]

What gets lost in this interpretation is the problem of the interplay of causes and effects in economic reality: neither by a rationalist logical nor by an ideological approach can this problem be adequately treated.

If we wish to interpret this causal interplay theoretically, i.e. if we would like to explain it, a change of perspective would seem necessary. Not an elimination of the sociological element but rather a radical 'sociologization' of economics is wanted. This is not to say that we must do away with the problem of price determination, but merely that it must be explicitly interpreted from the sociological angle and fitted into the context of sociological thought. All those matters that from the aspect of pure economics were seen as interference, friction, extra-economic factors, data, special problems and exceptions may from the sociological point of view acquire systematic relevance. Thus it is rather interesting to note that especially in the case of oligopoly, where the *social* phenomenon of competition was brought out even by the theorists of the neo-classical tradition, the confines of purely economic, static thinking are most clearly and visibly exploded, thereby evoking strong doubts about the usability of the neo-classical concept.[5] All that is most essential to a sociological interpretation of the economic complex comes most conspicuously to the fore in an analysis of the problem of oligopoly: we realize that a purely decision-logical treatment in the old style cannot get us anywhere; that any claim to methodological autonomy must remain most questionable; that in the face of conspicuous analogies in other sectors of social life (e.g. in political and military fields) any pretence to logical autonomy must fall; and that finally, as no closed domain of economics can be constituted in fact, theoretical autonomy cannot justifiably be proclaimed if we aim truly at an explanation of market phenomena. Here again, I think, it is obvious that a sociological

5. See especially the pioneering essay by Rothschild (1947). There the importance of the problem of oligopoly for neo-classical thinking is most clearly brought out, indicating an unmistakable change of perspective towards a sociological approach in economic theory.

interpretation of the price problem, that an examination of the causal interplay instead of 'meaningful' connections must lead us from the theory of value to an analysis of power.

Whilst pure economics, in a sort of ritual power-blindness, considered price determination primarily and principally as a value phenomenon, relegating all elements which could not be covered by the decision-logical apparatus to data, that very price formation process, viewed in sociological perspective, must appear as a social power problem pure and simple. Seen from this angle production, distribution, and the satisfaction of needs, appear as byproducts of a struggle for social predominance, for power position absorbing purchasing power, and as an outflow of the results of such conflicts: as the respective distribution of power in the market sphere, inseparable from the power structure in other spheres of society. The power phenomenon, regarded as a foreign body in the neo-classical concept, and quite rightly so, becomes the central question of an economic science that must be held to be an essential part of sociology.[6]

The injection of sociology into economics and the question of power

Economic theorists often used to feel disturbed by the unavoidable intrusion of problems of power into their scheme of thinking. If we are prepared to sacrifice the neo-classical value perspective, we shall accept the problem of power as the dominant question of economics as a social science. Viewed from this angle, the classical principle of competition, too, will undoubtedly be recognized as one approach to solving the question of power in society, at any rate as far as the economic sector is concerned, irrespective of whether this solution would appear desirable from some special point of view, such as the 'satisfaction of needs' or 'efficiency' (Galbraith, 1952, pp. 27 et seq.). Preoccupation with one aspect, viz. the satisfaction of needs, which was mainly derived from the neo-classical perspective, diverted attention from the task of subjecting to a causal analysis the fundamental changes in society

6. A consideration of the power question that transcends the neo-classical concept may already be found in the two articles by Preiser (1948) (included as Reading 6 in this volume); (1953); see also my article (1955).

(and in the economy) which had occurred since the days of classical economics: those changes in the social power structure which, after all, are decisive for everything else, including the so-called satisfaction of needs. Such an analysis contains the key to the integration of economics with political science and other parts of sociology. Even when dealing with the power problem in the economic realm economists usually moved within the strait jacket of an *a priori* adopted economic perspective in order to contribute ultimately to the solution of crypto-normative or pseudo-causal value problems (examining the causes of welfare, etc.). At best they aimed at an examination of explicitly normative or decision-logical value problems under more realistic premises.

In contrast to the power orientation of sociological thinking which aims at explanation, the economic value orientation introduces *a priori* and inevitably a teleological-final moment into the argument which, at best, leads to decision-logical, plan-theoretical formulations, but often goes on to normative and in the end to manifestly ideological phrasings.[7] Now, a theoretical inquiry that takes as its starting point the satisfaction of needs, or a postulated aim of the economy (or even attempts to introduce such a thesis by way of a matter of fact sounding definition of the economy) will most probably not produce any theory capable of serving as a basis for a *causal* explanation of the social process; it will merely lead to a system that tries laboriously to hide the analysis of meaningful connections behind pseudo-causal statements on the effects of dispositions of the economic subjects; effects which – curiously enough (and in spite of David Hume) – may be *logically* deduced from these dispositions. Within an edifice thus constructed it may well be possible to deploy empirical data for illustrative purposes; but their

7. Apparently this applies also to contributions in the field of game theory as exemplified in Richter's attempt (1954) to find a yardstick for reasonable or rational behaviour in the oligopoly situation and an 'equilibrium solution' to the question of competition in that situation. On the other hand, Nyblen (1951) appears to aim at an explanation of actual connections. But I believe the use he makes of game-theoretical techniques, though most ingeniously applied, merely serves as an ex-post interpretation of historical sequences of events.

essential utilization is, after all, determined by principles that are derived from the value perspective.

Of course, given the honest will to explain processes of social reality the sheer dead weight of the facts of social life will force us again and again – however value-orientated we may be – to tackle power phenomena in our theoretical approach. Even within neo-classical thought sociological problems keep intruding and eventually lead to a disruption of the neo-classical system, especially when it comes to questions of imperfect or monopolistic competition and of oligopoly. This often leads to a 'solution' of sociological problems with the aid of a surface sociology which is obviously derived from the *homo oeconomicus* fiction and the theory of rational conduct connected with it. Else there might occur a complete dissolution of theory into, on the one hand, a logically more or less exhaustive classification of possible market forms, market relations,[8] or market behaviour patterns without empirical revelance (nevertheless purporting to be a theory), and into empirical case analyses on the other hand, that no longer try to disguise the collapse of theoretical thought of neo-classical derivation and the transition to empiricism devoid of theory.

This outcome of earnest endeavour may not be the necessary effect of the complexity of present-day economic life but a result of the prevailing economic viewpoint, of the way in which the fundamental problems of economics are formulated. What is perhaps needed in the face of the patent inadequacy of all past attempts to get a theoretical hold on economic reality is not a supplementation of economic thinking by bringing in fragmentary theses from the other social sciences or the replacement of some sections in the traditional edifice of ideas; but rather a simple change of perspective, a deliberate revision of the fundamental economic approach. A change that radically does away with the distinctions between economic, political and sociological angles. Who indeed is forcing us to declare the pseudo-causal thinking of neo-classicism the only possible form of theoretical analysis? It is not unlikely that those who wish to honour and obey

8. See Triffin (1940), as well as Rothschild's critique of that work (p. 447). But where Triffin stands out from others with similar aims is in his scrupulous avoidance of any claim to empirical content.

traditions might even find some points of contact for a reinterpretation of the economic approach among the classics.

Seen without the blinkers of neo-classical thought, social reality appears to be a more or less conflict-laden concert of persons associated in social entities of various kinds who, according to their roles, occupy certain positions of power and who represent and promote certain interests (in the widest sense of the word). Society embodies a definite power structure, subject to more or less rapid change under the impact of the social power struggle, influencing the realization of emerging objectives according to the position of the persons aspiring to them and, as it were, 'canalizing' the conduct of those persons. At every stage of social development the most varied conflicts, convergences and identities of interests will obtain; they will dominate the social life of the community or fade into the background, according to the power constellations of the moment.

Among the social groups involved in this interplay we also find those enterprises and households as units of the market process that are usually the exclusive subjects of economic analysis. But to them should be added political parties, industrial and trade associations, government and administrative bodies etc., usually the concern of political science, and other groups that are treated in general sociology. Among the interests relevant to the concerted interaction of social life must be counted all those individual needs whose satisfaction – under conditions prevailing in a market economy – necessitates the purchase of goods or services. Group interests leading directly to such purchases (collective needs of public bodies, parties, churches, unions and associations of all kinds) equally belong to this category. But all these interests form merely a sector of the sum total of all effective interests – just as the economic units devoted to the production of various goods and services are a mere section of the social group structure. Any attempt at a theoretical isolation of consumer needs and economic entities as carriers of market relations is a hopeless undertaking and must, for obvious reasons, be paid for with a decline of scientific thinking into classification devoid of empirical content or empiricism devoid of theory; for such abstraction can be carried out only by classifying or describing. Such abstractions may seem justified to certain practical interests which tend towards a consumption-orientated way of thinking; but they will merely burden a theoretical interpretation of the processes.

Such a procedure is actually quite incomprehensible from a theoretical point of view. All these social entities – business firms, parties, unions, churches, government agencies etc. – are obviously faced with analogous problems. They could perhaps be roughly classified as internal and external power problems, questions of internal and external policy, of the formation of collective decisions, and the imposition of their objectives in the social field, without a clear distinction of these problems always being possible. A connection between internal power structure and external power position, between decision process and outward behaviour may always be taken for granted.[9] We note that the foreign policy problems of enterprises in a commercial–industrial society will surely often coincide to a large extent with their market problems, but by no means exclusively so, as we are today well aware, least of all in the case of large companies, the very firms that influence the market processes most decisively (National Resources Committee, 1949).

The fact that since its classical phase economic theory has made the price problem its central question, confining itself in essence to the analysis of commercial relations is, of course, no reason at all for an enterprise to confine its foreign policies to the market sector, especially as there are benefits to be reaped from interlocking financial and personal relationships between different enterprises even within the economic realm (in the usual sense of the word) – relationships that are also outside the range of price theory. On the internal front we find within all larger entities, in

9. Exponents of a pseudo-individualism in economic thinking who do not hesitate to identify the modern giants of the business world with the classical entrepreneur–capitalist as far as their outward behaviour is concerned are thus rightly criticized by Clark (1957); he holds a quasi-political analysis of economic entities to be necessary (p. 228), in the same way as Berle (1954), who considers the giant corporations to be quasi-political organizations. The outcome of decision-making in enterprises cannot be considered a constant independent of structural influences, nor can it be formulated as a simple principle to be accepted as plausible from a plan-theoretical aspect. A change in the power structure of economic units may fundamentally affect their policies.

enterprises, parties, unions etc., a growing bureaucratization bringing in its train problems of internal control. Here, too, we find no differences that would justify the autonomy of separate branches of science. But most important, the social interconnections between all these entities are such that in any analysis of, say, the determinants of the existing income distribution, of production, and the satisfaction of needs one can by no means confine oneself to the economic sector,[10] even if such an illusion may have been justifiable in former times when the model of perfect competition might still have been supposed to have had an explanatory value.

The economists of the classical period, in making the price problem – and with it the complex of problems of commercial relations between social entities of all kinds – the central theme of economics, no doubt acted on the belief that the price mechanism is the essential and solely pertinent system of social control for the economic sector. They assumed that all the major decisions of economic life, and therewith production, distribution and the satisfaction of needs were unequivocally determined by the mechanism of financial sanctions in the commercial sphere. Even accepting such a premise, the central problem of economics remains, of course, a question of power structure; but one regarding which one might rightly hope that its treatment in isolation, the pure analysis of the price mechanism, might be successfully accomplished. Free competition, in the opinion of some classical economists, was in many respects an ideal solution to the problems of social control in the economic realm.

The present level of our understanding of social reality, and in particular the changes in social structure that have since taken place, must make such concentration on the price problem seem absurd unless we wish to conserve a social Utopia. Even within the so-called economic sector (and defining its border-lines may well be deemed a daunting task) the price system must be regarded as a mere fragment of the system of social control holding sway in that domain (National Resources Committee, 1949). Even assuming the price mechanism to allow enterprises in conditions of less

10. For a methodologically orientated analysis of the significance of such general social interdependence, in particular in respect to the problems of underdeveloped countries, see Myrdal (1957).

developed industrial societies of the commercial type no latitude in their decision making – and I myself hold such an assumption to be untenable – it must be admitted that under conditions of a bureaucratic commercial industrial society of the modern type such latitude does exist, at least in large sectors of the economy, together with the existence of extra-commercial checks and controls that have in part a greater significance than the market system.

Further analysis of the present-day power structure will show quite plainly that it is impossible to draw a sharp line *vis-à-vis* the so-called political domain. Such demarcation is quite illusory even as far as price determination is concerned. The price mechanism becomes increasingly subject to influences from factors that are totally alien to classical and neo-classical thought and it is also losing much of its former significance for the allocation of economic resources. It may in consequence be more promising fully to acknowledge the dubious nature of the fundamental approach in economics. Instead of retaining it, with minor modifications, at all cost, a fundamental revision might be called for. [. . .]

If we are not satisfied to follow the 'flow of goods and money' on their course through the economy registering and extrapolating their quantitative properties in order to arrive at some projection relevant to economic practice; if we are suspicious of easily applied ad-hoc hypotheses and would rather adopt less modern-looking but otherwise definitely well-tried methods to arrive at a theoretical interpretation of social phenomena that underlie those 'flows': then we shall feel constrained to subject the sum total of society's power structure, with all its inherent configurations of interests, to our analysis; and we shall keep our eyes open for a general sociological theory that will contribute to an explanation of those phenomena in a manner that might seem old-fashioned, but that can ill be spared. [. . .]

References

AKERMAN, J. (1938), *Das Problem der sozialökonomischen Synthese*, Lund.
AKERMAN, J. (1939), *Ekonomisk Teori*, vol. 1, Leipzig.
AKERMAN, J. (1944), *Ekonomisk Teori*, vol. 2, Leipzig.

ALBERT, H. (1954), *Ökonomische Ideologie und politische Theorie*, Göttingen.

ALBERT, H. (1955), 'Macht und Zurechnung: Von der funktionellen zur institutionellen Verteilungstheorie', *Schmollers Jahrbuch*, vol. 75, no. 1, pp. 57–85.

ALBERT, H. (1958), 'Das Wertproblem in den Sozialwissenschaften', *Schweizerische Zeitschrift für Volkswirtschaft und Statistik*, vol. 94, no. 3, pp. 335–40.

BERLE, A. A. (1954), *The Twentieth-Century Capitalist Revolution*, Harcourt, Brace & World.

CLARK, J. M. (1957), *Economic Institutions and Human Welfare*, Knopf.

GALBRAITH, J. K. (1952), *American Capitalism: The Concept of Countervailing Power*, Houghton Mifflin.

HUTCHISON, T. W. (1937), 'Theoretische Ökonomie als Sprachsystem?', *Zeitschrift für Nationalökonomie*, vol. 8, no. 1, pp. 78–90.

HUTCHISON, T. W. (1938), *The Significance and Basic Postulates of Economic Theory*, Macmillan.

MYRDAL, G. (1932), *Das politische Element in der nationalökonomischen Doktrinbildung*, Berlin; translated as *The Political Element in the Development of Economic Doctrines*, Routledge & Kegan Paul, 1953.

MYRDAL, G. (1957), *Economic Theory and Underdeveloped Regions*, Methuen.

MYRDAL, G. (1958), *Value in Social Theory*, Routledge & Kegan Paul.

NATIONAL RESOURCES COMMITTEE (1949), 'The structure of controls', *The Structure of the American Economy*, Kelley; reprinted in R. Bendix and S. Lipset (eds.), *Class, Status and Power: A Reader in Social Stratification*, Free Press, 1953.

NYBLEN, G. (1951), *The Problem of Summation in Economic Science*, Lund.

PARSONS, T. (1955), 'Die Stellung der Soziologie innerhalb der Sozialwissenschaften' ('The role of sociology within the social sciences'), in W. Bendorf and G. Eisermann (eds.), *Einheit der Sozialwissenschaften* (Unity of the Social Sciences), Stuttgart.

PREISER, E. (1948), 'Besitz und Macht in der Distributionstheorie', *Synopsis, Festgabe für Alfred Weber*, Heidelberg.

PREISER, E. (1953), 'Erkenntniswert und Grenzen der Grenzproduktivitätstheorie', *Schweizerische Zeitschrift für Volkswirtschaft und Statistik*, vol. 89, no. 1, pp. 25–45.

RICHTER, R. (1954), *Das Konkurrenzproblem im Oligopol*, Berlin.

ROTHSCHILD, K. W. (1947), 'Price theory and oligopoly', *Econ. J.*; reprinted in *Readings in Price Theory*, Allen & Unwin, 1953.

SCHUMPETER, J. A. (1954), 'Marie Esprit Leon Walras', *Dogmenhistorische und biographische Aufsätze*, Tübingen.

TRIFFIN, R. (1940), *Monopolistic Competition and General Equilibrium Theory*, Oxford University Press.

2 E. Ronald Walker

Beyond the Market

Excerpts from E. Ronald Walker, *From Economic Theory to Policy*, University of Chicago Press, 1943, chapter 6, pp. 100–141.

Among the implicit psychological assumptions of conventional economic theory there is the supposition that people act only through the market. Other forms of behavior may be observed; but economic theory abstracts from them for the purposes of its analyses and assumes that people seek their ends only by buying and selling, hiring and borrowing. Or we may say that economic theory considers the pursuit of ends (financial and non-financial) which can be achieved through market activities and does not study human behavior in so far as it consists of the pursuit of other ends. For instance, going to church or doing physical exercises of a morning or agitating for a change in the divorce laws is usually regarded as 'non-economic' behavior, because these ends cannot be achieved through the market. Thus Professor Schumpeter draws a distinction between 'economic life', on the one hand, and political activities which 'do not aim immediately at the acquisition of goods through exchange or production,' on the other, although he admits that the distinction is not always clearly marked (Schumpeter, 1934, p. 5; 1939, vol. 1, p. 11).

It is not suggested there that the economist should enlarge his field of study to cover *all* such phenomena. But there are ends which may be pursued both inside the market and outside it. When the latter course is followed, we have a special type of behavior, which may be distinguished from those forms of behavior which are causally remote from the market, as well as from those that are observed in the market. This special type of behavior differs from non-economic behavior (as usually conceived) with regard to its ends and from market behavior with regard to its methods. In selecting the term 'extra-market operations' to represent this type of behavior, one hopes to convey both shades of meaning. Extra-market *activities* might be taken to cover all behavior outside the market; extra-market *operations* are only those extra-market activities which are directed toward ends which may be sought and are sought also through operations in the market. The term 'extra-market adjustments' might provide an attractive contrast with the adjustments which the market makes to given data and at the same time emphasize that we are concerned with responses to the same total situation as that to which the market adjusts itself. But the term 'operations' suggests a more active form of behavior than does the term 'adjustments'. As Veblen says, 'It is characteristic of man to do something' (1930, p. 74).[1]

Our principle of distinction between extra-market operations and other non-economic activities, therefore, is found in the impossibility of pursuing certain ends in the market, while our distinction between market operations and extra-market operations turns on the possibility of pursuing other ends outside the market as well as inside. According to Professor Robbins, 'in so far as the achievement of *any* end is dependent upon scarce means, it is germane to the preoccupations of the economist' (1937, p. 24); but the body of economic theory, as usually taught, deals only with the achievement of ends through market operations and generally ignores not only other methods of achieving those ends but also all ends which cannot be achieved in this way. In other words, the criterion of 'scarce means' is interpreted, in practice, to cover only goods and services which are exchanged in the market.

The study of extra-market operations, as defined above, is necessary on three grounds for economists who would advise on policy. In the first place practical men do not regard extra-market operations as lying outside the field of economic behavior, and

1. Veblen rejects 'the hedonistic conception of man' as 'a lightning calculator of pleasure and pains, who oscillates like a homogeneous globule of desire of happiness under the impulse of stimuli that shift him about the area, but leave him intact. . . . Self imposed in elementary space, he spins symmetrically about his own spiritual axis, until the parallelogram of forces bears down upon him, whereupon he follows the line of the resultant. When the force of the impact is spent, he comes to rest, a self-contained globule of desire as before.'

the economist is expected to show some competence to consider them. Second, any economic explanations or predictions which ignore the possibility of extra-market operations run the danger of being unrealistic. Finally, extra-market operations are an important source of change in the data of the market itself; and when we come to consider the possibility of a theory of economic development, which may aid the economist to predict data changes as well as market reactions to the data, we shall find that the theory of extra-market operations has something to contribute. The pressure of practical affairs makes it impossible for the economist to wait hopefully until some other specialist provides such a theory; but there are also two other good reasons why economists should themselves make the attempt. One reason is that a knowledge of how the market works is an important prerequisite to understanding why people reject its verdict and prefer to operate outside it. The other reason is that, although extreme cases of extra-market operations present a great contrast with market operations, it is, nevertheless, impossible to draw a hard and fast boundary between these two types of behavior. The one shades imperceptibly into the other.

Examples of extra-market operations

Some examples may render the last point clearer. Racketeering may be generally classed as an extra-market operation. The threat of violence to person or property is used as a means of extracting payments; and, although the payments are nominally for the service of protection, there is no misunderstanding as to their real nature. Even Marshall has observed that

the feverish pursuit of wealth may induce men, capable of great work, to drift into distinctly criminal courses. . . . The National Cash Register Company, whose technical achievements are in the first rank, has been convicted for malicious libels in regard to competitors; and for causing its agents to injure internal parts of rival machines when in use, and similar practices (Marshall, 1920, p. 537 and note).

We should class these as extra-market operations, along with some of John D. Rockefeller's attempts to prevent the construction of pipe lines in competition with the railways under his control: 'His agents frightened the farmers over whose lands the pipes must pass, by stories of poisonous leakages and unquenchable fires, and gangs of railway employees attacked the workmen laying the pipes' (Wells, 1932, p. 450). The sit-down strike is clearly an extra-market operation, amounting to the forcible occupation of the employer's property; and the use of pickets in ordinary strikes is also outside the market. The various methods used by arms manufacturers to discourage international agreement on disarmament may be regarded as extra-market operations designed to promote or maintain their commercial interests.

Nor should we hesitate to classify as extra-market operations the day-to-day attempts of businessmen and their organizations to obtain legislation favorable to themselves. This type of political business activity is an international phenomenon.

The government is not a neutral arbiter in economic matters, but tends to reflect the aims of those groups which are in the best position to influence governmental decisions. Few would deny that the policies of Canadian Governments since Confederation have been predominantly shaped by business men. . . . Permanent lobbies in Ottawa, innumerable special delegations, the molding of public opinion through newspapers and other media, contributions to party funds – all these investments have yielded an abundant return (Reynolds, 1940, p. 272).

Lobbying by various sectional interests, including large business units or organizations, has long been a feature of politics in the United States (Logan, 1929; Blaisdell, 1941). Not only the process of legislation but also the activities of regulatory bodies, such as the Interstate Commerce Commission, are subject to campaigns and various forms of pressure in the normal course of business. 'The recognized judicial character of its work does not render the Commission immune from efforts to influence its judgements. The struggles of contending economic groups and political influences give rise to actions in a court of law and to repeated efforts to obtain favourable decisions through the use of propaganda' (Herring, 1936, p. 194 and ch. 12).

In Australia organized producer interests are represented in Canberra when parliament is sitting, outside as well as inside the legislature. The Associated Chambers of Manufacturers – the principal protectionist pressure group – maintains a permanent office in the national capital; and the Associated Chambers of Commerce has followed this example. The reports of the Australian Tariff Board indicate the time, care and expense which businessmen devote to the preparation of evidence in support of, or opposition to, changes in rates of duty. Another form of political activity is to attempt to influence the regional distribution of defense contracts. State governments will readily view the granting of contracts to firms in their territory as a legitimate interpretation of the public interest and ally themselves with private interests to bring pressure to bear on the federal government.

In Great Britain, too, organized pressure groups are a prominent feature of the political scene. The National Farmers' Union, for instance, had a political fund amounting to over £68,000 in 1937, in addition to the still larger general fund. Dr Jennings gives many examples of the pressure exerted by this body on the government and on private members of parliament in connection with specific pieces of legislation (1940, p. 211). Other prominent business organizations in that country include the Mining Association, the Chamber of Shipping, the National Federation of Iron and Steel Manufacturers and the Federation of British Industries. To be effective they must not only perfect the technique of political influence but also compel the loyalty of the members whose 'interests' they represent. On the other hand, there are labor organizations with varying degrees of political power. The operations of these various organizations are designed, generally speaking, to alter the conditions of the market so that it will yield greater financial returns to the people they represent.

All these examples of political activity are sufficiently related to everyday business operations to warrant our description of them as attempts to gain ends similar to those that are also sought in the market; and they all involve operations *outside* the market. They may, therefore, be referred to as extra-market operations, in contrast to the market operations which are the customary subjects of economic theory. We may now consider some examples of borderline cases – forms of behavior which do not fall easily into either class. [. . .]

Borderline cases

Borderline cases are, for instance, those in which market activities of a sort are undertaken with the deliberate intention of modifying the conditions of the market or of obtaining some result outside the market. For instance, it might be argued that bribery is a market operation: 'Every man has his price.' The return asked of the corrupt official is often a small change in the law or the award of a public contract or preferential treatment in some regulatory activity of the government. In these cases the paying party is not content with the results of the market under existing conditions: he desires to alter the data of the market or to obtain direct benefits by means of the extra-market operations of another party; but in order to obtain the latter service he must make a market transaction.

Bribery is outside the law, but the same difficulty of definition arises with some actions which are strictly legal. For instance, the American Telephone and Telegraph Company has paid authors and arranged for the publication of books calculated to improve the public relations of the company and distributed many copies free (Danielian, 1939). This involved market activities; but it may be suggested that the acquisition of goods and services by exchange was of minor importance compared with the desire to influence public opinion. Again, the common practice of large industrial concerns of requiring their employees, as a condition of employment, to sell any patents to the company for a nominal fee involves only market activities. The purpose, however, is often to prevent technical improvements from becoming known to competitors, even though the company does not intend to adopt them itself. Patents are put to sleep in an attempt to control the development of a portion of the data of the market (Bernal, 1939; Hamilton, 1941b).

These borderline cases sometimes involve the intrusion of extra-market operations into the market in order to modify its workings; in other cases the methods of the market are extended into the field of politics and other extra-market activities. The result is a mixture of market and extra-market operations. When confronted by a concrete problem of this type, the procedure of the economist is to apply his market theory and to correct its results by a common-sense appraisal of the particular extra-market operations which are visible in the case under consideration. In problems in which extra-market operations dominate the scene and market theory has little or no relevance the economist has no technical competence at all. This is because he has no recognized theory of the purely extra-market operations. If he did possess such a theory, the mixed cases would call, not merely for the correction of market theory by common sense, but for a synthesis of market theory and the theory of extra-market operations. Such a synthesis can be achieved only by those who are masters of both theories. Thus the existence of borderline cases reinforces our argument that the economist should develop the theory of extra-market operations himself. [. . .]

Divisions of the theory of extra-market operations

The theory of extra-market operations falls into three divisions; an analysis of dissatisfactions with the market, a classification of the various types of extra-market operations and the ways in which they furnish greater satisfaction than can be achieved in the market alone, and finally, the conditions under which dissatisfaction with the market does or does not boil over into the available channels of extra-market operations. [. . .]

Dissatisfaction with the market

Dissatisfaction with the results of the market is a universal feature of economic life. [. . .]

Classification of extra-market operations

Given a strong impulse to reject the verdict of the market, an individual or firm (or, more generally, an economic unit) must consider the other means at its disposal. Similarly, a theory which is to guide our study of the facts must set out the various possible courses of action and indicate the conditions under which one is preferred to another. If we consider the methods by which various extra-market operations promise better results than can be obtained from the market under existing conditions, it should then be possible, in a particular concrete case, to determine which of the methods would be preferred, on the assumption that their relative efficiency is the only factor in choice. This involves abstraction from the social and psychological factors which to some extent control the use of extra-market operations. Some operations are illegal, while others, though not illegal, incur social disapproval. Some may be dismissed as too risky, yet others may exercise an attraction for particular persons because they give scope for exploratory behavior. These factors – the 'other things' which are not equal but which vary from time to time, from place to place, and from person to person – will be considered later. By abstracting from them at the present stage we should be able to see more clearly the *modus operandi* of extra-market operations.

But, since our exposition of the theory is to be kept in general terms, it will not be possible to study the actual processes in any detail. There is nothing to be gained by the construction of a theoretical model, showing all the details of an extra-market operation, in complete abstraction from the local facts which will largely determine its form. All we require at this stage is a classification of the principal types of extra-market operations and of the general channels through which they can improve upon the results obtainable from the market. In approaching a concrete problem we shall then know the avenues that should be explored; we shall be in a position to ask whether, under the actual conditions of the case, the best results can be achieved by an economic unit which adopts measures falling under one or more of the various types of extra-market operations which our general theory distinguishes.

The various extra-market operations can be classified on two different principles: either according to the form which the behavior takes (e.g. physical violence may be distinguished from agitating for a change in the law) or according to the channel through which results are to be achieved (e.g. making the market work more favorably may be contrasted with evading it altogether). It is useful to establish both classifications and to consider the position of particular actions in relation to each of them.

The second principle gives a smaller number of classes and may be studied first. The classes may be distinguished by asking what are the *intermediate* objectives of extra-market operations. By definition, the ultimate objectives are the same as are sought by market operations; but, in pursuing these ultimate objectives, economic units seek to achieve, inside or outside the market, certain intermediate objectives. In the case of market operations the intermediate objectives may be, for instance, a certain set of prices or scale of production. In the case of extra-market operations we may distinguish *four* intermediate objectives:

1. To circumvent the market and to obtain money, goods or services without offering anything in exchange.

2. To alter the external data of the market so that, without any change in the principles of market behavior, the resulting prices, production, incomes or the associated conditions of work etc., will be different from those obtainable with the original data.

3. To modify the principles of market behavior so that the same external market data will give rise to prices, production, incomes or associated conditions different from those reached with the former principles of behavior.

4. To influence the scope for extra-market operations by other economic units.

The last of these will be ignored in this division of the theory. It will be considered later, along with other factors which influence the actual use made of various possible extra-market operations. This reduces our classes to three.

The distinction between (2) and (3) is somewhat arbitrary, since the principles of behavior might be stated in the form of data: the ends sought by the various economic units and their methods of choosing between competing ends. But the distinction is commonly made in market theory, and it is equally convenient in the theory of extra-market operations. It may be noticed that the line between (3) and (1) might occasionally be difficult to establish, as when the principles of market behavior are modified to permit goods to be obtained for a 'nominal' payment.

But, generally speaking, the distinctions are clear enough. As an example of (1) we might instance transfers of wealth through fiscal policy, living on charity, or the profession of burglary. Examples of (2) are abundant: the formation of a cartel, the imposition of a customs duty, the prohibition of sales of alcohol. And under (3) we would classify coercion to modify price policy and the prevalence of generosity rather than self-interest in business relations.

Techniques of extra-market operations

Our other principle of classification turns on what people actually can do to achieve the above-mentioned intermediate objectives. There are so many different things which they can do that this classification might be developed in considerable detail. To be serviceable, however, it must be manageable. We therefore distinguish four major classes, which are intended to cover everything; and within each class we distinguish two subclasses, which do not, however, purport to exhaust all the possibilities of the class in which they fall. Some of the subclasses cover a wide range of activities.

1. Violence by one economic unit against another.
(a) Violence to person, including physical compulsion or restraint.
(b) Violence to property; forcible dispossession or destruction.

2. Specific instructions by one economic unit to another.
(a) Backed by individual power: including threats of violence or of damaging business policies, such as price-cutting or boycott.
(b) Backed by authority in an organization, including the power of the government or its agencies over the subjects of the state or the power of majority stockholders over others or the power of a bank over its debtors.

3. Informal influence (without explicit instructions or rules) of one economic unit over the decisions and behavior of another.
(a) Control of psychological conditions in which decisions are made, including the parade of power without direct threats, pressure for immediate decisions, appeals to sentiment.
(b) Control of relevant information.

4. Establishment (or alteration) of general rules, binding on other economic units.
(a) Enforced by an organization.
(b) Enforced by social approval or disapproval.

This classification may well be improved as a result of further study, particularly through its experimental use in dealing with concrete problems of extra-market operations. The latter is the real test; and, if we remain at the level of generalities, attempts to improve the classification will be directed toward symmetry and the avoidance of overlapping. But it does not follow that an elegant classification is a more useful analytical tool or that the borderline cases that can be imagined *a priori* will cause serious inconvenience in empirical investigations. Admittedly, the four classes, distinguished above, shade into one another; but overlapping is likely to cause less trouble than would gaps between the various classes. It will also be observed that operations falling into one class may react upon those falling in other classes.

Taking this classification as it is, we may now examine each class in relation to the three intermediate objectives already distinguished and illustrate the type of operation which may be brought under each class. We shall also express an opinion regarding the relative frequency or importance of the various types in practice, while recognizing that practice will be different in different places, times and circumstances.

1. Violence often involves the evasion, or even the destruction, of the market. Forcible appropriation of goods or money and the attacks of John D. Rockefeller's employees on the workers who were laying pipe lines are sufficient examples. But the destruction of industrial property is often to be regarded as an alteration of the data of the market, designed to make the market conditions more favorable in the future. The kidnapping or murder of a competitor (practised only in certain trades and countries) is also designed to alter the market data. It is difficult to see, however, how the practice of violence can achieve the third type of intermediate objective, namely, the modification of the principles of market behavior, without breaking up the process of exchange altogether. It is not proposed to investigate the technique or 'productivity' of violence here. Indeed, its study presents special difficulties and dangers – particularly where direct observation is required. And in any case the extent of its use will depend more on legal and moral controls than upon the rewards which it offers to those who employ it.

2. Specific instructions from one economic unit to another may theoretically apply to almost any form of activity. Accordingly, they may be designed to achieve any or all of the three intermediate objectives. When a bandit orders his victim to hand over his cash or demands a ransom, this is action to achieve market objectives without recourse to the market. So, too, when compensation is sought through a lawsuit. But the dissolution of a trust or labor union, by order of a court of law, alters the data of the market, so that future transactions will yield different results. And

when a city government resumes land at an arbitrarily fixed price, this involves a different principle of behavior from that usually observed in the real estate market.

The power to issue specific instructions is based, in the case of the bandit, on his superior armament and his willingness to use it. His threat of violence enables him to establish a relationship of authority over his victim. Other threats may serve in other circumstances, for instance, a large firm may order a small competitor to sell his business, *or else*. Here the power to issue an order rests on the superior resources of the large firm, which can ruin the small firm by price-cutting.

In the other examples mentioned, however, the specific instruction is issued by an authority constituted through an organization; and this may be regarded as the more normal type of extra-market operation within this class. The greatest of all organizations is, of course, the state; but less important organizations may have considerable powers over their members. Political parties, trade associations, religious organizations and labor unions are examples. But a similar relationship of authority may exist as a result of agreements between businessmen or financial relationships between firms and their customers. When one economic unit is heavily indebted to another, it is likely to receive instructions from it. This even happens in cases where one unit – say, a large processing works – is the only market for the produce of other units. These relationships of authority are similar to those that exist when individual units are bound by the rules of an organization.

The only distinction between class 2 and class 4 is that a specific instruction applies to a single occasion, whereas a general rule requires a definite form of behavior whenever the prescribed conditions are present. Apart from this there is no reason for considering separately the techniques of establishing an organization to issue instructions and one to enforce general rules. The problems which are common to both types of extra-market operations will be considered below under class 4.

3. Informal influence of one unit over another may have results similar to specific instructions, leading to the circumvention of the market, alteration of the data, or a modification of the principles of behavior. This is most clearly seen in the case of a parade

of force which, even in the absence of any overt threats or instructions, may induce the weaker unit to anticipate the wishes of the stronger, whatever they involve in terms of the three intermediate objectives distinguished above. But our second example, namely, pressure for quick decisions, is designed rather to modify the principles of behavior, making it less rational because there is not sufficient time to weigh all relevant considerations. An appeal to sentiment is usually directed to a similar objective.

Control of relevant information, including the spreading of false rumors, does not alter the fundamental conditions of the market, but it does alter the data available to the economic unit which it is intended to influence. From the viewpoint of the market conditions as a whole, the behavior of the economic unit is thereby rendered less 'rational', though this behavior may not be less rational in relation to the information at its disposal.

This class may also provide a convenient receptacle for cases where advice is offered by one individual to another, which is sometimes a profitable extra-market operation for the one that gives the advice. But it is introduced for the sake of completeness rather than for its probable importance in practice. Perhaps its chief interest from the theoretical viewpoint is that there are some market operations, such as advertising, which almost qualify for inclusion here. We have followed the convention of treating advertising as a market operation, because it is taken into account, more or less, in market theory. It is however, a favored method of achieving influence over the behavior of other economic units and might be regarded as being a borderline case between market and extra-market operations.

4. The establishment (or modification) of general rules is probably the largest of our four classes of extra-market operations and has come to be of particular interest with the growth of state 'intervention' in economic affairs. But it covers much more than attempts to influence legislation, as can be seen from the two subclasses which we have distinguished. General rules might also include personal habits; but these may be ignored, since they can rarely be altered by other economic units, except through social pressure.

Any of the intermediate objectives of extra-market operations may be gained through the application of rules. For instance, rules requiring the payment of taxes or contributions to other organizations or even charitable gifts achieve a transfer of wealth without any recourse to the market. Rules establishing import restrictions or the conditions on which capital may be borrowed or commodities which cannot be sold to the public or the legal hours of work or patent rights all determine in some degree the data of the market. Finally, rules may influence principles of behavior in the market: the one-price system as against higgling and price differentiation, hard bargaining as against 'economic chivalry' (Pigou, 1923, p. 323), maximization of profit as against regularity of operation.

Organizations as instruments

It is in this fourth class of extra-market operations that the study of technique will most repay the economist. Consider, first, the wide range of rules which can be enforced by organizations of all sorts, from the state down, and even by organizations extending beyond the state, such as international cartels. Since these organizations also provide the authority for a large number of specific directions, the study of their growth and functioning is particularly important in relation to extra-market operations.

As far as the state is concerned, the field is already occupied by the sciences of law, politics and administration; and the economist must draw upon them. But much of the ground must be worked over again, before the extra-market operations can be disentangled from other extra-market activities that are stimulated by another set of motives, for, despite Veblen's dictum that 'representative government means, chiefly, representation of business interests' (Veblen, 1940, p. 286), students of government have been chiefly concerned with forms and administration rather than with the technique by which businessmen may manipulate governments. And so with the study of law. It is said that 'one cannot examine nineteenth-century legislation without perceiving that organized pressure from groups having a common economic interest is the sole explanation of many things upon the statute book' (Pound, 1930, p. 113). Nevertheless, jurists do not generally envisage law as an instrument for the pursuit of business interests but as a system of social control. It is interesting to notice that the view of law favored by Dean Pound has much in common with the 'scarcity' definition of economics. 'The legal order . . . may well be thought of as a task or as a great series of tasks of social engineering; as an elimination of friction and precluding of waste, so far as possible, in the satisfaction of infinite human desires out of a relatively finite store of the material goods of existence' (Pound, 1930, p. 156). But extra-market operations to change or apply the law in the interests of a single economic unit might better be described as 'private engineering'. It is not the business of the economist to re-write jurisprudence. But, if the jurist does not provide the type of analysis needed for the study of these extra-market operations, the economist must also study the processes by which the legal order is modified, as well as those by which it affects or circumvents the market. Dr Odegard's study of the Anti-Saloon League illustrates the type of examination which might be undertaken on a larger scale, in connection with political movements more closely related to ordinary business objectives (Odegard, 1928).[2]

The sciences of law and government concentrate their attention upon the supreme organization, the state. But similar problems arise within all other formally constituted organizations, however small, which impose obligations on their members to obey general rules or explicit instructions. Sometimes the state itself supervises the exercise of authority within these organizations, such as restricting the demands made by a trade organization if they involve 'restraint of trade' or supporting the organization in disciplining its members, as in German cartel law. But there is a wide range of methods and activities in which the state, at least in democratic countries, takes no interest. By grouping different organizations under more or less homogeneous types, such as labor unions and trade associations, some general principles may be discovered regarding the methods of establishment, discipline, and choice of policy of each type.[3] But the range of variation between individual organizations is considerable.

It is particularly difficult to discern any uniformity in those organizations which are constituted by the direct relationships between one unit and another, such as banker and customer, factory and supplier of raw materials, employer and employee.

2. I have not yet had an opportunity to examine Clark (1939).
3. This has been attempted by many writers on labor unions.

For some purposes these organizations must be considered as single units in themselves, and we are not concerned with their *internal* relationships when they are acting as units. But, when an employer instructs his employees how to vote, he is dealing with them not as parts of his productive unit but as other economic units covered by his organization; and this is regarded as an extra-market operation. Similarly, if a bank requires a customer to employ non-union labor, this is a rule imposed by one economic unit upon another. The theory of extra-market operations can do little more than warn the economist not to ignore the possibility of such forms of behavior; there is little point in trying to formulate precise generalizations about them.

Social norms as instruments

Equally important in the control of human behavior are those less formal rules which rest upon social approval or disapproval and may never be promulgated by an overt organization. At present our knowledge of the origin and development of such codes and the extent to which they can be altered by policy is but fragmentary, especially as their patterns are by no means clearly established.

Attempts are made, of course, to control these codes through ethical teaching in the home, in school and in church; and the possibility arises that such teaching may be indirectly influenced by private or sectional interests. A Canadian historian has observed that in a period of rapid economic development in Canada, when the traditional mores were breaking down, 'religious denominations tended to act as a conservative force. In promoting the good, they were preserving the traditional. Thus, apart from financial considerations, their interests tended to become identified with the economically sheltered groups in the community.' (Clark, 1940, p. 212). But it is apparent that this type of extra-market operation does not, as a rule, promise results comparable with those that can be achieved through a change in the rules of a powerful organization.

Reviewing the various types of extra-market operations covered by our classification, the most important would appear to be specific instructions and rules, imposed by authority in a legally constituted organization. But, if there is little restriction upon the use of violence, this may be a highly 'productive' type of extra-market operation; and even an apparently peaceful community may give scope for the use of threats to back specific instructions. The choice of extra-market operations, however, does not depend upon their promised results alone. Account must also be taken of the limits of practicability, social controls, and other obstacles to action. These factors will now engage our attention. [. . .]

Social controls

There are strong deterrents to certain types of extra-market operations, which require consideration. Were it not for the obstacles which organized society places in the way of certain extra-market operations, the market itself would not be sufficiently developed to be a worthy object of study. In particular, the use of violence and threats must be strictly controlled if buying and selling are to be conducted in peace; and the history of market activities shows them growing up under the shadow of the church, the town and the state, as those authorities established some sort of law and order. On the other hand, the market cannot survive if a continued struggle for control of the state absorbs the energy of sectional groups, each desiring to use the authority of the state to circumvent the market or to alter its functioning. Similarly, a market requires for its proper functioning some restraints upon those 'doubtful' practices which benefit the few so long as they do not become general.

It would be false to view the legal and other controls upon extra-market operations as measures designed purely for the defence of the market. Business interests are not the only ones that may be damaged by the prevalence of violence, and few political theorists have sought a complete explanation of the state in men's desire to trade with one another. Nevertheless, confidence in the market as an institution and satisfaction with its results on the part of those who are successful are the natural allies of any system designed to limit the scope for violence and other practices which can be made to serve as extra-market operations.

The state is the supreme organization, but not the only one, which imposes controls upon extra-market operations. It is convenient to distinguish four types of rules which prevent or, on the other hand, favor recourse to particular extra-market operations:

(a) laws enforced by the state; (b) rules of other formal organizations, such as labor unions and trade associations; (c) the moral code endorsed by religious doctrines and taught by religious organizations; and (d) the social codes enforced by group approval and disapproval. The importance of laws enforced by the state is apparent from the history of labor unions; the right to combine has at different times been expressly forbidden and expressly guaranteed, and the same is true of certain union practices. Enforcement of laws is, of course, the important thing, not their enactment. This is abundantly illustrated by the attempts to control or prevent monopolies by legislation (see Hamilton, 1941a). The moral code endorsed by religion and the social codes enforced by group pressure help to determine the attitude toward violence, established property, coercion and fraud.

All these controls vary from place to place and from time to time. For instance, it is said (in Melbourne) that business morality is far 'lower' in Sydney than in other Australian cities. One finds, too, significant differences in the attitude of different churches to economic legislation. And the rules of the state and other organizations are subject to continuous revision in any country and vary from place to place. We have already raised the question of extra-market operations designed to modify these controls, as distinct operations designed to evade or alter the working of the market directly. We also find a parallel in the case of certain market activities which are designed not to maximize the immediate results obtainable in the market but to produce changes in the data, so that better results can be obtained in the future. In attempting to predict the extra-market operations which will be undertaken in given circumstances, we must take account, therefore, not only of the canalizing effect of the various rules which are effective in the time and place under consideration, but also of the possibility that economic units may be dissatisfied with existing rules (as well as with the market) and seek to alter them through extra-market activities. [. . .]

Conclusion

This completes our review of the many factors which may influence the extent and form of market operations. It does not provide a set of simple propositions formulated as general laws or a series of two-dimensional diagrams. Those who think that theories must be of that form may contest our claim to have presented, in outline, a theory of extra-market operations. But the simplicity of a theory and the possibility of setting it out as a few general laws depend upon the degree of abstraction, as well as upon the complexities of the real world. Economic theory of the usual type can be presented as a few simple laws only as long as it is confined to a very high level of abstraction. As soon as we begin to make the categories substantial instead of formal, even market theory becomes primarily a classification of the various factors which may operate in a concrete case.

It would not be impossible to construct a formal theory of extra-market operations, consisting of a few simple propositions, by abstracting from most of the complications reviewed in this chapter. For instance, we might construct a theory of the acquisition of goods by violence, as though that were the sole type of behavior. Any such theory, however, would be so remote from reality as to seem a mere caricature. We have chosen, therefore, to expound a theory at a somewhat lower level of abstraction, even though this involves giving the impression of a catalogue of possibilities rather than a simple model of a single process. And we have not depicted in any detail the actual mechanisms associated with each of the possible factors in extra-market operations, because these mechanisms are likely to vary so much according to time and place. [. . .]

The economic unit is confronted with the choice of several lines of conduct, according to the actual conditions. Some of these lines of conduct are those covered by the theory of the market and the others by the theory of extra-market operations. The two theories together cover the range of possibilities which are open in the specific instance under consideration; and the final decision will turn on their relative productivity, subject to the social controls already distinguished and the degree of rationality. By weighting all these elements in the situation, the economist can effect a synthesis of the two theories as applied to the particular case and attempt to judge which line of behavior is the most probable in the circumstances. Whether the quality of his judgement will be, on the whole, better after this procedure than if he took the findings of market theory alone and corrected them by the exercise of his unaided common sense must be tested by experience. At least the foregoing discussion suggests that the test is worth making.

References

BERNAL, J. D. (1939), *Social functions of Science*, Routledge & Kegan Paul.

BLAISDELL, D. C. (1941), 'Economic power and political pressures', *Temporary National Economic Committee Monographs*, no. 26.

CLARK, S. D. (1939), *The Canadian Manufacturers' Association: A Study in Political Pressure and Collective Bargaining*, University of Toronto Press.

CLARK, S. D. (1940), 'Economic expansion and the moral order', *Canad. J. econ. and polit. Sci.*, vol. 6, no. 2, pp. 203–25.

DANIELIAN, N. R. (1939), *American Telephone and Telegraph: The Story of Industrial Conquest*, Vanguard.

HAMILTON, W. H. (1941a), 'Anti-trust in action', *Temporary National Economic Committee Monographs*, no. 16.

HAMILTON, W. H. (1941b), 'Patents and free enterprise', *Temporary National Economic Committee Monographs*, no. 31.

HERRING, E. P. (1936), *Public Administration and the Public Interest*, Russell.

JENNINGS, W. I. (1940), *Parliament*, Cambridge University Press.

LOGAN, E. B. (1929), 'Lobbying', supplement to *Annals of American Academy of Political and Social Science*.

MARSHALL, A. (1920), *Industry and Trade*, Macmillan Co.

ODEGARD, P. H. (1928), *Pressure Politics*, Octagon Books.

PIGOU, A. C. (ed.) (1923), *Memorials of Alfred Marshall*, Kelley.

POUND, R. (1930), *Interpretations of Legal History*, Peter Smith.

REYNOLDS, L. G. (1940), *The Control of Competition in Canada*, Harvard University Press.

ROBBINS, L. (1937), *Essay on the Nature and Significance of Economic Science*, Macmillan Co., 2nd edn, first published 1935.

SCHUMPETER, J. H. (1934), *Theory of Economic Development*, Harvard University Press.

SCHUMPETER, J. H. (1939), *Business Cycles*, McGraw-Hill.

VEBLEN, T. (1930), *The Place of Science in Modern Civilisation*, Russell.

VEBLEN, T. (1940), *The Theory of Business Enterprise*, Kelley.

WELLS, H. G. (1932), *The Work, Wealth and Happiness of Mankind*, Heinemann.

3 F. Perroux

The Domination Effect and Modern Economic Theory[1]

F. Perroux, 'The domination effect and modern economic theory',
Social Research, vol. 17, 1950, pp. 188–206.

Economic life is something different from a network of exchange.
It is, rather, a network of forces. The economy is guided not only
by the search for gain, but also by that for power. The two motives
are seen to be intermingled in the policy of a firm or of a national
economy as soon as one asks for what period is the gain to be
maximized: the most prosperous undertakings are not those
which economize on candle ends and run off with the profits at
the end of the week.

There is nothing in this situation that the practical economist
does not know. Yet most academic economists develop their
analyses and present their recommendations as if they preferred
to ignore these facts. It seems to me possible to find an interpretation that is a little closer to reality yet imposes no disavowal
on our discipline. In order to express it I have constructed a tool
of analysis, which I hope may be regarded as the first of a series.
I call it, for lack of a better name, the *domination effect*.

Between any two economic units, A and B, the domination
effect is present when, in a definite field, unit A exercises on unit
B an irreversible or partially irreversible influence. The domination effect is the species of a genus: the asymmetries, which have
been little and poorly studied because they imperil the harmonious
and fragile logical edifice of general equilibrium.

For example, a business firm in many cases influences decisions

1. I wish to thank Mr Y. Mainguy, Director of the London branch of
the Institute of Applied Economic Sciences (Paris), Mr G. Rottier, Assistant
to the Director, and Mrs Margaret Copp, Technical Secretary, who
assumed jointly the task of translating this paper into English. To my
colleagues, Dr Eduard Heimann and Dr Felicia Deyrup, I am also indebted
for criticism and aid.

concerning price and quantity made by another firm, client or competitor, the inverse not being true or not to the same degree. Or an economic sector engenders a lowering or raising of costs and prices in another sector from which it does not receive influences comparable in breadth or intensity. Or one nation imposes on another goods or services or a general pattern of institutions of production and exchange. Such situations have been a persistent feature of the whole of economic history, yet while volumes have been written on the collaboration between equals through free exchange, virtually no attention has been devoted to the conditions and consequences of inequality.

The domination effect cannot be described purely and simply as either a difference in size or as a monopolistic regime. An economic unit exerting this effect does so through the combination of three elements: its relative dimensions, that is to say, the magnitude of its role in global supply and demand; its bargaining power, which is the power it can apply to fixing the conditions of exchange; and its place in the whole scheme or the nature of its operations. For a firm, as for a nation, these diverse elements do not amount to the same thing. The largest unit is not necessarily that which has the greatest bargaining power. If size and bargaining power are equal, the unit situated in a zone which is strategic for reasons relating to structure and combination of circumstances will prevail.

It is my aim in the following pages to show by establishing five fundamental propositions that the analysis of the domination effect is indispensable for (1) defining competition, (2) interpreting the life of the firm, (3) understanding the intermediary agencies of price determination, (4) understanding international trade, and (5) going beyond the inadequate model of Paretian equilibrium.

The working of competition cannot be defined except with reference to the domination effect

Though the books on competition would fill a library, and every elementary course in political economy produces its own definition, it is quite true, as J. M. Clark has recently stated, that we have neither a good idea nor a good theory of competition (1948,

p. 68). The situation appears paradoxical only to those who have not measured the endless difficulties of the usually admitted position.

In the literature devoted to competition we meet first the studies describing its modalities. Their inspiration is historical, sociological or juridical. They trace the different forms of competitive bargaining, from cut throat competition to the lowering of prices made possible by greater efficiency in production or improvement of the product, after mentioning in passing the use of influence and financial participation in the business wherein one must get collaboration or neutralize hostility. According to the season and necessity, the jurists and lawyers revise their categories of legal and illegal, fair and unfair, competition.

Another small group of studies directs attention mainly to what I propose to call *fundamental* competition. Whatever the form of economic organization and the social regime, individuals and firms are moved by the desire to better their lot; they display egotistical initiative and are capable of emulation. This competition, which has its roots in the more permanent human tendencies may change its direction and form, but it is doubtful whether it can ever be suppressed or nullified. Should fundamental competition ever become a subject for intensive research, the comparative sociology of the various types of economies would undoubtedly profit thereby.

A third group of expositions properly belongs to economists, who study competition in relation to prices and quantities. Economic science builds models of price determination. Price determination is considered complete as soon as competition is fairly strictly defined. It is so, under certain well-known conditions: if goods and services exchanged are homogeneous and perfectly and indefinitely divisible; if they move without resistance or friction within one industry or from one industry to another, under the influence of an alteration in the level of their remuneration – in other words, if they are fluid; and concretely, if labor, capital and consumers, in an economic space, move to the point where their economic advantage is maximized, meeting nothing that hinders or halts them. Thanks to these 'simplifications', a determinate price may be obtained, but it is one that can be achieved only in a static or stationary world.

Once such a world is rigorously constructed, it becomes impossible to transcend it. An economy that functions as a circular flow comes under no endogenous influence that could displace or deform its flow of goods and money. Under such a regime or the kindred regime of a quasi-stationary flow, where progressive modifications are possible in the sense that each of them can be absorbed without much trouble, the calculations of producers and consumers are marginal and the possible adaptations are marginal. The structures of the economic plans remain comparable in their main lines from one period to another, with only slight modifications in the margin of quantities whose arrangement constitutes the plans. In this model, competition shows none of the most characteristic stages, results, or links which are evident in the actual and dynamic world.

Actually, adaptations to changes in prices and costs take place in a universe where goods and services are not homogeneous, where indivisibility derives from numerous psychological, technical and institutional causes, and where viscosities hinder the movement of all factors and products. Important changes are wrought by entrepreneurs who take a chance on a new structure. These entrepreneurs anticipate *en bloc* a real demand which previously existed only in the form of potential demand; they bring to life desires which yesterday were latent and are today effective, because they have found the consumption good, the durable good, the production good or process for which people were dimly hoping. If these entrepreneurs manage to get the additional money or quasi-money (bank balances) which they need from the market, they upset the customary structure of production by attracting into the zone of their activity, labor and capital for which they can pay more than their less lively opponents. Unless these entrepreneurs have seriously miscalculated, they are the prime movers in the increase of real income, the improvement of quality, and the satisfaction of the requirements of diversity and variety. The exceptional profits which they collect then decline and eventually disappear under pressure from imitators and exhaustion of the new demand.

It is clear that these dynamic entrepreneurs exert more influence on the market than they receive from it. They do not treat the consumer as one equal treats another; they suggest to him or impose on him what he will be pleased to consume. They are not collaborators of unaggressive or static entrepreneurs; indeed, they deprive such entrepreneurs of their economic resources in order to achieve their own ends. They do not adapt themselves to the trends of their environment, but exercise an offensive strategy in the same or an opposite direction. They can truly be said to fix prices to the extent to which the new good which they produce, by cutting across the system of customary prices, modifies the general price level or the structure of its relative scales. To put into effect the economic innovation, as Joseph Schumpeter called it, the entrepreneur must exercise a domination effect on competitive enterprise, on the consumer and often also on the bank and the state.

There is nothing automatic or mechanical about the selection that takes place in actual dynamic competition. It does not exhaust itself in adjusting quantities; it can be understood only with reference to human decisions, that is, choices made by certain men that concern other men. Actual dynamic competition can be understood only by precise reference to a characteristic type of decision, the decision of the innovator. It cannot be studied without recourse to the domination effect which, though economically favorable to the whole society, must be won by a hard fight and maintained by unceasing effort. Competition that engenders economic progress does not occur between equal opponents; its field and its role presuppose inequality. Had we heeded the lessons of experience, we should long ago have understood that the evolution of capitalism can only be described around the central figure of the dynamic entrepreneur, who exercises innovation and domination effects at one and the same time.

The evolution of capitalism cannot be interpreted without an analysis of the dominant firm

In any period of history whatever, every industry and each branch of activity has firms that are dominant by reason of their size, their bargaining power, or the nature of their operations. Should the historian wish to renew his researches in this light, he would find much to add to what earlier monographs have said about firms or groups of firms. The economist need not assume the burden of the historian; his role is to elucidate the chain of cumulative effects whereby a firm is enabled to gain a position of dominance, once it has won an initial advantage or preferential position by a quick adaptation to the market. It is then in a position to pay the factors of production a higher price than kindred or analogous firms and possibly a price lower than their marginal productivity. It can sell the product at a figure above cost. It can proceed to an integration which gives it a certain independence with respect to the market for factors of production and credit. These links being present, the firm can buy less from outside sources in terms of quantity and value, and sell a greater quantity at a higher price. Its *terms of trade* become favorable and can be improved by conscious effort on its part. This linking of various aspects of the growth of a firm will never be revealed by considering the equilibrium or successive equilibriums of a firm of given structure.

The dominant firm which benefits from a surplus employs the mass of its undistributed profits as a strategic weapon to reinforce its position of dominance. A surplus allows a firm to shift the demand curve for its product, that is to say, to increase by means of sales and promotion policy the demand which it enjoys. By such methods the firm can alter, for its own benefit, the structure of competitive or allied firms by exerting influences that range from the simple act of observing to what can properly be called control. The sums of monetary capital which constitute the surplus of the dominant firm are handled according to aims and procedures about which classical economists have said almost nothing and which are more closely related to the art of war or belligerent sport than to the theory of contracts between parties equal or roughly equal in an environment of free exchange.

The same aspects of the situation are revealed by quite another approach. Inquiry into the area of the effectiveness which an entrepreneur's action exercises on economic quantities establishes that this activity occurs first in a *zone of free disposal*, which contains the quantities and prices of which the head of the firm is master; he chooses them and combines them to his taste. Second, it occurs in relation to a *plastic environment* formed from quantities and prices which the head of the firm can partially modify if he so wishes. And finally this action runs into a *parametrical environment*, formed from quantities and prices and institutions which the head of the firm must accept, whatever they are, without hope of transforming them. The practical economist who decides to undertake nothing that he cannot achieve makes on his own account (and more or less exactly) the distinctions which have just been suggested. The dominant firm enlarges the zone of plastic environment to its own advantage. Neighboring and competitive firms are influenced by its action and sometimes even the rules of the game imposed by the government are modified as a result of its pressure.

A glance at the history of capitalism confirms the relevance of this interpretation. At the dawn of modern economy, the great commercial firm developed through and for power as much as, if not more than, through and for gain. The firm used its surplus to obtain from benevolent and colluding public authorities the rules of the game most favorable to it, to make all possible use of insufficient and scarce transport, to coordinate, absorb and subordinate handicraft or small and medium-sized businesses. When it first started action the market had still to be created. The dominant firms and groups of dominant firms supported by the dominating power of the state then wove a network of forces wherein were formed the institutions which were generally molded and made flexible, until one could speak not too unreasonably of a network of free exchanges.

In contemporary capitalism, for large sectors the influence and role of the dominant firm are not subdued. The financial surplus of this firm gives it considerable freedom to maneuver with regard to its competitors, its customers, and even the state. It renders the firm relatively independent of the market for capital and for materials. Consumers react in a scattered way and the formula of consumer sovereignty becomes a mockery. At the same time the liberty of the buyer remains appreciably greater than if he were held in the vice of a dictatorial plan; he is largely safeguarded by disagreement and conflict among the 'great' even though these great do not derive their power from the multitude except very indirectly.

The forms of monopoly can be usefully regrouped from the point of view of the domination effect

Pure and complete competition is unreal. It leads directly to the model of a stationary economy. If we relax the rigor of the conditions which define it, if we take certain liberties with the abstract assumptions underlying it, we can define a regime of workable competition which is nearer the actual forms of competition. In a real market, approximately competitive, the price is but roughly determined. The indetermination proceeds from many causes: the abilities of the parties to the calculations are of unequal precision and breadth; the parties have not the same capacity to evaluate and accept risk; and they start with unequal weapons in the debate whereby they strive to make the opponent agree to the maximum concessions.

The cattle markets of our village yield, in this respect, valuable indications. The earlier Austrians, particularly Böhm-Bawerk, made no mistake about this. Those who jeer at the 'metaphysical horses' dear to the great founders of the Vienna School succeed only in revealing their own poor capacity for investigation. The premathematical forms of exchange and price analysis had the virtue of avoiding any portrayal of economic life as a mechanical adjustment of quantities: they took it for what it actually was, a set of decisions and plans, elaborated by men and altered by colloquies of a dialectical nature. The earlier economists acknowledged bargaining, and consequently the working of the domination effect in a competitive price formation. Their thinking was much closer to the most recent interpretations of strategy than are the mechanisitic models of equilibrium.

Workable competition does not exclude some differences of size, bargaining power and kind of operations. In other words, the constituents of the domination effect are not excluded. With differences of degree only, these constituents are found in all forms of monopoly.

The monopolist of supply offers the price and the quantity which, considered together, yield maximum return. His pretension is limited only by the elasticity of demand. Asymmetry and irreversibility are obvious. The monopolist commands supply which is not, with regard to its size and quality, submitted to the consumer's decision. If the monopolist raises around his industry such barriers that newcomers are kept away, he exerts a domination effect on his potential competitors. Monopoly price is determined in a sense quite different from that of the determination of competitive price. Since, by definition, the monopolist commands supply, external pressures do not act on the side of supply to draw the price to a determinate level. Since the decisions of a monopolist are actually dynamic, he may choose to reduce his earnings in one period in order to increase them during the next. Thus, his price depends on the strategy he chooses.

In the case of bilateral monopoly, it can be taken as demonstrated that price is determined only if the bargaining powers of the two parties are equal, or if, from the start of the discussion in which the terms of the bargain are fixed, the inequality of powers is given and remains constant till the end. Such cases are of the greatest rarity. In all other cases, the domination effect is obvious: the terms of the bargain are fixed on a point which is not that of equal concessions. In bilateral monopoly, price is determined – when it is determined – by equality between the bargaining powers of the parties, not by the pressure of a large number of decisions on the part of scattered suppliers and consumers. This kind of determination is again quite different from those described above. If the state makes the bargaining powers of the parties less unequal, it makes the determination of the price more certain, but only by employing a strategy rather difficult to define and execute.

Where there is an oligopoly, price is most generally fixed by one or another of the following four strategies: elimination (one party aims to put others out of the market); influence (one party attempts to alter the others' decisions on price and output); adaptation (one party takes for granted and as unalterable the others' decisions and endeavors to adjust his own decisions to them); agreement (the parties decide to cease fighting and to settle their particular policies by common agreement, in order to get the maximum benefits of joint action).

In most cases, the domination effect, understood as the irreversibility of the influence of one firm on another or others, is present. If the price is to be determined, there must be either an exceptional set of chance circumstances, or a more or less exact equality of forces.

In the case of competition with product differentiation, it is also possible to spot the domination effect: a firm can capture the sales or part of the sales of a rival firm by undertaking to incur selling and advertising costs.

Actually, one does not meet any of these types in their pure forms. They are intermixed, and their tangling opens a wide area to the domination effect.

The result of this realistic interpretation of market structure is that it is impossible, in the modern economy, to think of the network of exchange as independent of a network of forces. Pure exchange appears as a limiting case; any actual exchange involves a struggle between private influences and the public power, the state being bound by nature and by right to arbitrate in the public interest, that is, to limit and guide the struggle in an effort to achieve the best result. A democratic state can act only with shrewd strategy, holding coercion in reserve as long as possible. It will manipulate public opinion, and resort to threats and pressures and monetary expenditures in order to avoid a show of force.

Contemporary market structures impose on the state two attitudes which, under a parliamentary regime, it does not like either to avow frankly or to define precisely. It must, on the one hand, acknowledge the existence of intermediate economic bodies. On the other hand, it is bound to arbitrate the disputes between these bodies through a higher power than that of the parties, and in the name of an ideal which is not, or does not seem to be, born of a class or a coalition. The day the parliamentary state acknowledges that it is subject to these exigencies, it will be tantamount to saying, however unpalatable the terminology, that corporativism contains a kernel of truth.

If, in its own sphere, the state does not exert on economic life more influence than it is subject to, it faces the threat of spreading instability, waste, and indetermination. The right exercise of the domination effect by the state is an indispensable corrective in an economic world where the domination effect operates between private firms and bodies.

Deliberate disregard of the domination effect prevents one from seeing the major difficulty in the transformations of capitalism and of the modern state. Dominant units prefer not to hear about domination effect. They would go on exerting their one-sided influence to their own advantage, if no one doubted that the economy works through an automatic price system and a spontaneous equilibrium of markets. Indeed, the explanations put forth by some adherents of *laissez faire* are really excuses and must be regarded as no more than clever ways of domination.

The concept of the dominant economy elucidates the play of international trade [2]

The foregoing analysis finds its best application in the field of international trade. It is generally accepted that external economic relations do not follow the rules of pure competition, in fact, not even the rules of workable competition. Such terms as 'dominant economies' and 'key countries' are in common enough use. Many economists, however, do not accept the implications of these terms, and persist in describing the international exchange of goods, services, and capital as taking place in a world of perfect competition and free prices. The moral and scholarly level of these writers precludes any suggestion that they are the conscious perpetrators of an intellectual trick and a social fraud. They are nevertheless unintentionally fostering a misunderstanding which their talents equip them to clarify. It is relatively easy to consider nations equal within the covers of a textbook. But one has to acknowledge their great inequalities when the job at hand is to establish the voting rules of an international body, or set up an organization for the equalization of exchange rates and the distribution of investment, or to determine the content and limits of the global responsibilities of the major partners in relation to their own internal policies.

The protracted use of unsuitable analytical tools is due to a faulty concept of the nation in the economic sphere. All the efforts of an earlier liberalism tended to demonstrate that there was no such thing as overall supply and demand from the United States, England and France, but only individual supplies and demands from Americans, English and French. This was perhaps an inevitable reaction to the oversimplification of mercantilism and the lust and greed of governments. But it concealed certain important aspects of reality which the facts have compelled us to

2. See my paper (Perroux, 1948).

discover anew. A national economy is essentially a group of groups, coordinated by the state, monopolist of public coercion. It has been so since the birth of modern nations, and is still so, unchanged by the practices of democracy. The relations between national economies, as well as the relations between economic units inside the nation, can therefore be correctly interpreted only if we are fully aware of the interrelations that exist between a network of free exchanges and a network of unequal forces.

The economic evolution of the world has resulted from a succession of dominant economies, each in turn taking the lead in international activity and influence. From 1815 to 1848, western Europe played the leading role because it had a monopoly of science and a 'monopoly of power'. Throughout the nineteenth century the British economy was the dominant economy in the world. From the seventies on, Germany was dominant in respect to certain other Continental countries and in certain specified fields. In the twentieth century, the United States economy has clearly been and still is the internationally dominant economy. There is no need to justify the choice of this example to elucidate the analysis of the domination effect, but it is important first to clarify one point.

The notion of dominant economy is so rich and expressive that it covers widely different experiences and realities. In many cases, the dominant economy exerts its characteristic irreversible and asymmetrical influence mainly by the use of means alien to a market economy (extra-market operations). This type of dominant economy may take any one of the various forms described below:

The occupying economy in its relations with the occupied economy. In this case the domination is deliberate. It emerges in the setting up of institutional rules of operation that put the occupied economy at the service of the war aims of the occupying economy. Germany and Japan, at the time of their first successes, demonstrated how an economy, which an apparent and temporary victory made dominant, used its hold on the economic resources of the subjugated territories through currency manipulation, the molding of institutional structures, and control of public opinion.

The home economy in its relations with the colonial economy.
The home economy exerts a domination effect on the economies which it has conquered and organized. This effect results from the inequalities of power and experience between highly capitalistic firms and closed or non-capitalistic economies. These inequalities make it easier for the home country to impose the rules of the game. The trade between home country and colonies is monopolistic, quasi-monopolistic or regulated. Industrialization of the overseas territory is retarded or promoted according to the interests of the home firms. Labor forces in the dominated economy are employed by methods based on open or concealed coercion. The theory of a colonial or imperial economy, even of the economy of a union, should be entirely reconstructed, assigning to the domination effect that central role which it merits.

The totalitarian economy in its relations with satellite economies.
The policy of the Third Reich in the Danube area offers ample material for study. The planning of external trade and the rigid control of exports and imports by the autarchic state imposes heavy burdens on the national populations affected. Such measures lend efficacy to the distinction between two sectors – essential and non-essential goods – whereby the autarchy, closed to the outside world, paves the way for its expansion. The partial vassalization of economies essential to the dominant economy is often effected by means of unbalanced clearings. International payments follow the channels of bilateral agreements negotiated by the leading economy with each of the satellite economies. The debtor position of the dominant economy allows it to exert an insistent pressure on the vassalized economies, to make them accept imports of such a nature and in such quantity as to be fully in accord with the interest of the leading partner. Once it has won the war, the leading economy can shape the economies of minor allies or defeated adversaries in conformity with its own expansion pattern by methods more like the usual technique of exchange and marketing.

The action of the Soviet Union in the territories under its control proceeds from an ideology different from that of National Socialism but still related to the domination effect. Satellite economies, accepting the gospel of 'popular democracy', set up and enforce dictatorial planning. This planning breaks down the economic and social structures at variance with those developed by the Soviet economy and eliminates social classes undesirable for a collectivist regime. It then tends to get coordinated with the plans of the dominant economy. In so far as it works, this long process of adjustment results in a system of production and exchange widely different from that which is the outcome of a supranational collaboration of economies still following, at least in part, the rules of a market economy.

The above types of dominant economies are cited only by way of contrast with the type to be considered in greater detail – that is, the dominant economy which exerts its domination effect through operations compatible with the logic of the firm, of the price system in a regime of workable competition, and of the market considered as a network of exchange between relatively independent centers of calculation. In this set-up the state is supposed not to aim at extending its power, but at increasing the welfare of the people. Governments and firms pay attention to prices and quantities, and try to obtain the largest quantity of goods and services at the lowest cost (or to sell the largest quantity at the highest prices). They strive to maximize their economic advantage, considered in terms of goods in trade.

Even under these conditions and subject to these reservations, there have been national economies throughout the history of modern capitalism which have exerted a domination effect on groups of other countries with regard to a given good or several groups of goods. When a national economy, owing to its general configuration, the character of the government and of its firms and groups of firms, exerts in a special way asymmetrical and irreversible influences, it is suitable to call it the dominant economy. This is convenient, though not wholly accurate, for domination effects are met in every quarter of international life.

It is easy to point out the three main constituents of the domination effect (bargaining power and size and nature of activities) in the economy of the United States. The picture, however, can be elaborated. In particular, it is proper to distinguish between economic causes of the domination effect and the historical circumstances extending and intensifying it. But here as elsewhere, it is more essential to understand function than to describe structure. Any internationally dominant economy is a relatively autonomous center of economic development. It exerts more influence on whole groups of countries than it receives.

This fact was clearly evident during the Great Depression. In the course of a few years, the supply of dollars in the world market dropped by 63 per cent (75 per cent, if we take into account dollar obligations of debtor countries), with a resultant paralysis of the mechanism of international payments. Currently, the adjustment of foreign balances with the United States suffers from the inelasticity of reciprocal demand, and will continue to do so for an indefinite future. In other words, the income and price elasticity of the American demand for imports from the rest of the world and the income and price elasticity of the demand of the rest of the world for imports from the United States are such that the disequilibrium of trade balances is persistent and the devaluations of European currencies of doubtful efficacy. It is probable that there will be some adjustment between these elasticities in the long run. But a more or less balanced trade will not be possible until the dominant economy, having grown fully conscious of its responsibilities, pursues a deliberate policy directed toward the development of imports and of international investment.

The responsibilities of the United States are clear, for her economy is subject to three kinds of instability which tend to spread throughout the world. First, it works through huge investments, thanks to a series of big businesses, typical of certain sectors. It is thus especially sensitive to cyclical disturbances. Second, it is the center of a wide and strong speculative market, the fluctuations of which are reflected in entrepreneurial and consumer expectations. Lastly, although the United States is still the motherland of dynamic businessmen and of a widespread spirit of enterprise, it suffers from the constant criticism of capitalism, for it is being subjected to attack at the very time when it finds itself with no new frontiers and without the resources of a mass immigration. Without accepting Alvin Hansen's stagnationist thesis, we can see that some grounds exist for believing that the confidence in the logic and in the actual functioning of capitalism is no longer intact and unshaken.

The internationally dominant economy is further obligated to bear part of the costs of an international salvage operation, which will protect the essential basis of a free market economy whose disappearance would hinder and reduce the domination effect it exerts.

The model of adjusting dominating and dominated economies gives a more realistic view of the economic life than does the Paretian equilibrium model[3]

The data out of which the Paretian equilibrium is constructed do not result from any deliberate plan of the state: the institutions and the pattern of distribution are regarded as given, and the analyst is not concerned with determination of the implicit domination effects allowed by these institutions and this distribution for the profit of certain social groups as opposed to others. In such a theoretical system, the choices are made by a large number of units, comparable in size and power, whose economic horizons do not overlap and whose economic plans are made compatible by the pricing system. Thus, the domination effect cannot be exerted by any unit toward another or by any group of units toward another.

This scheme, however, is divorced from reality. In actual economic life, economic units and groups of units work out plans that are dominating and dominated with regard to one another. The plans of units which are rendered compatible among themselves and with the plans of the other units by the price system are those of the most passive units; they are mainly the consumers and the small entrepreneurs. Their choices are influenced by the pressure of dominant units: big businesses, business groups, government. These units endeavor to make the plans subordinated to them compatible with each other by the use – confessed or not – of a forgotten economic commodity: coercion.

Let us assume an economic space in the most abstract sense, a set of relations belonging to the economic order. Then let us assume various plans of economic units – P_1, P_2, ... P_n – and that the domination effect is exerted from P_1 to P_n.

If P_1 influences the other plans by selling a larger quantity of a given quality at the same price, or an equal quantity of a better quality at the same price, or an equal quantity of the same quality at a lower price, we have the situation which is closest to economic

3. See my paper (1949).

competition. The domination effect is not left out, but it is exerted through the means most consistent with the free market.

There are, however, three other possible situations where this is not the case: (1) P_1 imposes a quantity on P_2, that is, compels the agent who has drawn up P_2 to modify his calculations of maximization; (2) P_1 imposes on P_2 the maximum and minimum of one of its constituent quantities, which differ from those envisaged by the author of P_2, to the same effect as in the first case; (3) P_1 compels a harmonization of P_2, P_3, ... P_n before they start operations, by eliminating their most obvious incompatibilities.

It is immediately apparent how many concrete cases fall into one or another of these categories, the dominant plan being either the plan of one state with regard to plans of other states, or that of one state with regard to other private groups, or that of a private group with regard to individual units.

The action of P_1 on P_2 ... P_n is kept within limits. In an economy obeying the rule of rationality, the cost of coercion is justified only by its efficiency. Moreover, dominated plans may have their own productive capacity and their bargaining power increased by the influence of the dominating plan. And finally, in any assumption, units which draw up plans that are immediately dominated react by developing strategies of defensive adaptation and strategies of grouping. When one adds that, in a dynamic economy, invention and innovation, either technical, economic, political or social, are always at work, it is evident that the opportunities for shifting, halting or reversing the domination effect are innumerable.

In a scheme of this nature, the partial or overall adjustments seem in any case to be the consequence of a network of forces between unequally powerful partners. In its principle, this scheme appears much closer to the real world than is the Paretian model or even the more perfected schemes based on the same fundamental premises.

The domination effect, far from being a rarity found only after long searching, can be discerned almost anywhere in the relations between individual units and unified groups of production and trade. Competition is not a regime which leaves out economic domination, but one where the domination effect is kept in check, directed, and utilized, with the object of achieving a better economic result.

Liberalism no longer appears as a natural order, but as a rule of the game, broadly defined and usually observed. There is no human society possible where such rules are not established and respected. But the content of the byelaws, the choice of the umpire, the determination of the powers and the regular application of the decisions of this umpire are incomparably more decisive than the spontaneities of equilibrium and the effects of automatisms.

References

CLARK, J. M. (1948), *Alternative to Serfdom*, Blackwell.
PERROUX, F. (1948), 'Esquisse d'une théorie de l'économie dominante' *Économie Appliquée*, vol. 1, no. 2/3, pp. 243–300.
PERROUX, F. (1949), 'Les macrodécisions', *Économie Appliquée*, vol. 2, no. 2/3, pp. 321–54.

Part Two The Concept of Economic Power

To recognize the importance of power in economic relations is just a first step; it does not solve the problem how the influence of power is to be included in the analytical framework. In fact, social and economic power is a multi-dimensional phenomenon which is not easily defined and still less easily measured. The modern theories of strategic games and bargaining have by necessity come up against the problem of power, and the contribution by Harsanyi gives a glimpse of the many aspects which the power concept involves and of the difficulties which would have to be surmounted, if an *accurate* measurement of the strength of power were to be attained.

Harsanyi deals with social power in general. In economic theory proper the problem of power began to creep in when one came up against the market forms of bilateral monopoly (in the commodity sector) and collective bargaining (on the labour market). Pen shows the difficulties and contradictions in which economic theory became involved when it had to deal with these market forms. A solution of these problems requires the explicit recognition of power influences. In doing this Pen discusses the essential characteristics of economic power and its relation to other forms of power.

Some poignant remarks on the concept of economic power are also contained in the contribution by Galbraith (Reading 10).

4 J. Harsanyi

The Dimension and Measurement of Social Power

Excerpts from J. Harsanyi, 'Measurement of social power, opportunity costs and the theory of two-person bargaining games', *Behavioral Science*, vol. 7, 1962, no. 1, pp. 67–80.

Introduction

Recent papers by Simon, by March and by Dahl have suggested measuring person A's power over person B in terms of its actual or potential *effects*, that is, in terms of the changes that A causes or can cause in B's behavior. As Dahl puts it, A has power over B to the extent to which 'he can get B to do something that B would not otherwise do'.

As Simon and March have obtained very similar results, I shall restrict myself largely to summarizing Dahl's main conclusions. Dahl distinguishes the following constituents of the power relation:

1. The *base* of power, i.e. the resources (economic assets, constitutional prerogatives, military forces, popular prestige, etc.) that A can use to influence B's behavior.

2. The *means* of power, i.e. the specific actions (promises, threats, public appeals, etc.) by which A can make actual use of these resources to influence B's behavior.

3. The *scope* of power, i.e. the set of specific actions that A, by using his means of power, can get B to perform.

4. The *amount* of power, i.e. the net increase in the probability of B's actually performing some specific action X, due to A's using his means of power against B.

If A has power over several individuals, Dahl adds a fifth constituent:

5. The set of individuals over whom A has power – this we shall call the *extension* of A's power.

Dahl points out that the power of two individuals can be compared in any of these five dimensions. Other things being equal, an individual's power is greater: (1) the greater his power base, (2) the more means of power available to him, and the greater (3) the scope, (4) the amount, and (5) the extension of his power. But Dahl proposes to use only the last three variables for the formal definition and measurement of social power. He argues that what we primarily mean by great social power is an ability to influence many people (extension) in many respects (scope) and with a high probability (amount of power). In contrast, a large power base or numerous means of power are not direct measures of the extent of the influence or power that one person can exert over other persons; they are only instruments by which great power can be achieved and maintained, and are indicators from which we can normally *infer* the likely possession of great power by an individual.

Among the three variables of scope, amount and extension, amount of power is the crucial one, in terms of which the other two can be defined. For the scope of A's power over B is simply the set of specific actions X with respect to which A has a non-zero amount of power over B, i.e. the set of those actions X for which A can achieve a non-zero increase in the probability of these actions actually being performed by B. Similarly, the extension of A's power is the set of specific individuals over whom A has power of non-zero scope and amount.

While the amount of power is a difference of two probabilities, and therefore is directly given as a *real number*,[1] all other dimensions of power are directly given as lists of specific objects (e.g. a list of specific resources, a list of specific actions by A or by B, or a list of specific individuals over whom A has power). But Dahl and March suggest that at least in certain situations it will be worthwhile to develop straight numerical measures for them by appropriate aggregating procedures – essentially by counting the num-

1. But as the probability that B will actually perform a specific action X suggested by A will in general be different for different actions X and for different individuals B, the total amount of A's power (or even the amount of A's power over a given individual B) will also have to be described by a vector rather than by a single number, except if some sort of aggregation procedure is used.

ber of comparable items in a given list, and possibly by assigning different weights to items of unequal importance (e.g. we may give more 'marks' for power over an important individual than for power over a less important one). In other cases we may divide up a given list into several sublists and may assign a separate numerical measure to each of them, without necessarily aggregating all these numbers into a single figure. That is, we may characterize a given dimension of power not by a single number, but rather by a set of several numbers, i.e. a vector. (For instance, we may describe the extension of President de Gaulle's power by listing the numbers (or percentages) of deputies, of army officers of various ranks, of electors, etc. who support him, without trying to combine all these figures into one index number.)

Two additional dimensions of social power

A quantitative characterization of a power relation, however, in my view must include two more variables not mentioned in Dahl's list:

6. The opportunity costs to A of attempting to influence B's behavior, i.e. the opportunity costs of using his power over B (and of acquiring this power over B in the first place if A does not yet possess the required power), which we shall call the *costs* of A's power over B; and

7. The opportunity costs to B of refusing to do what A wants him to do, i.e. of refusing to yield to A's attempt to influence his behavior. As these opportunity costs measure the strength of B's incentives for yielding to A's influence, we shall call them the *strength* of A's power over B.[2]

More precisely, the *costs* of A's power over B will be defined as the *expected value* (actuarial value) of the costs of his attempts to influence B. It will be a weighted average of the net total costs that A would incur if his attempt were successful (e.g. the costs of rewarding B), and of the net total costs that A would incur if his attempt were unsuccessful (e.g. the costs of punishing B).

2. Of course, instead of taking the opportunity costs (i.e. the net disadvantages) associated for B with non-compliance, we could just as well take the net advantages associated for him with compliance – they both amount to the same thing.

Other things being equal, A's power over B is greater the smaller the costs of A's power and the greater the strength of A's power.

Both of these two cost variables may be expressed either in physical units (e.g. it may cost A so many bottles of beer or so many working hours to get B to adopt a given policy X; and again it may cost B so many bottles of beer or so many years' imprisonment if he does not adopt policy X), in monetary units (e.g. A's or B's relevant costs may amount to so many actual dollars, or at least may be equivalent to a loss of so many dollars for him), or in utility units. (In view of the theoretical problems connected with interpersonal comparisons of utility, and of the difficulties associated with utility measurement even for one individual, in practice the costs and the strength of power will usually be expressed in physical or in monetary units.[3] But for the purposes of theoretical analysis the use of utility costs sometimes has important advantages, as we shall see.)

Unlike the power base and the means of power, which need not be included in the definition of the power relation, both the costs of power and the strength of power are essential ingredients of the definition of power. A's power over B should be defined not merely as an ability by A to get B to do X with a certain probability p, but rather as an ability by A to achieve this at a certain total cost u to himself, by convincing B that B would have to bear the total cost v if he did not do X.

The costs of power

One of the main purposes for which social scientists use the concept of A's power over B is for the description of the policy possibilities open to A. If we want to know the situation (or environment) which A faces as a decision-maker, we must know whether he can or cannot get B to perform a certain action X, and more specifically how sure he can be (in a probability sense) that

3. A good deal of recent experimental work shows that it is possible, at least under certain conditions, to measure the utilities that a given individual assigns to various alternatives. Interpersonal comparisons of utility can also be given operationally meaningful interpretation. Note, however, that the main conclusions of this paper, in particular Theorems 1 and 2, do not require interpersonal utility comparisons.

B will actually perform this action. But a realistic description of A's policy possibilities must include not only A's ability or inability to get B to perform a certain action X, but also the *costs* that A has to bear in order to achieve this result. If two individuals are in a position to exert the same influence over other individuals, but if one can achieve this influence only at the cost of great efforts and/or financial or other sacrifices, while the other can achieve it free of any such costs, we cannot say in any useful sense that their power is equally great. Any meaningful comparison must be in terms of the influence that two individuals can achieve at comparable costs, or in terms of the costs they have to bear in order to achieve comparable degrees of influence.

For instance, it is misleading to say that two political candidates have the same power over two comparable constituencies if one needs much more electioneering effort and expenditure to achieve a given majority, even if in the end both achieve the same majorities; or that two businessmen have the same power over the city government if one can achieve favorable treatment by city officials only at the price of large donations to party funds, while the other can get the same favorable treatment just for the asking.

Of course, a power concept which disregards the costs of power is most inaccurate when the costs of using a given power become very high or even prohibitive. For instance, suppose that an army commander becomes a prisoner of enemy troops, who try to force him at gun point to give a radio order to his army units to withdraw from a certain area. He may very well have the power to give a contrary order, both in the sense of having the physical ability to do so and in the sense of there being a very good chance of his order being actually obeyed by his army units – but he can use this power only at the cost of his life. Though the scope, the amount and the extension of his power over his soldiers would still be very great, it would clearly be very misleading in this situation to call him a powerful individual in the same sense as before his capture.

To conclude, a realistic quantitative description of A's power over B must include, as an essential dimension of this power relation, the costs to A of attempting to influence B's behavior.

The strength of power

While the costs of power must be included in the definition of our power concept in order to ensure its descriptive validity, the variable of *strength* of power must be included to ensure the usefulness of our power concept for explanatory purposes.

As March has pointed out about the concept of influence, one of the main analytical tasks of such concepts as influence or power (which essentially is an ability to exert influence) is to serve as *intervening variables* in the analysis of individual or social decision-making. Therefore we need a power or influence concept which enables us in the relevant cases to explain a decision by a given private individual or by an official of a social organization, in terms of the power or influence that another individual or some social group has over him. But fundamentally, the analysis of any human decision must be in terms of the variables on the basis of which the decision-maker concerned actually makes his decision – that is, in terms of the advantages and disadvantages he associates with alternative policies available to him. In order to explain why B adopts a certain policy X in accordance with A's wishes, we must know what *difference it makes* for B whether A is his friend or his enemy – or more generally, we must know the *opportunity costs* to B of not adopting policy X. Hence, if our power concept is to serve us as an explanatory intervening variable in the analysis of B's decision to comply with A's wishes, our power concept must include as one of its essential dimensions the opportunity costs to B of non-compliance, which measure the strength of B's incentives to compliance and which we have called the strength of A's power over B.

For instance, if we want to explain the decision of Senator Knowland to support a certain bill of the Eisenhower administration we must find out, among other things, which particular individuals or social groups influenced his decision, and to what extent. Now suppose that we have strong reasons to assume that it was President Eisenhower's personal intervention which made Senator Knowland change his mind and decide to support the bill in question. Then we still have to explain *how* the variables governing the Senator's decision were actually affected by the President's intervention. Did the President make a promise to him, i.e. did he attach new *advantages*, from the Senator's point of view, to the policy of supporting the bill? Or did the President make a threat, i.e. did he attach new *disadvantages* to the policy of opposing the bill? Or did the President supply new information, pointing out certain already *existing* advantages and/or disadvantages associated with these two policies, which the Senator had been insufficiently aware of before? In any case we must explain how the President's intervention increased the opportunity costs that Senator Knowland came to associate with opposing the bill.

If we cannot supply this information, then the mere existence of an influence or power relationship between President Eisenhower and Senator Knowland will not *explain* the latter's decision to support the bill. It will only pose a *problem* concerning this decision. (Why on earth did he comply with the President's request to support the bill, when it is known that he had many reasons to oppose it, and did actually oppose it for a while?)

There seem to be four main ways by which a given actor A can manipulate the incentives or opportunity costs of another actor B:

1. A may provide certain *new* advantages or disadvantages for B, subject to *no condition*. For instance, he may provide certain facilities for B which make it easier or less expensive for B to follow certain particular policy objectives desirable to A. (For example, country A may be able to induce country B to attack some third country C, simply by supplying arms to B, even if A supplies these arms 'without any strings attached' – and in particular without making it a condition of her arms deliveries that B will actually attack C.) Or A may withdraw from B certain facilities that could help B in attaining policy objectives undesirable to A. More generally, A may provide for B goods or services complementary to some particular policy goal X, or competitive to policy goals alternative to X, so as to increase for B the net utility of X, or to decrease the net utility of its alternatives; or A may achieve similar results by depriving B of goods or services either competitive to X or complementary to its alternatives.[4]

4. Case 1 is discussed in somewhat greater detail because power based on providing services or disservices without any conditions attached is often overlooked in the literature. For our purposes, the distinction between

2. *A* may set up *rewards* and *punishments*, i.e. *new* advantages and disadvantages subject to certain *conditions* as to *B*'s future behavior.

3. *A* may supply *information* (or misinformation) on (allegedly) already *existing* advantages and/or disadvantages connected with various alternative policies open to *B*.

4. *A* may rely on his legitimate *authority* over *B*, or on *B*'s personal *affection* for *A*, which make *B* attach *direct disutility* to the very act of disobeying *A*.

Of course, in a situation where *A* has certain power over *B*, either party can be mistaken about the true opportunity costs to him of various alternatives. Therefore both in discussing the costs of *A*'s power over *B*, and in discussing the strength of his power, we must distinguish between *objective* costs and *perceived* costs – between what these costs actually are and what the individual bearing these costs thinks them to be. For the purpose of a formal definition of the power relation, the *costs* of *A*'s power over *B* have to be stated as the *objective* costs that an attempt to influence *B* would actually entail upon *A*, while the *strength* of *A*'s power over *B* has to be stated in terms of the costs of non-compliance as *perceived* by *B* himself. The reason is that the costs of *A*'s power serve to describe the objective policy possibilities open to *A*, whereas the strength of *A*'s power serves to explain *B*'s subjective motivation for compliant behavior. (Of course, a full description of a given power situation would require listing both objective and perceived costs for both participants.)

The strength of power, and the amount of power in Dahl's sense

Clearly, in general the greater the *strength* of *A*'s power over *B*, the greater will be *A*'s *amount* of power over *B* with respect to action *X*. The relationship between these two variables will take a particularly simple mathematical form if the strength of *A*'s power is measured in *utility* terms, i.e. in terms of the disutility costs to *B* of noncompliance.

We shall use the following model. *A* wants *B* to perform action

---

unconditional advantages or disadvantages on the one hand, and conditional rewards or punishments on the other hand, is important because the latter lend themselves to *bargaining* much more easily than the former do.

X. But B associates disutility x with doing X. Nevertheless B would perform X with probability p_1 (i.e. would adopt the mixed strategy $s[p_1]$ assigning probability p_1 to doing X and probability $1-p_1$ to not doing X), even in the absence of A's intervention.[5] B would adopt this strategy because if he completely refused to do X (i.e. if he adopted the mixed strategy $s[0]$) he would obtain only the utility payoff u_0; while if he did X with probability p_1 (i.e. if he adopted strategy $s[p_1]$), then he would obtain the higher utility payoff u_1, making his total expected utility $u_1 - p_1 x > u_0$.

Now A intervenes and persuades B that B will obtain the still higher utility payoff u_2 if he agrees to do action X with a certain probability $p_2 > p_1$ (i.e. if he adopts strategy $s[p_2]$), making his total expected utility $u_2 - p_2 x$. In view of this, B does adopt strategy $s[p_2]$.

Under these assumptions, obviously the *amount* of A's power over B will be the difference $\triangle p = p_2 - p_1$, while the *strength* of A's power over B will be the difference $u_2 - u_1$. As $p_2 \leqslant 1$, we must have $\triangle p \leqslant 1 - p_1$. Moreover, by assumption $\triangle p \geqslant 0$.

If B tries to maximize his expected utility, then he will adopt strategy $s[p_2]$ only if

$$u_2 - p_2 x \geqslant u_1 - p_1 x, \qquad\qquad 1$$

that is, if

$$\Delta p = p_2 - p_1 \leqslant \frac{u_2 - u_1}{x} = \frac{\Delta u}{x}. \qquad\qquad 2$$

This gives us:

Theorem 1

The maximum *amount* of power that A can achieve over B with respect to action X tends to be equal to the *strength* of A's power over B (as expressed in utility units) divided by the disutility to B of doing action X – except that this maximum amount of power cannot be more than the amount of power corresponding to B's doing action X with probability *one*.

The strength of A's power over B divided by the disutility to B of doing X may be called the *relative strength* of A's power over B. Accordingly, we obtain:

5. We follow Dahl in considering the more general case where B would do action X with some probability p_1 (which of course may be zero), even in the absence of A's intervention.

Theorem 2

The maximum *amount* of power that A can achieve over B with respect to action X tends to be equal to the *relative strength* of A's power over B with respect to action X (except that, again, this maximum amount of power cannot be more than the amount of power corresponding to B's doing action X with probability one).

Of course, in the real world we seldom observe B to use a randomized mixed strategy of form s[p], in a literal sense. What we do find is that, if we watch B's behavior over a series of comparable occasions, he will comply with A's wishes in some proportion p of all occasions and will fail to comply in the remaining proportion 1−p of the occasions. [. . .]

Power in a schedule sense

We have just seen that the greater the strength of a person's power over other persons the greater the amount of his power over them tends to be. But likewise, the greater the strength of a person's power over other people, the greater both the scope and the extension of his power over these people. That is, the stronger incentives he can provide for compliance, the larger the number of specific actions he can get other people to perform for him will be, and the larger the number of individuals he can get to perform these actions.

But while the scope, the amount and the extension of his power are all functions of the *strength* of his power over all individuals, the strength of his power is itself a function of the *costs* of power he is prepared to bear. The greater efforts and sacrifices he is prepared to make, the stronger incentives for compliance he will be able to provide and the greater will be the strength of his power over them.

Therefore, a given individual's power can be described not only by stating the specific values of the five dimensions of his power (whether as single numbers, or as vectors, or as lists of specific items), but also by specifying the mathematical *functions* or *schedules* that connect the costs of his power with the other four dimensions. When power is defined in terms of the specific values of the five power variables we shall speak of power in a *point* sense, and when power is defined in terms of the functions or schedules connecting the other four power variables with the costs of power we shall speak of power in a *schedule* sense.[6]

Power in a schedule sense can be regarded as a 'production function' describing how a given individual can 'transform' different amounts of his resources (of his working time, his money, his political rights, his popularity, etc.) into social power of various dimensions (of various strengths, scopes, amounts and extensions). The common-sense notion of social power makes it an *ability* to achieve certain things – an ability that the person concerned is free to use or to leave unused. It seems to me that this notion of power as an ability is better captured by our concept of power in a schedule sense than it is by the concept of power in a point sense. (The latter seems to better correspond to the common-sense notion of actually exerted *influence*, rather than to that of power as such.)

If a person's power is given in a mere schedule sense, then we can state the specific values of his five power dimensions only if we are also told how much of his different resources he is actually prepared to use in order to obtain social power of various dimensions – that is, if besides his power schedules we know also his *utility function*. Whereas his power defined in a schedule sense indicates the conditions under which his environment is ready to 'supply' power to him, it is his utility function which determines his 'demand' for power under various alternative conditions.

Bilateral power and the 'blackmailer's fallacy'

So far we have tacitly assumed that, in situations where A has power over B, A is always in a position to determine, by his unilateral decision, the incentives he will provide for B's compliance, as well as the degree of compliance he will try to enforce. Situations in which this is actually the case may be called unilateral power situations. But it very often happens that not only can A exert pressure on B in order to get him to adopt certain policies, but B can do the same to A. In particular, B may be able to press A for increased rewards and/or decreased penalties, and for relaxing the standards of compliance required from him and used in administering rewards and penalties to him. Situations of this

6. In analogy to the distinction in economic theory between demand or supply in a point sense and in a schedule sense.

type we shall call bilateral or reciprocal power situations. In such situations, both the extent of B's compliant behavior (i.e. the scope and the amount of A's power over B) and the net incentives that A can provide for B (i.e. the net strength of A's power over B) will become matters of explicit or implicit *bargaining* between the two parties.

Of the four ways in which A can increase his strength of power discussed previously, we tend to obtain unilateral power situations in cases 1, 3 and 4, where A's power over B is based on providing *unconditional* advantages or disadvantages for B, on conveying information or misinformation to him, or on having legitimate authority over B and/or enjoying B's personal affection (though there are also exceptions where these cases give rise to bilateral power). For example, it is usually largely a matter for A's personal discretion whether he provides certain facilities for B, whether he discloses certain pieces of information to him, or whether he gives him an order as his legitimate superior. In case 2, on the other hand, when A's power over B is based on A's ability to set up rewards and/or punishments for B *conditional* upon B's behavior, normally we find bilateral power situations (though again there are important exceptions). Here B can exert pressure on A by withholding his compliance, even though compliance would be much more profitable than non-compliance. He may also be able to exert pressure on A by making the costs of a conflict (including the costs of punishing B for non-compliance) very high to A.

For bilateral power situations Theorem 1 and Theorem 2 do not hold true. For these conclusions have been completely dependent on the assumption that if a certain strategy s_1, involving some given degree of compliance by B, is more profitable to B than any alternative strategy s_2 involving a lesser degree of compliance (or none at all), then B will always choose strategy s_1 and will never choose strategy s_2 – not even as a result of dissatisfaction with the terms A offers in return for B's cooperation. While in unilateral power situations this assumption is perfectly legitimate (as it amounts to no more than assuming that B tries to maximize his utility or expected utility), in bilateral power situations this assumption would involve what I propose to call the 'blackmailer's fallacy'.

A would-be blackmailer A once argued that as he was in a position to cause damage worth $1000 to a certain rich man B, he should be able to extract from B *any* ransom r short of $1000, because after payment of $r < \$1000$, B would still be better off than if he had to suffer the full $1000 damage.

But this argument is clearly fallacious. By similar reasoning, B could also have argued that A would accept *any* ransom r larger than nil, because after accepting a ransom $r > \$0$, A would still be better off than if no agreement were reached and he did not receive anything at all. What both of these arguments really show is that in any bargaining between two rational bargainers, the outcome must fall between what may be called the two parties' *concession limits*, which are defined by each party's refusal to accept any agreement that would make him actually worse off than he would be in the conflict situation. But the two arguments in themselves say nothing about where the two parties' agreement point will actually lie *between* these two limits. They certainly do not allow the inference that this agreement point will actually coincide or nearly coincide with one party's concession limit. (Only if we know the two parties' attitude towards risk-taking, and in particular towards risking a conflict rather than accepting unfavorable terms, can we make any predictions about where their agreement point will lie between the two concession limits.)

Either party's actual behavior will be a resultant of two opposing psychological forces. On the one hand, for example, B will admittedly have some incentive for agreeing to any ransom payment less than $1000. But B will also know that A will likewise have some incentive for accepting any ransom payment greater than zero, and this fact will make B expect to get away with a ransom payment of much less than $1000. This expectation in turn will provide B with some incentive to resist any ransom payment too close to $1000. Any realistic theory of B's behavior must take full account of *both* of these psychological forces – both of B's motives for compliance, and of the reasons which make him expect some concessions on A's part which will render full compliance on his own part unnecessary.

The Zeuthen–Nash theory and the strength of power in bilateral power situations

For analysis of the two parties' behavior in bilateral power situations, and in particular for quantitative assessment of the two opposite psychological forces governing each party's degree of compliance, we shall use the Zeuthen–Nash theory of the two-person bargaining game. Our analysis will be based on the following model.

Just as in the model discussed earlier, A wants B to perform action X. But B associates disutility x with doing X. Nevertheless B would perform X with probability p_1, i.e. would use the mixed strategy $s[p_1]$, even in the absence of A's intervention. This would happen because if B completely refused to do X (i.e. if he adopted strategy $s[0]$) he would obtain only the utility pay-off u_0 – while if he did X with probability p_1 (i.e. if he adopted strategy $s[p_1]$) then he would obtain the higher utility payoff u_1, making his total expected utility $u_1 - p_1 x > u_0$.

If B completely refused to do X, then A's utility level would be u_0^*. If B did perform X (with probability 1), then A's utility would increase by the amount x^*. Accordingly, if B did X only with probability p_1 then A's expected utility would be $u_0^* + p_1 x^*$.

Now A intervenes and offers B a reward R if B will increase the probability of his doing action X from p_1 to some mutually agreed figure p_2 (i.e. if B adopts strategy $s[p_2]$). In utility units, this reward R would represent a gain r for B, while providing this reward would cost A the amount r^*. Hence, if the two parties can agree on some probability p_2, then A's total expected utility will be

$$u_2^* = u_2^*(p_2) = u_0^* - r^* + p_2 x^* \qquad 3$$

whereas B's total expected utility will be

$$u_2 = u_2(p_2) = u_1 + r - p_2 x. \qquad 4$$

A also sets up the penalty T for B if B refuses to sufficiently increase the probability of his performing action X. In utility units, this penalty T would cause a loss t to B, while enforcing this penalty would cost A the amount t^*. Hence, if the two parties could not agree on the value of p_2, A's total expected utility would be

$$u_3^* = u_0^* - t^* + p_1 x^* \qquad 5$$

(assuming that B would still perform X with probability p_1), whereas B's total expected utility would be

$$u_3 = u_1 - t - p_1 x.\qquad\qquad 6$$

More generally, we may assume that in a conflict situation *both* parties would use retaliatory strategies against each other, A using strategy T_A and B using strategy T_B. In such a case t should be redefined as the *total loss* that B would suffer in the conflict situation, including both the damages caused to him by his opponent's retaliatory strategy T_A, and the costs to him of his own retaliatory strategy T_B. Similarly, t^* should be redefined as the *total loss* that A would suffer in the conflict situation. But otherwise our conclusions retain their validity.

Now, what will be the equilibrium value of the probability p_2 which tends to be agreed upon in bargaining between two rational bargainers?

We already know that it must lie between the p_2 values corresponding to the two parties' concession limits. A's concession limit is reached when $u_2^* = u_3^*$. By 3 and 5, the corresponding p_2 value is

$$p_2^A = p_1 + \frac{r^* - t^*}{x^*}.\qquad\qquad 7$$

With $p_2 = p_2^A$, A's total expected utility would be

$$u_2^*(p_2^A) = u_3^* = u_0^* - t^* + p_1 x^*,\qquad\qquad 8$$

while B's total expected utility would be

$$u_2(p_2^A) = u_1 + r - \frac{x}{x^*}(r^* - t^*) - p_1 x.\qquad\qquad 9$$

On the other hand, B's concession limit is reached when $u_2 = u_3$. By 4 and 6 the corresponding p_2 value is

$$p_2^B = p_1 + \frac{r + t}{x}.\qquad\qquad 10$$

With $p_2 = p_2^B$, A's total expected utility would be

$$u_2^*(p_2^B) = u_0^* - r^* + \frac{x^*}{x}(r + t) + p_1 x^*,\qquad\qquad 11$$

while B's total expected utility would be

$$u_2(p_2^B) = u_3 = u_1 - t - p_1 x.\qquad\qquad 12$$

It is easy to see (Figure 1) that in the utility plane $\{u^*, u\}$ for the two parties, all possible agreement points $U(p) = [u_2^*(p_2), u_2(p_2)]$ must lie on the straight-line interval connecting the two parties' concession limit points, $M = U(p_2^A) = [u_2^*(p_2^A), u_2(p_2^A)]$ and $L = U(p_2^B) = [u_2^*(p_2^B), u_2(p_2^B)]$. (The two parties' payoffs in the conflict situation are indicated by the conflict point $C = [u_3^*, u_3]$.)

When the locus of all possible agreement points U is a straight line, the Zeuthen–Nash solution takes a particularly simple mathematical form; it is located simply at the mid-point of the distance between the two concession-limit points L and M (i.e. at S).[7]

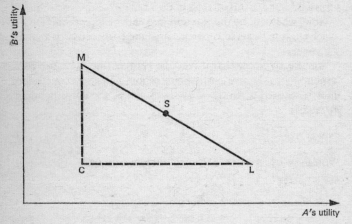

Figure 1 Zeuthen–Nash utility plane

Hence, at the solution point S, A must obtain the expected utility

$$u_4^* = \frac{1}{2}[u_2^*(p_2^A) + u_2^*(p_2^B)]$$

$$= u_0^* - \frac{r^* + t^*}{2} + \frac{x^*}{2x}(r+t) + p_1 x^*, \qquad 13$$

7. This is obviously true in the special case where the game is perfectly symmetric with respect to the two players. Generally the result follows from the invariance of the Zeuthen–Nash solution with respect to order-preserving linear transformations.

where the last equality follows from **8** and **11**; while B must obtain the expected utility

$$u_4 = \frac{1}{2}[u_2(p_2^A) + u_2(p_2^B)]$$

$$= u_1 + \frac{r-t}{2} - \frac{x}{2x^*}(r^*-t^*) - p_1 x. \qquad \textbf{14}$$

If we set $u_4^* = u_2^*(p_2)$ and $u_4 = u_2(p_2)$, by **13** and **3** (or by **14** and **4**) we obtain, as the equilibrium value of p_2 corresponding to the solution point S, the expression

$$p_2 = p_1 + \frac{r+t}{2x} + \frac{r^*-t^*}{2x^*} \qquad \textbf{15}$$

subject, of course, to the requirement that always

$$p_2 \leqslant 1. \qquad \textbf{15a}$$

The Zeuthen–Nash theory also tells us that A will choose the reward R he offers B in such a way as to maximize the expression

$$\Delta r = \frac{r}{x} - \frac{r^*}{x^*}$$

which measures, from A's point of view, the value of R as an incentive, less the cost of providing R for B. Moreover, A will select the penalty T in such a way as to maximize the expression

$$\Delta t = \frac{t}{x} - \frac{t^*}{x^*}$$

which again measures, from A's point of view, the value of T as a deterrent, less the cost of administering T to B. This is so because, according to **13**, A will maximize his own final utility payoff u_4^*, by means of maximizing Δr and Δt.

In the more general case where both parties would use retaliatory strategies in the event of a conflict, A (in order to maximize his own final payoff u_4^*) would again try to select his own retaliatory strategy T_A so as to *maximize* Δt when B's strategy T_B is given. On the other hand, B (in order to maximize his own final payoff u_4) would try to select his own retaliatory strategy T_B so as to *minimize* Δt when A's strategy T_A is given. Hence the equilibrium choice of T_A and T_B will be such as to make Δt take its maximum value.

Now clearly, if B adopts strategy $s[p_2]$ corresponding to the p_2 value defined by **15**, then the *amount* of A's power over B with respect to action X will become

$$\Delta p = p_2 - p_1 = \frac{1}{2}\left(\frac{r+t}{x} - \frac{t^*-r^*}{x^*}\right).\qquad\qquad\textbf{16}$$

But of course the value of Δp must be consistent with **15a**. Hence **16** is subject to the restriction that

$$\Delta p \leqslant 1 - p_1.\qquad\qquad\textbf{16a}$$

Let X^* denote A's action of *tolerating* B's failure to perform action X on one occasion. (We shall call action X^* the complementary action to action X.) Now suppose that A and B agree that B will perform action X with probability p_2, i.e. that B will *not* perform action X, with probability $1-p_2$. This will mean that A will have to tolerate B's not performing action X, i.e. that A will have to perform action X^*, with probability $1-p_2$. That is, technically, A and B will agree on a *jointly randomized* mixed strategy under which, with probability p_2, B will perform action X while A will *not* perform the complementary action X^* – whereas, with probability $1-p_2$, A will perform action X^* while B will *not* perform action X.

Thus, while A's power over B will primarily consist in A's ability to get B to perform action X with a certain probability p_2; B's power over A will primarily consist in B's ability to get A to perform the complementary action X^* with probability $1-p_2$.

On any given occasion where A performs action X^* (i.e. tolerates B's *not* performing action X), A will lose the utility gain x^* that he would derive from B's performing action X. Therefore A will associate disutility x^* with performing action X^*.

In equation **16**, the sum $r+t$ is the sum of the *reward* B would obtain for compliance, and of the *penalty* he would suffer for non-compliance, both expressed in utility terms. This sum measures the *difference it would make* for B to have A as his enemy instead of having him as his friend. It represents the total opportunity costs to B of choosing non-compliance leading to the conflict situation instead of choosing compliance, i.e. some strategy $s[p_2]$ acceptable to A. In brief, it represents the *opportunity costs* *of a conflict*, from B's point of view. In our terminology, it measures the (gross) *absolute strength* of A's power over B. Accordingly, the quotient $(r+t)/x$ measures the *gross relative strength* of A's power over B with respect to action X.

The difference t^*-r^* is the difference between the costs to A of *punishing* B and the costs to A of *rewarding* B, both again expressed in utility terms. This difference measures the difference it would make for A to have B as an enemy instead of having him as a friend. It represents the net opportunity costs to A of choosing the conflict situation rather than performing action X^* with a probability $1-p_2$ acceptable to B, i.e. rather than tolerating B to follow some strategy $s[p_2]$ acceptable to B. (In computing these opportunity costs, r^* has to be deducted from t^*, because in case of a conflict, A of course would save the costs of rewarding B.) In brief, this difference measures the *opportunity costs of a conflict*, this time from A's point of view. In our terminology, it measures the *gross absolute strength* of B's power over A. Moreover, as x^* is the disutility to A of performing action X^*, the quotient $(t^*-r^*)/x^*$ measures the *gross relative strength* of B's power over A with respect to action X^*.

Finally, the difference $(r+t)/x-(t^*-r^*)/x^*$ is the difference between the gross relative strength of A's power over B with respect to action X, and the gross relative strength of B's power over A with respect to the complementary action X^*. It may be called the *net strength* of A's power over B with respect to action X. This gives us:

Theorem 3

If both parties follow the rationality postulates of the Zeuthen–Nash theory of the two-person bargaining game, then in bilateral power situations the *amount* of A's power over B with respect to some action X tends to be equal to *half* the *net strength* of A's power over B with respect to the same action X – this net strength being defined as the difference between the gross relative strength of A's power over B with respect to action X and the gross relative strength of B's power over A with respect to the complementary action X^*. (But this theorem is subject to the qualification that the amount of A's power over B cannot be so great as to make the probability of *B*'s performing action *X* become greater than *unity*.)

In empirical applications the amount-of-power concept in Theorem 3 (and in Theorem 1) must be reinterpreted in terms of empirical *frequencies*, instead of theoretical *probabilities*. [. . .]

5 J. Pen

Bilateral Monopoly, Bargaining and the Concept of
Economic Power

Excerpts from J. Pen, *The Wage Rate under Collective Bargaining*,
Harvard University Press, 1959, chapter 5, pp. 91–105, 207–9.

The 'determinateness' of the contract

In the literature on bilateral monopoly two main trends may be
discerned. The first tries to explain price making in a fashion similar to that used for prices under competition, that is to say, by
employing supply and demand functions, marginal cost and
revenue functions and the like. These attempts have not led to
anything more than limited solutions, which are based on too
narrow assumptions to be of any use to our problem; they have
also led to a number of mistaken ideas. The second trend, which
has been quite fruitless, regards price making as 'indeterminate',
in particular because power relations play a part in it. Before
investigating the significance of this latter point of view, we shall
give a short survey of the first group of attempts. Besides the two
trends mentioned there are a number of rather isolated theories
which analyse the bargaining process (Zeuthen 1930, Hicks 1935).

A very simple solution was offered in the past by Cournot
(1838, see Hicks, 1935). A monopolistic seller of iron ore supplies
his product to a monopolistic steelmaker. When doing so he
fixes the price of the ore; the steelmaker in his turn fixes the price
of the steel. Both suppliers are monopolistic price fixers with
regard to their customer(s); the price of the ore and that of the
steel are represented by the respective optima (Cournot's point)
of the two entrepreneurs. It will be clear that this reasoning,
although sound in itself, cannot offer much help for the situation
which we have in mind. Cournot leaves out of consideration the
fact that the monopolistic buyer of the iron ore will try to follow
a price policy of his own, not only with regard to his customers
but also with regard to his supplier. Despite his monopsonistic
position the steelmaker is represented as a 'price taker', who

passively submits to the price which the supplier of the ore dictates to him. Therefore Cournot's solution is very limited; it fails if the monopsonist offers counterpressure, and is quite useless for our problem of wage bargaining.

Nevertheless, Cournot's reasoning has been applied to the labor market by Wicksell. According to him, price making under a bilaterally monopolistic exchange of goods is indeterminate, but matters are different on the labor market. There the supplier determines the wage rate because, as Wicksell says, 'if the manufacturer can fix the wage, then, contrary to what may be assumed, the worker has no monopoly' (1927). What with Cournot was a limited but not incorrect solution has become in the case of Wicksell a mistaken idea, and a curious one at that: it is deduced from the concept of bilateral monopoly that the supplier acts as a price fixer; the bilateral character of the monopoly is left out of consideration on principle here, and not by implication, as is the case with Cournot.

The article in which Wicksell explains this opinion has an introduction by Schumpeter (1927). In this the latter goes a stage further than Wicksell and has *both* monopolists acting as price takers. At every given wage rate the workers will supply that quantity of labor which they deem fit; the employers will demand *their* optimum quantity. There is equilibrium – in his view – only when these two amounts coincide. As a result the wage rate is determinate.

Schumpeter's reasoning is also to be encountered in Schneider (1932).[1] It amounts to the fact that the wage is determined by the point of intersection of the supply and demand curves. This idea excels in simplicity, but it does not do justice to the particular properties of the bilaterally monopolistic relation. For it is supposed here that both parties will aim at a wage rate at which

1. Schumpeter's point is called a pseudo-equilibrium by Henderson (1940). Henderson's point is not clear; on the one hand he postulates that 'both parties will choose to cease dealings' when they stumble on the point of intersection of supply and demand but on the other hand he rightly says 'each party would gain by having a more favourable price'. The pseudo-equilibrium would only be reached 'by accident' (p. 242). The first theory quoted, namely that Schumpeter's point represents the terminal point of the negotiations (even if the parties would have to stumble on it by chance) is quite untrue.

neither unemployment nor an unsaturated demand for labor will occur. Under perfect competition the mechanism of the market ensures the achievement of this wage rate, and the parties react by quantity adjustment. But under bilateral monopoly both parties are aiming at a price of their own, and they need not wish by any means to avoid unemployment and unsaturated demand at all costs. It is, however, conceivable. If the union lets its wage policy be governed completely by the wish to absorb all the workers, it will in fact aim at the wage indicated by Schumpeter. And if the employers are not inclined to force down the wage below this level – and this, too, is a very special assumption – the parties will reach agreement on that wage which is given by the point of intersection of the supply curve and the demand curve. This wage is then equal to that under perfect competition, assuming that the action of the union has not deformed the supply curve.

It thus emerges that Schumpeter's reasoning can be saved, but only at the cost of an unrealistic narrowing of the objectives of the union and of the employers. It cannot, however, be assumed that in its wage policy the union will let itself be led purely and simply by the fear of unemployment; and the hypothesis that the wage policy of the employers is inspired by this fear is quite illogical. As a result of this, the determination of the wage rate, as Schumpeter sees it, loses practically all its importance for us.

A solution of the problem put forward by many writers is that in which both parties aim at the greatest possible collective profit. Edgeworth, who as a good utilitarian considered this solution particularly attractive, already pointed out that somewhere on the contract curve a point must lie at which the sum of the utilities of both parties is maximal (1881, p. 53). However, it is dubious whether the addition of these magnitudes is permissible. Totting up ophelimities which are felt by various subjects seems a very precarious artifice. In view of this, this solution of the problem has already become irrelevant so far as the labor market is concerned. Even in the case of two businessmen who are aiming at maximum joint profits, the reasoning concentrates on a very special case, and does not make any contribution towards an explanation of price making in all other cases. Added to this is the fact that in accordance with the accepted opinion the price is still indeterminate even if the parties are aiming at maximum collective profit. In that case only the sales are determined by the point of intersection of marginal revenue curves (Bowley, 1928, p. 254; Tintner, 1939, p. 265; Bilimovič, 1943, p. 329; Fellner, 1947, p. 329; Hoffman, 1942, p. 304).[2] And that is obvious, too: in their efforts to achieve collective profit, one can regard the two monopolists together as one enterprise, at least viewed outwardly. But inwardly the problem of how the joint profit must be divided still remains. This division is determined by the price, and therefore a further arrangement must be made between the monopolists about this price.

Put in this way, it emerges that the above solution of the bilateral monopoly on the labor market is particularly interesting to those who want to place workers and employers in one community of interests. Therefore it is not surprising that a number of Italian theoreticians, with the corporative organization of society in mind, have occupied themselves with this reasoning.[3] For our purpose it is unimportant, if only, as mentioned above, because the addition of the two ophelimities is difficult to conceive.

The starting point of the reasoning can be particularized still further. For instance, Bilimovič makes the assumption that both parties are aiming at the point of 'the same minimal negative deviations from the absolute maximum.'[4] It seems to us that such strange casuistry can contribute little to an understanding of bilateral monopoly, and is rather a proof of the unsatisfactory state of the theory on this point.[5]

In the above we reviewed various attempts to arrive at a determination of the price under bilateral monopoly. It proves that they have contributed practically nothing. The prevailing opinion

2. However, with Edgeworth the utilitarian point corresponds to one single price, since the price vector intersects the contract curve only at one point.

3. Bilimovič (1943, p. 317) names them as Masci, Di Nardi and Jarraccone.

4. Bilimovič (p. 352) seems to derive this and other constructions from Jarraccone.

5. As a curiosity another view may be mentioned, namely that the price lies halfway between the limits of the contract zone. This idea, which may be found in Schäffle (1873; quoted by Bilimovič, p. 315) proves also to have some attraction for Zeuthen (1930).

is therefore that the price is 'indeterminate'.[6] What does this mean? The first meaning which could be attached to the expression 'an indeterminate phenomenon' is that the phenomenon is indefinite, in the sense that no causes led to its occurrence. Interpreted in this way 'an indeterminate phenomenon' would be synonymous with 'a non-existent phenomenon', since every existing phenomenon is brought about by causes. In that case the pronouncement that the price under bilateral monopoly is indeterminate would be equivalent to saying that no price can come into being under bilateral monopoly. The wording by which Edgeworth describes bilateral monopoly points to some extent in the direction of this view: 'undecidable opposition of interests, deadlock, ἄκριτος ἔρις και ταραχή' (p. 29). Now it is of course possible that the bargaining process leads to nothing more than an 'irrational, wild and turbulent' struggle, without a decision ever being taken or a contract being realized, but this case can safely be left out of consideration, since within the contract zone both parties have an interest in the contract. For that matter, if no contract is concluded, Edgeworth's reasoning, which results in the contract zone, no longer has the slightest point. Therefore 'indeterminate' may definitely not be interpreted as meaning 'not determined by causes'.

A second meaning[7] which may be attached to the word 'indeterminate' is approximately equal to 'unpredictable'. We have not encountered this meaning explicitly in the literature, but we would mention it because it seems to us that Zeuthen, in whose opinion bilateral monopoly is in no way indeterminate, possibly holds such a view. In this train of thought a determinate phenomenon displays regularity in the sense that the phenomenon tends towards a certain value. In other words, if a sufficiently large number of cases are examined, the frequency distribution will display a sharp peak. Against this there is the 'indeterminate'

6. Besides the publications of Edgeworth (1881), Bowley (1928), Tintner (1939), Henderson (1940) and Bilimović (1943) mentioned above, this opinion also finds expression among others in Menger (1871), Marshall (1890), Böhm-Bawerk (1888), Nichol (1942), von Stackelberg (1934, 1945) and Stigler (1947).

7. The meaning in which the term is used in ethics (namely in connection with freedom of will, in which 'free' actions are set against 'determinate' ones) can be left out of consideration here.

phenomenon, which is 'erratic' and 'incalculable', which does not tend towards a certain value and which therefore is unpredictable.

It is difficult to combat this view, since it is nowhere explicitly defended. All we shall say about it is that if desired one could use such terminology, but that in that case various phenomena, which up to now have definitely been regarded as 'determinate', will have to be considered 'indeterminate'. In particular we have in mind price making under perfect competition, in which erratic and incalculable factors may also occur, making the price more or less unpredictable. Therefore this view of the concept is unsuitable.

The third and usual meaning is that of mathematics. A system of equations is determinate when it contains as many equations as variables. If there are too few equations, the variables are indeterminate, that is, they remain unknown, and can assume various values without coming into conflict with the system of equations. In this case the system of equations is not enough to determine the variables.

The term 'indeterminate' is used in this sense by most economists. It then means nothing more than that their system of equations, that is, their theory, is inadequate to offer an explanation of the magnitudes to be examined.

A typical example of this is the 'theory of limits' of bilateral monopoly. By confining oneself to the formulation of a theory on the price limits, one signifies that the price between these limits is not explained by this theory; this is implied in the concept of 'limit'. It is superfluous to explain once more that the price is indeterminate within these limits; this merely amounts to saying that the investigation has been broken off before it came to a successful conclusion.

Therefore with this meaning of the term 'indeterminate' it must be borne in mind that indeterminateness is not a property of the price in itself; like every phenomenon, the price is determined by its causes. The indeterminateness of the price proceeds from the imperfect theory with which the phenomenon has been approached.

As matters stand, an answer must be given to the questions of why so great a majority of economists have given up their attempts to explain prices under bilateral monopoly when they have come halfway. This answer is difficult to give, since it differs from case to case. As regards Edgeworth, whose view has strongly influenced the ideas of others, the cause of his agnosticism is perhaps to be found in the distaste which this utilitarian rationalist felt for the 'clogged and underground procedure', as he described the struggle for power. What others called 'the art of bargaining' was for him a long string of 'incalculable and often disreputable accidents', with which he wanted to have nothing to do (p. 46). In others, such as Böhm, the lack of interest in the bargaining process may perhaps be attributed to the fact that the newly discovered theory of marginal pairs, which was applied with such enthusiasm to the attachmentless market, does not hold water in the case of bilateral monopoly. With still others the impression that the problem could not be tackled either with supply and demand curves,[8] or by means of the marginal cost concept or marginal revenue, probably led to an agnostic attitude. Another important point is that economists are accustomed to dealing with maximum and minimum problems, while price making under bilateral monopoly, at least at first sight, contains neither a maximum nor a minimum problem. This point has been illustrated by Morgenstern, who describes the state of the theory in the following striking, though somewhat exaggerated manner:

in this case [bilateral monopoly] no trick whatever will help us to disguise the fundamental fact that, while each of the participants wishes to maximize his own gain, the problem as a whole is not a maximum problem. It is a situation not taken care of anywhere in current economic theory. It is not even treated in classical mathematics. Furthermore, this kind of problem does not occur in mechanics, from which economic theory has taken its images, concepts and logical methods (1948, p. 12).[9]

All these causes have probably contributed to the present situation, in which we do not have at our disposal a theory of bilateral monopoly. The authors who adopt the point of view of 'indeterminateness', however, suggest an entirely different explanation.

8. For instance, Jevons (1882, p. 153). 'The laws of supply and demand do not apply . . . there may arise a deadlock.'
9. The situation is painted too blackly here, for Zeuthen, followed by Denis, has already done important work on this subject, while Hicks had also undertaken an attempt – in our opinion not particularly successful – to analyse the struggle for power.

In so far as they try to make excuses for the gap in their theory, they hint that the analysis of the bargaining process is not the task of the economist, in other words that by doing so one exceeds the bounds of economics. For instance, Scitovszky says of bilateral trade agreements (which of course represent a contract under bilateral monopoly) '[they] are a matter of higgling and bargaining, and have little interest for the economist' (1949, p. 378).

These views have also given rise to a couple of variants. The first is that price making under bilateral monopoly belongs to the field of psychology. Now it may be admitted that psychological factors play a major part in the bargaining process. However, this is no reason to banish the explanation of the price from economics, since the latter after all still has the task of showing how these psychological factors lead to a certain price. In 'ordinary' price making, too, psychological factors play a part in the final analysis. The bond between psychological factors – which can be regarded as data in themselves – and the price is definitely a subject of study for economics. But also the 'psychological' factors themselves, which formally belong to the data of economics, may in our opinion not entirely be handled as such. This would lead to fruitless formalism, and especially so with respect to the bargaining process. The psychological factors which occur are so closely interwoven with economic magnitudes that too strict a separation is undesirable. Moreover, if bilateral monopoly is referred to the psychologists, it is not unlikely that it will not be dealt with any more. In the manuals of psychology, at least as far as we know, no references to our problem are to be found up to now.

The second variant of the view that bilateral monopoly does not belong in economics is that which is based on the belief that price making is governed by power factors (Bilimovič, 1943, p. 317; Tintner, 1939, p. 270; Stackelberg, 1934, p. 27; Bowley, 1928, p. 569; Stigler, 1947, p. 100), while these power factors form a datum for economics.[10] This view is still more debatable than the

10. A typical pronouncement from Tintner (1939, p. 270) 'Other non-economic, especially political, forces will create the bargaining power of the two monopolists, which in turn determines the price within the range indicated.'

preceding variant, in the first place because it is more widespread, and in the second place because it offers ample opportunity for confusing economic and non-economic power. The concept of power, which in our opinion cannot only be of good service but even is indispensable to a correct treatment of bilateral monopoly, falls into discredit through such confusion.[11] It is therefore important to examine this concept in somewhat greater detail, which will be done in the following section.

To conclude this section, reference may be made to the consequences of the view that under bilateral monopoly the contract is 'indeterminate'. If one foregoes an explanation of the prices and wages achieved by bargaining, one cannot of course indicate the external limit of wage policy. In that case one can at most remark that the wage increase cannot exceed the limit of the contract zone. As a result, the whole question of wage determination is left in the air. Anyone who considers bilateral monopoly a curiosity can abandon it without much difficulty and leave it unsolved or push it off on to other branches of science (with the danger that these will not solve it either). On the other hand, anyone who realizes that when the union appears on the scene wage determination takes place in circumstances of (untrue) bilateral monopoly must leave bilateral monopoly unexplained, at the same time dropping the wage theory, which is after all one of the cornerstones of a complete economic theory.

The concept of power

The concept of 'power' can be defined very generally as the capacity of a subject to have his own way. This use of words is purely formal, for power is also concerned when the subject's will does not encounter a single external obstacle. The term comes closer to common usage when one postulates as an element of the concept of power that in having one's own way an external resistance, a counterpressure, must be overcome. Finally, the concept of power can be still more closely delineated by positing that this external resistance must consist of the will of one or more other subjects. The latter is not strictly necessary; one can speak

11. Lindblom (1948, p. 396) has even advocated dropping the concept of 'bargaining power', since it is meaningless and harmful.

of the power which man has over nature, but for the present study so wide a use of the word is less suitable. Thus in what follows 'power' is used in the sense of the capacity of a subject to carry through his will against that of another subject (or other subjects). Therefore the concept of power means a relationship between subjects, a social relationship. (If we speak of 'social power', this concept, if it is not to be a pleonasm, must be narrower than the concept of power defined here.)

With regard to this concept of power further distinctions must be made. To do so two possible criteria may be used: the first concerns the origin of the power, the second the consequences (and possibly the aim) of the exercise of power. If these two criteria are not kept separate, confusion may arise.

Depending on the criterion chosen, the concept of 'economic power' may be defined as power which originates in economic relations or as power which is directed towards economic relations. Both definitions are possible, but in our opinion the second is not a suitable starting point for an economic analysis. We shall now try to demonstrate this by means of Eucken's concept of power (1944, p. 236).

Eucken does not define his concept of power, but illustrates it by a number of examples, this being in full accordance with his method of 'pointing up'. These examples concern among other things the relationship between the ancient Greek and his slaves, between the state and its subjects in a 'centralized total economy' and between the banking house of Fugger and the princes dependent on that house. In all three cases Eucken believes that there is some question of 'economic power'. What does this pronouncement tell us? Only this: that subjects exercise power over other subjects, and that this power is directed towards the satisfaction of wants of the first-mentioned subjects. Despite the fact that this exercise of power is in an economic direction, the nature of it is totally different in the three cases, so different, in fact, that an all-embracing concept cannot be of the least analytical service. Eucken's concept of power contains so many heterogeneous elements that without exaggeration it may be called amorphous. If an attempt is made to study the three situations described above, this leads to three theories alongside one another, in which the concept of power is quite different in content on each occasion. In our opinion this amorphous nature damns such a concept of economic power.[12]

If we desire to characterize the nature of power, we must pay attention to the origin of that power. Of course this does not mean to say that the objectives and the consequences of the exercise of power are irrelevant, but only that the general concept of power should be split up into elements by means of the factors on which the power is based. The suitability of this procedure must emerge from what follows. We shall approach the matter in the following fashion: from the general concept of power those particular concepts of power will be split off which relate to economic data. When doing this we shall try to give a full classification of the forms of power. . . . The classification proceeds from the nature of the power, that is, from the sanctions which the subject can apply to impose his will on the subject to be overcome.

The classification of the non-economic forms of power (seven in number) is as follows:

1. *Physical power:* this is based on the threat or use of physical force.

2. *Personal power:* this is based on personal ascendancy. A typical example of personal power is the father-child relationship. The father can impose his will on the child; frequently the child will accede to the wishes of the father, although this is against his own will, so as to avoid the displeasure of the father. This displeasure is then the sanction (of course physical sanctions may also play a part in this relationship). From this case must be distinguished that of voluntary compliance by the child with the wishes of his father, because the child is convinced that father 'knows best'. Here the father does not exercise power, but authority, because there is no opposition from the will of the child. For our present purpose – splitting off non-economic forms of power – the distinction between power and authority is unimportant, but it parallels another distinction, which is of value to

12. Further details about the unsuitability of the amorphous concept of power (especially in Weber and Oppenheimer) are discussed by van der Tempel (1927, p. 24).

our problem, namely that between internal and external limitation of actions. In the second case the actions of the child are determined internally; the child submits to the will of the father, even without methods of coercion. In the first case the actions of the child are determined externally; the child does as the father wishes, because otherwise sanctions will follow, which he wishes to avoid. This is the exercise of power.

3. *Social power:* this is based on respect for the social position of the subject. A typical example is that of the village doctor, who can exercise power through his social position. As in the case of personal power – from which, incidentally, social power is often difficult to distinguish – authority and power often merge into one.[13] An example of the exercise of social power which has been discussed in the literature of economics is Schumpeter's country servant girl who, because of her submissiveness towards her 'master', is prepared to accept a low wage (1916, p. 23). In this instance personal and social power are obviously closely inter-related: the distinction becomes more of a nuance than a fundamental difference.

4. *Administrative and organizational power:* this form of power is based on the rules of an organization or administrative body: a business, an association, and so on. The power relation only applies in so far as the subjects keep to these rules; the sanction on the exercise of power is the expulsion of the recalcitrant subject from the organization. A typical example is the relationship between a foreman and a worker. The hierarchy of the civil service is also an example, but the military hierarchy is not, because there is no question here of a voluntary acceptance of rules; the rules themselves are also a subject of coercion in the military hierarchy.

5. *State power:* this is the power which the state exercises *qualitate qua* and which is based on the sanctions which the state has at its disposal *qualitate qua.* These sanctions are exercised via bailiffs, police officers, soldiers, prison and so on. This form of power as manifested in modern society can usually be easily and sharply

13. A particular and in practice very important form of social power is based on the presumed relations between the powerful subject and the supernatural. Both authority and power may proceed from this.

delineated from other forms of power. Behind state power lies physical power: this is the basis on which state power ultimately rests.

6. *Legal power:* this proceeds from a legal relationship which is often based on an agreement. If, after concluding a tenancy agreement, the landlord wishes to put the tenant out of the house, the latter can counter this wish by means of the agreement. This form of power must be clearly distinguished from economic power; the distinction becomes obvious when the nature of the sanctions is considered. In the case of legal power, the sanctions – in modern society at least – are exercised via the state: bailiffs and police officers. Therefore in the final analysis legal power is based on state power.

7. *Political power:* this is the exercise of power by citizens in respect of the state. It is organized under a system of rules which is sanctioned by the power of the state. Therefore political power and state power are the opposite of each other, but at the same time political power is based on state power. A typical example is the power of the elector.[14]

This seems to be a complete classification of the non-economic forms of power. It may perhaps be inadequate for sociological purposes, but it is of sufficient assistance for investigating whether a phenomenon of power is a datum for economics or an economic phenomenon. In this connection reference may be made to two points. In the first place, the exercise of power may be complicated because of the fact that various forms of power are applied simultaneously. In the second place – and this complication can more easily lead to a misunderstanding than the first one – the exercise of power may be indirect. Let us assume that subject A wishes to exercise power over subject B. There is no direct relationship between the two subjects which can give rise to a direct exercise of power. Now let us further assume that such a relationship *does* exist between subjects C and B, and that A succeeds in using C for his purposes. The exercise of power by

14. Furthermore a subject can influence the state by power which is *not* based on these rules, such as personal power over a congressman or a mayor. Since our classification is based on the origin of power, we do not call this political power.

A over B is then built up out of two elements: the influence (and possibly power) exerted by A over C, and that exercised by C over B. To give an example of this, a group of electors combined in a political party can exert influence on the actions of the state. This power is political in nature. If this group uses its political power to wrest certain measures out of the state, in this way – indirectly – it can exercise power over the subjects who are affected by the power of the state. Here the exercise of power consists of two links: political power and state power. This example has been deliberately chosen because the distinction mentioned is not made in common usage, so that sometimes confusion occurs.

The indirect exercise of power can also run via more than two links. The power of the press is a good example of this. The press exercises what one might call social power over its readers, but it is debatable whether this is really power, because the will of the reader is not conquered but transformed (in the actions of the reader there is not an external but an internal limitation). In the second link, however, power may well be present: the public, influenced by the press, starts to exercise political influence, for instance. As a result the state comes into action, so that state power is exercised and certain subjects are compelled to do something. Thus the power of the press over these subjects is built up out of various forms of power occurring one after the other.

The forms of power mentioned here are of a non-economic nature; they are data for economics. When we split these forms of power off from the concept of power in general, economic power remains. The question now is to define the nature of this form of power.[15]

Economic power originates in economic relations. The typical 'economic situation', the starting point of economic science, is that in which the subject who has a series of unsatisfied wants is faced with the relatively scarce means of satisfying these wants. In this situation economic power can be exercised if the means on

15. Perhaps unnecessarily it may be repeated that it is immaterial to the form of power what the aim of the exercise of power is. Fiscal policy of the state has of course economic consequences and objectives, but still one cannot say that here the state is exercising economic power; to say this would point to an amorphous concept of power.

which the subject must rely for the satisfaction of his wants are in the hands of another subject. For this situation it is of course necessary that the needy subject A should in fact be dependent on the means which are in the hand of the 'powerful' subject B, and that A cannot cover his needs elsewhere, or at least not as well. Therefore dependence of a certain subject is the first requisite of the power relation.[16] The sanction on the exercise of power is that B withholds the scarce means from A. As a result the satisfaction of A's wants is affected, and therefore, to avoid this, he will be prepared to make concessions to B. From this follows the second condition for the exercise of power. B must be able to retain the goods[17] or, to be more exact, he must convey to A the impression that he possesses the possibility of retention.

If A is convinced that B is unable to withhold the goods, he will interpret B's threat to do so as an idle one, and then he will not be prepared to make any concessions; in this situation B cannot impose his will on A, and no exercise of power is possible.

These two elements – the dependence of the subject to be overcome and the possibility of retention by the 'powerful' subject – form the basis of economic power. All exercise of economic power is based directly or indirectly on the relation in which these two elements are present. Conversely, in the analysis of any problem of economic power attention will have to be paid to these two elements.

An understanding of the concept of power can be considerably deepened by defining the two elements quantitatively. The dependence is of course a quantitative concept in itself. The possibility of retention can easily be made into one by considering the

16. In the literature the concept of power is sometimes interpreted differently. For instance, Preiser has drawn up a theory of power under perfect competition, whilst the very characteristic of this state of affairs is that the subjects can change partners freely and without loss. Preiser regards the supply and demand elasticities as the criteria of the power, as a result of which he obtains a sound theory which, however, tells us little that is new, because economics long ago succeeded in giving a full explanation of price making under perfect competition. In our opinion such a concept of power is superfluous (Preiser, 1948, p. 333). Dunlop also interprets the concept of power in such a way that under perfect competition power may occur.

17. By 'goods' services and money must also be understood in this context.

sacrifice which B makes by not letting A have the good, but by withholding it (and either keeping it himself or letting a third party have it). If retention entails no sacrifice for B, he is obviously in a very strong position *vis-à-vis* A, the greater the sacrifice, the weaker B's position is, and when the sacrifice has become prohibitive and excludes retention, B cannot exercise any power, in so far as A realizes the actual situation sufficiently. Now the sacrifice which B makes by retaining the good is obviously nothing more than the dependence of B on A. Therefore economic power is based on the extent to which the subject to be overcome is dependent on the 'powerful' subject, and on the extent to which the 'powerful' subject is independent of the subject to be overcome.

In this way the basis of economic power has been described quantitatively. But is the economic power of a subject over another subject completely quantified by the two elements mentioned above? According to Slichter this is in fact the case. He defines the concept of 'bargaining power' as 'the cost to A of imposing a loss upon B' (1940, p. 57).[18] Here the cost to A is the dependence felt by the 'powerful' subject and the 'loss' the dependence felt by the subject to be overcome on the opposite party. Slichter therefore thinks that the bargaining power is completely determined by these two factors; in other words, if these two magnitudes are established, Slichter believes that the outcome of the exercise of power can be deduced.[19]

Evidently in this view the importance of the two above mentioned factors is overestimated. That this must be the case follows

18. Slichter uses the letters A and B in the opposite way to us. The fact that he does not speak of 'economic power', but of 'bargaining power', means little because, also according to Slichter's concept of power, power can very easily be exercised without it being preceded by an actual bargaining process. Bargaining can assume the rudimentary form of an imposition of will.

19. It should be further commented on Slichter's definition that it suffers from the same drawback as a not unusual definition of the economic principle, namely, that both the combined magnitudes are undefined. Instead of: 'the greatest utility at the least sacrifice' read 'the greatest utility at a given sacrifice' or 'a given utility at the least sacrifice'. In Slichter's definition the word 'given' should be inserted before the word 'loss'.

from the very fact that, as already mentioned, the point at issue is not the size of the sacrifice which the 'powerful' subject makes in the event of his accomplishing his possibility of retention, but the impression which his threat makes on the opposite party. And, although this impression does have something to do with the size of the sacrifice which the 'powerful' subject makes in the event of accomplishment of the threat, this connection is not a simple one and is in any case determined by other factors, such as the faint-heartedness of the subject to be overcome. Also all those factors which are summarized under the heading of 'ability to bargain' determine the result of the exercise of power. There is no question of the concept of power being given quantitatively by the two elements mentioned above.

To obtain a more complete picture of this concept of power an analysis of the bargaining process is necessary. The points under discussion in the present context consist of the indication of the basis of economic power, the delineation of the economic form of power as against other forms of power, and the answering of the question whether economic power may be interpreted as a datum for economics. The first two points have already been discussed; the latter question must now be answered. To do so it will suffice if we show that at least the dependence discussed above does not form a datum; whatever might be the result of the study of the other factors which determine the exercise of power, the answer to this question is then in the negative in any case.

It is easy to see that this dependence does not form a datum and is quite accessible to economic analysis when it is realized that it is based on two grounds.

The first of these is the want which the dependent subject feels in general with regard to the good in question. According to the current opinion this want can be accepted as a datum in so far as it is a direct one, for instance the want that a consumer feels for a consumer good. But a producer also has 'wants', he attaches ophelimity to means of production, and this ophelimity is not a datum, but is examined by economic theory (the marginal productivity theory!).

The second ground on which the dependence is based is the fact that the goods which are necessary for the satisfaction of the dependent subject's wants are not obtainable – or as easily obtainable – from other subjects than the 'powerful' subject himself.

Therefore an incomplete possibility of substitution of possible opposite parties must be present. This possibility of substitution is determined by a series of phenomena which have been treated for years in economics, in particular during discussion of the form of the market. There are close links between the form of the market and dependence, and thus between form of the market and power. On the strength of the above, economic power may definitely not be treated as a datum for economics. Consequently, the theory which states that bilateral monopoly is 'indeterminate' because the power factor plays a part in it, is condemned. [. . .]

References

AMERICAN ECONOMIC ASSOCIATION (1947), *Papers and Proceedings of the American Economic Association.*

BILIMOVIČ, A. (1943), 'Der Preis bei beiderseitigem Monopol', *Weltwirtschaftliches Archiv*, vol. 57, no. 2, pp. 312–63.

BÖHM-BAWERK, E. (1888), *Positive Theorie des Kapitals*, Jena, 4th edn, 1921.

BOWLEY, A. L. (1928), 'Bilateral monopoly', *Econ. J.*, vol. 38, no. 152, pp. 651–9.

COURNOT, A. (1838), 'Recherches sur les principes mathématiques de la théorie des richesses', Paris.

EDGEWORTH, F. Y. (1881), *Mathematical Psychics*, Kelley.

EUCKEN, W. (1944), *Die Grundlagen der Nationalökonomie*, Berlin.

FELLNER, W. (1947), 'Prices and wages under bilateral monopoly', *Q.J. Econ.*, vol. 61, no. 4, pp. 503–32.

HENDERSON, A. M. (1940), 'A further note on the problem of bilateral monopoly', *J. polit. Econ*, vol. 61, no. 4, pp. 238–43.

HICKS, J. R. (1935), 'Annual survey of economic theory', *Econometrica*, vol. 3, no. 1, pp. 1–20.

HOFFMAN, A. C. (1942), *Elements of Modern Economics* (ed. A. Meyers), Prentice-Hall.

JEVONS, W. S. (1882), *The State in Relation to Labour*, Macmillan.

LINDBLOM, C. E. (1948), 'Bargaining power in price and wage determination', *Q.J. Econ.*, vol. 62, no. 3, pp, 396–417.

MARSHALL, A. (1890), *Principles*, Macmillan.

MENGER, C. (1871), *Grundsätze der Volkwirtschaftslehre*, Vienna,

MORGENSTERN, O. (1948), 'Oligopoly, monopolistic competition and the theory of games', *Amer. Econ. Rev.*, vol. 38, no. 2, pp. 10–18.

NICHOL, A. J. (1942), 'Monopoly supply and monopsony demand', *J. polit. Econ.*, vol. 50, no. 6, pp. 861–79.

PREISER, E. (1948), 'Besitz und Macht in der Distributionstheorie', *Synopsis, Festgabe für Alfred Weber*, Heidelberg.

SCHÄFFLE, A. (1873), *Das gesellschaftliche System der menschlichen Wirtschaft*, Tübingen.

SCHNEIDER, E. (1932), *Reine Theorie monopolistischer Wirtschaftsformen*, Tübingen.

SCHUMPETER, J. (1916), 'Das Grundprinzip der Verteilungstheorie', *Archiv fur Sozialwissenschaft und Sozialpolitik*, vol. 42, no. 1, pp. 1–88.

SCHUMPETER, J. (1927), 'Zur Einführung der folgenden Arbeit Knut Wicksells', *Archiv für Sozialwissenschaft und Sozialpolitik*, vol. 58, no. 2, pp. 238–51.

SCITOVSZKY, T. DE (1949), 'A reconsideration of the theory of tariffs', *Readings in the Theory of International Trade*, Allen & Unwin.

SLICHTER, S. (1940), 'The impact of social security legislation upon mobility and enterprise', *Amer. Econ. Rev.*, vol. 30, no. 1, pt. 2, pp. 44–60.

STACKELBERG, H. VON (1934), *Marktform und Gleichgewicht*, Berlin.

STACKELBERG, H. VON (1945), *Grundlagen der theoretischen Volkswirtschaftslehre*, Berne.

STIGLER, G. J. (1947), *The Theory of Price*, Collier-Macmillan.

TEMPEL, J. VAN DER (1927), *Macht en economische wet*, Haarlem.

TINTNER, G. (1939), 'Note on the problem of bilateral monopoly' *J. polit. Econ.* vol. 47, no. 2, pp. 263–70.

WICKSELL, K. (1927), 'Mathematische Nationalökonomie', *Archiv für Sozialwissenschaft und Sozialpolitik*, vol. 58, no. 2, pp. 252–81.

ZEUTHEN, F. (1930), *Problems of Monopoly and Economic Warfare*, Routledge & Kegan Paul.

Part Three Property, Big Business and Power

One of the most important sources of inequality and economic power in private enterprise economies is the accumulation of wealth and the formation of big business. The uneven distribution of wealth means that individuals enter into economic transactions under very different economic pressures. Thus the behaviour which an individual can afford to adopt in the market will depend on the amount of property he owns. Without the use of any actual force the unequal initial positions will lead to very unequal results for the participants in the market. This aspect of economic power – the ways in which possession of wealth affects the 'laws' of the market – is treated, within the framework of competition theory, by Preiser.

The momentum of productive and decision-making power in big business extends, however, far beyond the immediate advantages arising from a strong market position. The power can be used to mould institutions and public opinion in various ways with the aim of strengthening one's position. Reagan's contribution affords a good general insight into the main channels of big business influence. Though his illustrations are drawn from US experience, the general picture applies to other countries as well.

A few concrete examples of the devices which can be used to influence the political decision process are contained in the excerpt from Lynch. They are based on evidence given to the US Temporary National Economic Committee. This monumental Congressional investigation into the concentration of economic power, which lasted from 1938 to 1941, and which produced – at a cost of more than one million pre-war dollars –

thirty-seven volumes of testimony and forty-three monographs on specific problems, did not get that amount of public attention which it deserves. The outbreak of war diverted all energies in a different direction. The passage from Lynch refers to pre-war cases of political interference by big insurance companies.

The theme of big business influence, which is the essence of the contributions by Reagan and Lynch, also comes up in the Readings from Brady and Galbraith in the following section (Part Four).

6 E. Preiser

Property, Power and the Distribution of Income

E. Preiser, 'Property and power in the theory of distribution', *International Economic Papers*, no. 2, 1952, pp. 206–20. Translated from the German by J. Kahane.

In his celebrated debate with the supporters of the concept of power in the theory of distribution, Böhm-Bawerk maintained two theses. One was that power exerts its influence not outside and against, but within and through economic laws; the other, that its effects are not lasting. We shall develop the problem. which concerns us here on the basis of these two assertions. We shall begin with the first (1914, p. 230).

We take it for granted nowadays that the conditions of power in a society constitute a datum which, in itself, explains neither the process nor the results of the distribution of income. In effect, to conceive of power as a direct causal factor of distribution means forgoing any explanation. In a market economy distribution is a market process resulting from price formation. It needs to be shown, therefore, how power manifests itself in the market and, ever since Böhm-Bawerk chose monopoly as an example on which to demonstrate its effects, there is general agreement that the conceptual tool for the study of economic power is the market form. The reasoning is that power manifests itself in monopolistic positions, and that only one market form excludes 'the domination by one part' *a priori*, namely by definition – and that is the market form of atomistic competition amongst both buyers and sellers. On the other hand, almost as much unanimity prevails in denying, explicitly or implicitly, the thesis that the power derived from the *possession of property*, too, can influence distribution. It is argued that the distribution of property influences the distribution of incomes amongst persons, but not that amongst the factors of production; furthermore, that only the latter is properly a subject of economic theory, whereas the former belongs to the field of sociology and statistics.

Let us look a little closer into this argument. The question of the personal distribution of income is one of the size of the income accruing to each individual, whereas the theory of the functional distribution of income is concerned with the distribution of the total yield, the so-called social product, among the factors of production which jointly determine the social product. Since we are here concerned only with the principle, we shall limit our argument to two factors of production, labour and land. We shall consider land to represent all the material factors of production.[1] The study of functional distribution will, then, reveal the shares accruing to 'labour' (not to the labourer) and 'land' (not to the landowner). The theory of functional distribution is thus by no means a theory of the distribution of incomes amongst individuals, but one of the repartition amongst factors of production. The incomes of the individuals can be ascertained only when we know the amounts of labour or of land, or of labour *and* land, at the disposal of each person.

However, this clear-cut distinction between functional and personal distribution becomes untenable as soon as we consider the previously mentioned case of monopoly. Monopoly is undoubtedly a relationship between persons and not between 'factors'; nor can there be any doubt that the study of monopoly is a specific task of economic theory, and may not be relegated to the theory of the personal distribution of income. The classification of 'functional' and 'personal' distribution of income is, in this case, at once revealed as inadequate, both terminologically and in substance. What is needed is a twofold distinction: first, between the theory of distribution and sociology (or statistics), and second, within the theory itself.

The sociologist regards the shares accruing to units of labour and of land as data and investigates the distribution of these units in society. Multiplication by the share accruing to each unit gives him the income of the individual or of the social group. The

1. We need not discuss here whether there is, in reality, only *one* factor of production. It all depends on the way we pose the problem. If we want to study the processes of production and the size of the relative shares in the product, it is convenient to work with the concept of several coordinated factors of production. On the other hand, in a complete theory of the distribution of income there is only *one* factor, namely labour; the rest are *means* of production. Herein I agree entirely with Conrad (1931, 1934).

theory of distribution, on the other hand, is concerned with the share itself. The first step is to calculate the appropriate shares from the productive importance of each factor of production, by imputing the marginal product. This is the very essence of what is called 'functional distribution'. The next step consists in proving that the owner of the factor of production really receives the marginal product, and at this stage the person replaces the factor. However, so long as this person really does receive the marginal product – which happens only under perfect competition – the use of the term 'functional distribution of income' is still justified. *We must, however, note right away that the function of each factor of production determines the size of its income only by virtue of the existence of one particular market form.* This is a market form which eliminates all elements other than productivity which might influence the distribution of income, and which, too, gives rise to the opinion that this is the 'natural' distribution, and that any other distribution would be an artificial deviation which could not last. But, for all its virtues, perfect competition is in no way more natural than any other market form. As soon as we introduce a fresh datum, e.g. an employers' monopsony in the labour market, there can no longer be any question of wages being determined by productivity.

It is therefore not surprising that economic theory has increasingly shaken off the constrictive analysis of the pure theory of marginal productivity, and has learned afresh to regard the process of distribution as a market phenomenon, namely as the formation of the prices of the means of production, or in other words, of the goods and services supplied to the entrepreneur, where marginal productivity is only one of several determining factors. There are, then, two successive parts to the theory of distribution. The first, disregarding all sociological data, considers the division of the *product* amongst the *factors of production* solely from the point of view of the dependence of the product on the contribution of each factor. The second, on the other hand, studies the mechanism of the distribution of *income* between *persons*, and must obviously take account of all the elements which influence the formation of the prices of all the goods and services supplied by these persons. One may doubt whether this second part still deserves the name of a functional theory of distribution. We shall, nevertheless, call it so in order to avoid confusion, and so as to stress, by retaining the customary designation, the contrast to the personal distribution of income (which is a problem of sociology and statistics).[2]

2. Economic literature is by no means clear on the concept of functional distribution, and in view of the twofold nature of the problem to which we have pointed, it could hardly be otherwise. The theory of imputation sets the problem in its own way. Thus Landauer (1923, pp. 22–3) defines functional distribution unequivocally as 'the distribution of the joint product amongst the separate factors . . . but not the distribution of the proceeds amongst the representatives of the factors'. He maintains that functional distribution is 'in no way a real distribution of actual goods, but merely a matter of accountancy, namely the imputation of the yield'; and that functional distribution does not determine 'the shares of individuals . . . but those of the factors of production' (p. 24). On p. 71 he declares right out that the essential content of a theory of functional distribution is nothing but a theory of imputation. This does indeed yield economic laws valid for any economy, whatever its economic order may be; and these laws must be observed by any rational economic policy (pp. 65–6). The setting of the problem leaves no place for any element of power; the theory of functional 'distribution' is, in reality, a part of the theory of production which shows the importance of the individual factors in the formation of the total product.

At the same time the static analysis, at any rate, looks to the theory of functional distribution for the laws governing the *distribution of incomes* as well. Here the difficulties begin. One *must* prove, as against the theoreticians of power, that neither the interference of non-economic forces, e.g. minimum wage legislation (p. 33), nor the influence of monopolies (p. 57) can, in the long run, affect the distribution of income; and that, on the contrary, the static 'normal case' is that of 'free competition', where the 'functional yield' prevails (p. 63). Whether or not this thesis can be proved, the problem itself is now set in a different manner: the question is no longer one of accounting, but of actual distribution. This shift of ground becomes apparent in the – not always explicit, but in any case *de facto* – addition of a fresh datum, namely the market form. In contrast to the data previously employed (available amount of factors of production and demand schedules), this new datum is an element of the social order.

Clark (1908) already makes it clear that functional theory in fact has in view the actual distribution of income; Hans Mayer, the latest representative of the theory of imputation in its strictest form, explicitly identifies the problem of functional distribution with that of ascertaining 'the laws governing the formation of the prices of the means of production'. This really means carrying the theory of functional distribution beyond the framework of the theory of imputation, and marginal productivity then becomes but *one* element amongst others determining functional distribution. If we find that Mayer himself, and Schumpeter, too (1916), nevertheless attribute the

The market form, then, is one of the elements influencing functional distribution; but it is not the only one. The subsequent discussion aims at showing that – contrary to prevailing opinion – *the distribution of property, too*, exercises an influence which affects not only the personal, but also the functional distribution of income. The distribution of property obviously does not exert its influence directly, and we must therefore again look for the medium through which it affects the formation of prices. This medium is the elasticity of supply and demand. As this is clearly the most ordinary matter, susceptible to give rise not to contradiction but rather to a compassionate smile, our only task is to demonstrate the far-reaching importance of this point.

Before going more closely into this, let us concentrate our attention for a moment on Böhm-Bawerk's *second thesis*. This asserts that distribution rates forcibly imposed by the exertion of power cannot be of a lasting nature. Its proof is based on the example of a rise in wages above marginal productivity which has been imposed by trade-union action. Böhm-Bawerk argues that this could, indeed, have a momentary success, but that it would induce employers to change over to production methods involving greater capital intensity; the competition of now redundant workers would then, again, depress wages to a rate corresponding to marginal productivity. Power, in Böhm-Bawerk's argument, thus is defeated by the operation of 'economic motives' and by the counteracting forces of a 'purely economic nature'; the 'natural' distribution, that is the distribution according to marginal productivity, comes into force again. Even those who make certain reservations with respect to this particular method of proof are unlikely to question the substance of the argument – the less so since Böhm-Bawerk carefully lists all the special circumstances in which an imposed rise in wages is later, as it were, legitimized through the course of events (1914, p. 294).

But does this example really prove the general thesis that power must fail in the long run? Böhm-Bawerk did indeed mention – though he did not develop – the contrary case of a monopsony

decisive role to this one element, then we must not overlook their limiting assumptions: they assume atomistic competition and a given stock of factors of production. We shall later have to revert to the importance of just this latter point.

on the labour market. Here, too, he could have pointed to counteracting forces which, at least in one case, would render the dictates of power ineffective in the long run. This special case is that of a locally limited monopoly. He could, furthermore, have pointed out that if employers in an industry have a collective monopoly of the demand for labour, this is generally but a reply to a collective monopoly of labour supply. Assuming, however, a unilateral collective monopoly of demand for labour, without local limitation, there would be no counteracting forces of a 'purely economic nature', for, whilst the employer can react to a rise in wages by adopting different methods of production, the worker possesses no means of evading the effects of a fall in wages. Therefore a wage rate *lower* than the marginal product could be maintained for much longer than a wage rate *higher* than the marginal product. The worker does not, indeed, lack the 'motive' to oppose such action, but he does lack the means of making his opposition effective by changing his economic activity. The weakness of Böhm-Bawerk's concept of the ephemeral nature of the effects of power becomes quite obvious in a generalized formulation. Such a general formula would, in effect, say that every monopoly calls forth counteracting forces which remove the monopolistic price and thus cancel the monopoly itself – an assertion which is obviously wrong.

If, nevertheless, the distribution of income does by and large correspond to marginal productivity, the reason lies not in the counteracting forces of a 'purely economic nature' called forth by every monopoly, but simply in the fact that a comprehensive monopoly is inconceivable in the case of any of the three large classes of income receivers. Power as a phenomenon of the market form may thus be able to influence distribution locally, and for a short time even over the whole market; nevertheless, it is, in effect, of little importance for the long-term distribution of the social product. All the more important is the second aspect of economic power: the distribution of property.

Our previous discussion has shown that the distribution of property is bound to be significant not only for the personal but also for the functional distribution of income, since it is just his lack of property which prevents the worker from reacting to an unfavourable wage structure in a manner similar to that adopted by the employer in the opposite case. Böhm-Bawerk had already pointed out that during a wage struggle the employer could hold his breath longer. Of greater importance is the fact that later, too, when the wage struggle has been decided, the employer is able to rearrange his economic activity, whereas the worker cannot do so.

This fact is quite independent of the existence or non-existence of a monopoly, whether unilateral or bilateral. *What matters here is the elasticity of supply and demand.* This may strengthen or weaken a monopolistic position, but it is of significance even in the total absence of monopolies.[3] For this reason we shall assume perfect competition on both sides of the market, i.e. we shall exclude power in so far as it is an attribute of monopolistic elements in the market, and shall concern ourselves only with the nature and the effects of power in so far as it finds expression in the elasticity of supply and demand.

Unfortunately, we lack a succinct term – corresponding to that of 'market form' (*Marktform*) – to describe the market constellations which will now concern us. We shall have to revert to the general concept of 'market situation' (*Marktlage*), although this is too wide for our problem. 'Market situation' describes the situation resulting from the momentary relationship of supply and demand; it is thus conditioned both by the *position* of the two curves and by their *shape*, i.e. the elasticity. In fact, we are here interested only in the latter. Moreover, the market situation is – to a far greater degree than the market form – a fleeting phenomenon. It is subject to constant change, especially as regards the relative position of the two curves. The shape of the curves is more stable and sometimes reveals characteristics connected with more fundamental causes. This is particularly the

3. On the significance of elasticities for the effectiveness of economic power see Eucken (1944, pp. 315–16). It is true that Eucken always regards the market form as the basis of power; the elasticity of supply and of demand strengthens or weakens already existing positions of economic power, but it does not – as in our argument – constitute a second, completely independent, element *apart* from the market form.

case with the supply of labour which can be typically elastic or typically rigid. It is this case which concerns us, and when, therefore, we speak simply of 'market situation' this term must be understood in the specific sense of a curve whose shape is typical, and not merely temporary and accidental.

Sociologists and psychologists, when discussing the social question and, in particular, wage questions, always deal at length with the special position of the supply of labour in a capitalist economy. The worker cannot 'wait', the urgency of his supply is great, and his position is therefore necessarily weaker than that of his employer. Economists do, indeed, note all this as a special feature of the labour market, yet do not accord it any significance for the functional distribution of income, since the mechanism of price formation is affected neither by the position of the curves nor by their shape. Oppenheimer is the only writer to have built his theory around this state of affairs: the possibility of cutting off the supply of land, and secondarily also that of the manufactured means of production, confers on the property-owning class a 'buyers' monopoly' relative to the worker who is under constant pressure of supply (1924, 1926). With reference to the particular form in which Oppenheimer chose to present his thesis, it has rightly been objected that there could be no question of a capitalists' 'buyers' monopoly', and that profit could not be explained as a monopoly rent.[4] But this objection does not invalidate Oppenheimer's main idea. Even if there is no monopsony in the strict sense, the fact remains that, when supply is greatly pressed, the buyer acquires a preponderance which places him in a position similar to that of a monopsonist. One would not expect this to have no bearing on the functional distribution of income; indeed, at first sight one may marvel at the self-confidence with which economists disregard this idea and cling to the thesis of marginal productivity. However, this is formally justified, for – as we shall soon see – the worker still receives the marginal product of his labour. Nevertheless, the distribution of incomes is drastically altered according to the elasticity of supply.[5]

4. Particularly Schumpeter.
5. Whether profit itself can be similarly deduced is quite a different question. The fact that wages coincide with the marginal product, and that therefore there can be no profit at the margin of production, is no counter-

Let us draw the labour supply curves for the cases of high and of low elasticity.

Greatly simplified, the curve of elastic supply would rise from left to right, whilst the curve of rigid supply would be at right

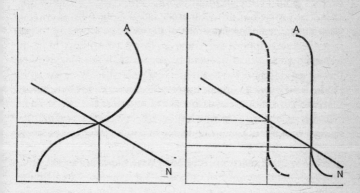

Figure 1

angles to the abscissa. In reality, both curves reveal other characteristic features. Both will turn back when the wage level reaches a certain height: at very high wages the supply of labour recedes, whether it is otherwise elastic or rigid. Furthermore, the two curves will probably have a small vertical section in common, immediately below the point where they begin to turn back; this is a section where the wage rate is without influence on the supply of labour. Below this, however, they will differ fundamentally: in one case supply will react strongly to changes in wage rates, diminishing with falling wages and increasing with rising wages; in the other case the labour supply remains constant, because the worker offering his services has no means of reacting. Finally, at very low wages, the curves will diverge completely: if the labour supply is elastic, it will vanish almost entirely; if it is rigid, supply will increase – even if the number of workers remains constant –

---

argument, for the intramarginal surplus, too, represents profit or rent. But several other objections can be raised against Oppenheimer's derivation, so that, even if his basic idea is granted, a different theoretical construction is required.

because at exceptionally low wages even those members of the family who do not normally work for pay will be forced to seek employment and earnings outside the home.

The exact course of the curves, and in particular the end sections both at the top and at the bottom do not, however, affect our problem. For the intermediate, i.e. the most prevalent wage rates, the decisive sections of the curves correspond to the simplified description given above. If we now insert in both diagrams an identical demand curve, we shall see immediately that the equilibrium wage rate is higher when the labour supply is elastic than when it is rigid. Employment is indeed lower, but in this case this is not the consequence of an artificially raised wage rate, i.e. of a wage rate which does not correctly represent the scarcity of labour. The lower degree of employment corresponds to the essential facts of the case, for supply *is* really lower. The position is quite different from one where wages are raised, say, by trade-union action or by the state's *fiat* decree. Other things being equal, such a rise would bring about involuntary unemployment, because wages would not correspond to the actual position of the curves.[6] In our case, however, wages are conditioned by the data, and in so far as the lower degree of employment is to be regarded as unemployment at all, it could only be a question of voluntary, and not involuntary, unemployment. Elasticity of supply thus acts like the reduction of a rigid supply: we need only move the curve of rigid supply to the left in order to get the same wage and the same degree of employment as with elastic supply.

This discussion enables us, in the first place, to draw an important general conclusion. When the market situation is different the price naturally is different, too. But generally we think in this connection only of the relative *position* of the demand and supply curves, which, in reality, shifts constantly and leads to dynamic price changes. Here, however, prices are different even under static conditions according to the *shape* of the curves. These shapes are conditioned by the data of a static system, too; and that holds for all markets. The shape of the supply curve for manufactured goods – which, of course, coincides with the

6. This requires no complicated chain of argument. It suffices to point out that the marginal producer cannot pay the increased wages and that his production therefore ceases.

marginal cost curve – is unequivocally determined by the given technical conditions. In the markets for the factors of production sociological data replace technical data, but economists are apt to forget this fact. Economists usually start by assuming that there is, of each factor of production, a definite stock which has to be placed. Prices then result from the quantitative relations between the factors of production, e.g. from the given quantitative proportion between labour and land, for marginal productivity is merely the reflection of the relative scarcity of the factors of production. The concept of a stock means, in effect, starting out with a rigid supply curve; but in reality the supply curve could just as well be elastic. True, we have to deal with amounts of labour and of land; not, however, with naturally given amounts *awaiting* disposal, but with amounts which first *have to be placed* at the disposal of production. The measure in which they are so placed depends on sociological data.[7]

Sociological data obviously exert an influence on all markets, and on both sides of the market, i.e. both on supply and on demand. These data form the bases of the reflections of the persons acting in the markets, reflections which formally accord with Gossen's second law, and result in quite definite decisions. There are, for instance, certain things which greatly affect the demand of housewives for domestic help: whether or not hard times have accustomed them to do their own housework if need be, the size of their husband's income, and so on. As the case may be, their

7. The supporters of the theory of marginal productivity appear to take the assumption of a given stock of factors of production for granted. They start, on the one side, from marginal utility functions, or the functions of demand; on the other side, from absolute quantities of the factors of production. These they describe as 'the total material and personal means of production within an economy, distributed amongst the great mass of their owners who, actuated solely by the desire to get the highest compensation for the employment of their means of production, seek to direct them into the most profitable uses' (Mayer, 1928, p. 1225). Labour, too, appears as a datum, just like the forces of nature; it is sold to the highest bidder, and its price falls until the whole 'stock' has been placed (Schumpeter, 1916). As we have seen, this is in fact true only in certain definite circumstances, namely in the case of the propertyless worker. Just as there is a demand function (and a technical production function), so, too, there exists a function of the supply of factors of production; and it is by no means self-evident that this should – graphically – be a line at right angles to the abscissa.

demand will be either elastic or rigid, and under given conditions of supply wages will accordingly be lower or higher quite independently of the market system, e.g. even under perfect competition on both sides of the market. Returning to our general example, we may ask: What is it that lies behind the varying elasticity of the supply of labour? There are a number of elements which may influence elasticity. But above all else we are here face to face with the stark question of sheer physical survival, the question whether there is some other means by which to keep above water. In this context, paramount importance attaches to the distribution of property – in our example the distribution of land among the economic subjects. Where labour is completely divorced from ownership of land, the supply of labour is rigid; wherever the worker owns a certain amount of land, the labour supply is elastic, and the wage rate will be higher quite irrespective of the market form. *Behind the elasticity of supply lies the power embodied in property*, and this foundation is much more stable than, say, a collective monopoly of the workers which could limit the supply of labour only by artificial means, and, by its very nature, only temporarily.

Having demonstrated that an elastic supply of labour brings with it higher wages, we have still only taken the first step. If we want to know what happens to the functional distribution of income we must inquire into the total result, and doubts may arise here, if only because employment will be lower. Let us illustrate the position graphically.

The right-hand part of Figure 2, *ABCE*, shows, according to Clark's method, the yield – or the income – obtained by cultivating a given area of land with a given number of workers. *BC* is the marginal product of the labour applied along *AB*; *ABCD* represents total wages and *DCE* the rent (the intramarginal profit). The distribution of property is immaterial here, but it will be convenient to assume, in the first place, that the functional distribution of income coincides with the personal one, i.e. that the wages are earned by workers owning no property, and that the rent accrues to an idle class of landowners.

In order to study the effects of the distribution of property, let us alter the figure a little. Assume that half the land belongs to the workers, and assume that they arrange their work in such a manner that they devote half their time to the cultivation of their own soil, and the other half to working other people's land for wages. To illustrate this, let us displace *FB* to the left of point *A*, making *AH = FB*. The figure *ABCE* is now replaced by *HFGEI*; the two are equal both absolutely, and in their sections. The

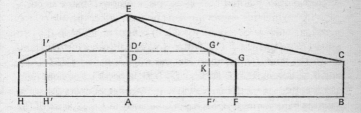

Figure 2

difference between the two figures lies, at first, simply in the fact that half the rent, namely *IDE*, now accrues to the workers in their capacity as landowners.

At the same time, however, the functional distribution has altered. The labour supply, hitherto rigid, grows elastic, i.e. it diminishes. Let the marginal product of labour rise to *H'I'* or *F'G'*. Employment, and with it the social product, are reduced. The absolute amount of wages (*H'F'G'I'*) may rise, remain constant, or fall (we must naturally regard as 'wages' also that part – *H'AD'I'* – which the landowning workers must impute to themselves as the specific yield of their labour). In any case, labour's share in the social product has increased, while the share of land has decreased. The influence of the distribution of property is not exhausted by the fact that the worker, too, now draws rent: wage rates and the share of wages in the social product rise – i.e. the distribution of property affects not only the personal but also the functional distribution of income.[8] Since employment has dim-

8. At the end of his discussion, Böhm-Bawerk writes (1914, pp. 299–300): 'Since power can permanently displace the "data" of the functional rules of distribution, it is possible to effect interventions in the field of personal distribution, the effects of which need not be limited in time. If a government, by land grants, turns proletarians into landowners, then they and their successors, without foreseeable end, will find their personal incomes

inished, the total income of the landowning worker ($H'I'ED'G'F'$) is indeed not as large as it would be were he to maintain his previous labour supply ($HIEDGF$), in spite of the altered distribution of property; on the other hand, he has to work fewer hours. The change in the functional distribution has presented the worker with a rent, and, in addition, with greater leisure. It is, or course, possible that he will use his additional leisure to cultivate his own land more intensively than other people's: the marginal product of labour would, in that case, differ in the two areas (HI as against $F'G'$). If the worker cultivates his own land up to the limit HI, his total income will consist of $HIED'G'F'$, and if we assume that $F'FGK = DKG'D'$, it becomes evident that, as an employee of the landowner, the worker pockets the same wage as before, and that his leisure is clearly at the expense of the landowner's (already halved) rent, which is now reduced from EDG to $ED'G'$.

A few supplementary remarks may serve to consolidate this result and to mark its importance for the theory of distribution and for the problem of economic power in general.

As regards the theory of distribution, our result in no way contradicts the basic idea on which rests the prevailing explanation of the distribution of income. Our result fits into the theory of marginal productivity, so far as the latter does not try to be more than it is by its own nature, namely an instrument of theoretical analysis for explaining the relative levels of income. Whatever the shape of the supply curve, wages correspond to marginal productivity, or to the relative scarcity of labour as a factor of production. This scarcity is not artificially introduced as in the case of a collective labour monopoly, where the distribution brought about by the temporary withdrawal of labour, namely a wage rate *higher* than marginal productivity, conflicts with the factual proportions of land and labour; and which must lead in one way or another to involuntary unemployment, and – other conditions being equal – can have no lasting existence. On

increased by ground rents, and this irrespective of the dividing line drawn in functional distribution between ground rent and wages.' We would add: quite true, but this dividing line itself is altered in favour of the new landowners!

the other hand, the scarcity of labour is not due to natural, i.e. physical causes, but to social causes. This social scarcity may coincide with natural scarcity – in the case of rigid supply – but it need not necessarily do so. *Even if, physically, just the same number of workers exists, and just the same quantity of land, the different distribution of property will create a greater scarcity of the amount of labour which comes on offer, and it is the latter – not the number of workers in itself – which is decisive.* What matters is indeed the relative scarcity of the factors of production, and the correction to be made to the theory of marginal productivity consists simply in this: that such scarcity is not a natural, but a social phenomenon. It depends on the distribution of property, and the degree of stability of this social datum determines the degree of stability of the distribution of income based upon it.

Our result thus agrees with the theory of marginal productivity in so far as the latter represents a formal principle, but there is disagreement as soon as that theory claims to reveal the 'natural' distribution. We have already pointed out in our first section that the functional theory is not content with explaining the imputation of yields to the factors, but also purports to explain the incomes received by the owners of these factors, for which purpose it draws on the hypothesis of atomistic competition. The theory thus switches from the field of natural economic laws to social considerations, i.e. in this case to the market economy. But such a μετάβασις εἰς ἄλλο γένος entails consideration of all the factors which influence supply and demand. If the supply conditions of the factors of production were to be studied as lovingly as the conditions of demand, the functional theory would encounter the problems of differences in elasticity and would thereby be led to consider the distribution of property (perhaps other data, too – we have merely singled out an especially striking one). This, however, destroys the concept of a natural distribution which is supposed always to enjoy a final triumph over 'power'. Natural distribution could be allowed to vanquish the power embodied in monopolies, because this power is said to affect the distribution of income only partially and temporarily, without altering the given scarcity relations of the stocks of factors of production. Now, however, power appears as a datum affecting this very scarcity relation, and there is no force urging a move away from the given distribution of incomes towards that legendary 'natural' distribution.[9]

All this needs to be fully appreciated together with yet another fact which tends to be presented as incidental only. namely, that it is not scarcity of land which is the immediate cause of the landowner's income, but private ownership of (scarce) land. It will then be seen that sociological data rightly deserve a prominent place in the theory of the distribution of incomes. At the same time, such a point of view would lead to the disappearance of the seemingly unbridgeable conflict between the theory of marginal productivity and those theories of distribution which, basing themselves on labour as the sole factor of production, trace all rent incomes to the simple fact that scarce and essential means of production are in private ownership, and that the owners are in a position to obtain a price for the sale of their use.[10]

9. The confusion of the (formal) idea of imputation with the concept of a (real) 'natural' distribution is common to nearly all the supporters of the theories of imputation and marginal productivity. This is true of Böhm-Bawerk no less than of Clark and their successors; only Wicksell (1913) really does use marginal analysis only as a formal principle. *The idea of a natural distribution is a dogma.* With Clark, this shows itself in his conviction that the natural distribution is also the just one; with all the others, in the more or less explicit notion that the natural distribution is the only rational distribution, and that therefore the spontaneous economic forces tend towards its realization. This distribution is regarded as rational because, with given needs and given amounts of factors of production, there is only *one* valuation of the factors of production – and, therefore, in a market economy, only *one* distribution – which meets the requirement of a maximum social product. But the idea that only that distribution is rational which maximizes the social product, is no less dogmatic than Clark's view that only that distribution is just which accords to each factor of production its own marginal product. Rational economic action is not identical with the pursuit of the maximum income which leads to the maximum social product. In our example the social product diminishes with the increasing elasticity of the labour supply, yet all economic agents are acting entirely rationally, i.e. in the sense of the maximum individual satisfaction of wants. The difference is that the data have altered, and with them the distribution. The new distribution is certainly 'rational', but it is no longer 'natural' or 'purely economic' since, at least in part, it is determined by power.

10. It would be erroneous to object that we may, here, be digressing unconsciously into the personal distribution of incomes. This type of theory is just as much concerned with functional distribution as is the theory of marginal productivity; it merely refrains from turning the 'rent-getter' into a 'product-creator' (Clark), or speaking of 'productive contribution', etc.

These theories, which, too, must employ marginal productivity or relative scarcity to explain the relative levels of incomes, need not imply any sort of social indictment. Similarly, the theory of marginal productivity should divest itself of any suspicion of an apologetic attitude by discarding the concept of a 'natural' distribution. It is a concept which is just as erroneous as that of the theoreticians of power against whom it is directed.

We can now proceed to the last question, that of *the concept of economic power* and its manifestations. We have kept this to the end, because the end of a paper is the proper place for any conceptual discussion which aims at being more than a provisional definition. By confronting 'power' and 'economic law', Böhm-Bawerk formulated a contrast which, in his own view, does not exist, since power – in the form of monopoly – is interwoven into the context of economic laws. It is all the more remarkable that he himself should have reverted to this contrast: for him, power is and remains an 'artificial' and 'arbitrary' incursion of social forces, which is ultimately wrecked on the 'natural economic laws'. Böhm-Bawerk thus perverted the relationship between data and economic processes into a conflict between two opposing forces; this explains how he came to apply the same yardstick to two such different things as the power positions of private persons and the power of the state. We exclude *a priori* any discussion of state power, for the question of the scope and the limitations of governmental economic policy obviously has no bearing on our present problem.[11]

What, then, do we mean by power when we speak of 'economic power', of the power of private economic agents? Since all economic activity aims at the acquisition of an income, private power means, first, simply the ability to appropriate goods.[12] In this sense *all* economic agents have power. It can be measured in terms of that very ability, which in turn depends on the magnitude of a person's qualifications and property. This, however, is clearly a matter of the purely personal distribution of income, which

11. Another way of setting the problem, which differs completely from ours, is that of Salz (1930), who discusses the sociological conflict between the concepts of power and of economy.

12. The economic power of the state could similarly be defined as the ability to influence the data and the economic processes.

does not set us any further problems. What interests us is the problem of power in connection with functional distribution, and for this we require a narrower concept which will reveal the influence of power on the mechanism of the distribution of income. In other words, we are no longer concerned with noting that high qualifications and great wealth confer on their owner a larger income, and thus more 'power' than low qualifications and little wealth would do; we now ask whether, and how far, 'power' affects income *per hour of work* and *per unit of wealth*.

Max Weber has given us a useful criterion: we may think of power as the opportunity of enforcing our own will *even against resistance* in some social context (in this case, within the mechanism of the market). This could be either in attack or in defence, i.e. with the purpose of raising our income or preventing a reduction in our income.[13] From this point of view power presupposes that the economic agent has the possibility of stipulating conditions, that he may accept or refuse offers, that he can evade pressure; such a possibility presupposes in its turn either qualifications higher than average, i.e. some specifically rare skill, or a material basis such as ownership of material goods or of certain rights. In this sense there can obviously only be one group *without* power, namely the propertyless wage earner.[14] In relation to him all other economic agents have power. This does not manifest itself in the rent which their wealth yields them – for this concerns only the personal distribution – but in the different position on the labour market: an essentially rigid supply faces an essen-

13. Landauer rightly stresses that economic power manifests itself in the process of exchange (1923, pp. 10–11). But his thesis that *every* income from economic exchange is a gain due to economic power is inconsistent, since he himself regards the possibility of exercising 'social coercion' as the essence of economic power (p. 14). Were this element missing, the concept of power would indeed be of no value. Böhm-Bawerk was thus quite right in pointing out that the slogan 'power' really meant 'domination by one part' (1914, p. 233).

14. Lack of property and no-more-than-average qualifications generally go hand in hand; if they have no property at all, it is difficult even for the gifted to acquire higher qualifications. On the other hand, exceptional qualifications, whether innate or acquired, act like property: they raise their owner's 'economic power'. Wherever we simply speak of 'property' in the following pages, we mean to include higher-than-average qualifications.

tially elastic demand.[15] This situation confers on the buyer a position similar to that he would enjoy were he to possess a buyer's monopoly, i.e. a monopsony. In the following, we shall use the term 'monopoly' to cover both monopoly in its strict sense and monopsony; and we shall designate as *quasi-monopoly* the typical market situation described here, which is defined by certain elasticities. It is the first manifestation of economic power.[16]

Quasi-monopoly is only a special case amongst the numerous market situations in which the changing position and shape of the demand and supply curves favour or handicap now one party and now the other. Obviously, a rigid demand, too, can find itself exposed to the pressure of a quasi-monopoly: every shortage of essential goods offers an example. Up to a point every market situation is a power situation. There is no sense, however, in linking the idea of economic power with all these merely dynamic fluctuations of market situations. We must confine ourselves to statics, and here our example of the labour market is the only one in which functional distribution is actually affected by the power of property.

Apart from this the distribution of property plays no part in the

15. The objection that the interdependence between landowner and worker is reciprocal, misses the point. We need not even consider the extreme case of the landowner who, renouncing all help, himself cultivates all or part of his land, while the worker lacks the possibility of such 'autarchy'. As long as land is at all scarce in relation to labour, labour will be on offer and rent will arise. Rents may fall and may perhaps no longer provide a livelihood for the landowner. But his very existence is never threatened. In any case, elasticity of demand does not mean that the employer always has the upper hand in a wage struggle; his demand may, momentarily, be very rigid. But eventually he can react by changing his methods of production, or in other ways. That is why we say that demand is 'essentially' elastic; we could also have said 'in the long run'.

16. We begin to appreciate now that the trade unions cannot be classed amongst the other collective monopolies, although their actions may be studied by the methods proper to the theory of monopoly. The trade unions, too, do indeed eliminate competition. But even if they are successful, they do not create a privileged position amongst parties otherwise equal (as is the case in entrepreneurs' monopolies of supply); rather do they, in the first place, try to compensate for the specific lack of power of the propertyless worker.

static analysis. A person's wealth may be large or small (and thus yield a large or a small personal income), but so long as perfect competition prevails no one can enforce his will against opposition, except on the labour market. This follows from the definition of perfect competition and requires no further proof. Apart from quasi-monopoly, economic power manifests itself only in monopolistic market forms, i.e. in all systems other than that of atomistic competition.

Let us sum up: 'quasi-monopoly' and 'monopoly' (in the widest sense, which includes all market forms other than atomistic competition) are the economic categories within which economic power manifests itself. This power rests, on the one hand, on ownership of material goods, on the other hand, on privileged market positions. Both are elements of the economic order; they are social data and, jointly with the natural, technical and psychological data, they determine the functional distribution of income. These social data act indirectly through monopoly and quasi-monopoly which directly determine prices – so far as the latter can ever be unequivocally determined at all. We know that this is not always the case. There are gaps in the system of interdependence – one need only think of bilateral monopoly or of an imperfect market – and here we must consider one final manifestation of economic power: the personal ability to succeed. This works directly by threat or suggestion. It does not rest on circumstances exterior to the individual, e.g. his social position, but on his entirely personal ability to influence the motives of the contracting party.[17] It will suffice to mention the struggle between trade unions and employers' associations in order to appreciate the scope and significance of this direct manifestation of power. Nevertheless, whatever the importance of this personal element, its effectiveness rests on the power inherent in the objective facts of the social order: a trade union's chance of success in the battle of wits, too, will be the greater the 'richer', i.e. the more powerful it is.[18]

17. See Jöhr (1943, p. 233).
18. The attempt at exact formulation reveals a difficulty due to the ambiguity of the word 'power', which belongs to the unhappy class of verbal abstracts. 'Power' means 'being able to do something', and we thus defined 'economic power' as the ability of individuals to influence

Quasi-monopolistic or monopolistic positions of privilege remain the fundamental conditions for economic power, however the latter may manifest itself. They confer on their owner power, not only in the personal, but also in the functional distribution of income. If, in conclusion, we are to draw a lesson applicable to economic policy, then it is the following: an economic policy aiming at social justice must not limit itself to fighting monopolies, but must also pay attention to quasi-monopolies. Any measures tending to equalize the distribution of property fall under this heading. Any policy which helps the man without property to acquire property, gives him not only a share in rent; it increases

the distribution of income in a certain way (Power 1). This ability rests on certain conditions, it has a basis, a foundation, a point of departure as distinct from this ability; the latter might be called 'power situation', 'power position' or 'power relationship', but in fact it is loosely also called 'power' (Power 2). We say 'knowledge *is* power', when in reality it only *confers* power. The logical relationship is clear: the power relationship as a social datum confers on those it favours the ability to act in a certain way; they possess a position of power and exercise power. Language, however, turns this into the simple statement that they have power, which can and does refer equally to the ability (Power 1) and the power situation (Power 2).

The power founded purely on personality, i.e. the ability to influence the motives of the contracting party, affords a specially peculiar case. Here Power 1 and Power 2 coincide, the ability is not based on a separate social position of power, but is itself a datum, and this datum has a direct influence on the distribution of income. It is indeed itself, as we have seen, not quite independent of objectively based positions of power. Viewed comprehensively, the phenomenon of economic power in relation to the functional distribution of income may be represented schematically as follows:

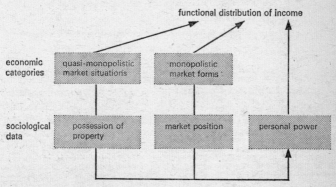

the elasticity of the supply of labour with the result of raising the share of labour in the social product and reducing that of the income from property. Employment, and with it the social product, will indeed be less, but there will be more leisure. All in all, with shorter hours of work, the income of those who work *and* own will rise, whilst the income of those who *merely* own will fall.

References

BÖHM-BAWERK, E. (1914), 'Macht oder ökonomisches Gesetz?', *Gesammelte Schriften von E. von Böhm-Bawerk* (ed. F. X. Weiss, 1924), Vienna.

CLARK, J. B. (1908), *The Distribution of Wealth*, Macmillan Co.

CONRAD, O. (1931), *Der Mechanismus der Verkehrswirtschaft*, Jena.

CONRAD, O. (1934), *Die Todsünde der Nationalökonomie*, Leipzig and Vienna.

EUCKEN, W. (1944), *Die Grundlagen der Nationalökonomie*, Berlin.

JÖHR, A. (1943), *Theoretische Grundlagen der Wirtschaftspolitik*, St Gallen.

LANDAUER, C. (1923), *Grundprobleme der funktionellen Verteilung des wirtschaftlichen Wertes*, Jena.

MAYER, H. (1928), 'Zurechnung', *Handwörterbuch der Staatswissenschaften*, 4th edn, vol. 8, pp. 1206–28.

OPPENHEIMER, F. (1924), *Theorie der reinen und politischen Ökonomie* (*System der Soziologie 3*), 5th edn, Berlin.

OPPENHEIMER, F. (1926), *Wert und Kapitalprofit*, 3rd edn, Jena.

SALZ, A. (1930), *Macht und Wirtschaftsgesetz*, Leipzig.

SCHUMPETER, J. (1916), 'Das Grundprinzip der Verteilungstheorie', *Archiv für Sozialwissenschaft und Sozialpolitik*, vol. 42, no. 1, pp. 1–88.

WICKSELL, K. (1913), *Vorlesungen über Nationalökonomie*, vol. 1, Jena.

7 M. D. Reagan

Business Power and Influence

Excerpts from M. D. Reagan, *The Managed Economy*,
Oxford University Press, 1963, chapter 6, pp. 99–120.

Economic impact

Corporate decisions on wages, prices, dividends and investment
directly affect important public economic goals: economic
growth, full employment, price stability. These decisions are
made, however, on criteria of the firm's welfare rather than of
the whole economy. And, it must be said, to some extent they
must be so made as the system now stands, even if the individual
firm wished to use broader criteria. The reasons are threefold:
first, the price system is a better device for achieving an equilibrium for supply and demand of individual products than for
achieving a national equilibrium of investment, savings and
consumption. Second, individual firms lack the knowledge of the
whole system's needs that would be requisite to meshing their
own decisions with those needs. And, third, the legal and customary obligations of management are not to the public but to
stockholders.

It is at least a working hypothesis among economists that
investment decisions bulk large among the determinants of
national prosperity. When investment increases, all economic
activity is stimulated; when investment declines, so do employment and the rate of production. Now suppose that a firm – say,
the National Widget Company – has had a ten-year record of a
7 per cent annual increase in the sale of widgets, and that it has,
accordingly, invested six million dollars per year to increase its
capacity to keep pace with rising demand. But suppose that this
year, because of a decline in automobile sales, let us say, people
have less money to spend and are only buying the same number
of widgets as last year. The finance committee of National
Widget's board of directors is advised by the president that

further investment in increased capacity is not warranted at this time. The finance committee accepts his judgement, and the six million dollars is not spent this year.

From the viewpoint of the National Widget management, this is a perfectly rational, responsible decision. Rational, because of the changed demand situation; responsible, because the stockholders' funds should not be spent unproductively. From the viewpoint of national stabilization, however, these virtues turn into corresponding vices. The rational requirement in a situation of generally declining investment and demand is to increase expenditures – to prime the pump. Nationally responsible action would consist in the finance committee saying that, while the firm did not need the investment, the economy did, and making the investment on that basis. But, to come full circle, this would be foolish from a supply-demand, profit-oriented, stockholder-responsibility viewpoint, which is the viewpoint embedded in our psychology and our institutions. The good of the national economy and the good of the firm are in short-run opposition. Only a very visible hand can bring the two together.

This situation is the typical one. It places management in a most unenviable dilemma. Collectively, business decisions of this kind have great impact on the economy, and businessmen are generally as anxious to operate in a full-profit situation as are wage-earners. Severally, the vast majority of firms cannot afford to invest when the return will not be immediate; and they cannot have sufficient impact individually for their decisions to matter very much. The businessman in this situation is more to be pitied than censured, unless he lobbies against effective action by those who are in a position to have a measurable, prosperity-inducing impact: the governmental authorities.

But the divided impotence of most businesses and their collective impact upon stabilization and growth is only one part of the story. The other part, and perhaps the more crucial one from the standpoint of public policy, concerns the firms that are large enough to have individual effects on the economy. For we have today two economies: the traditional market economy in which price competition prevails and the individual producer has little power; and the oligopolistic economy of the giants, in which the scope of managerial discretion is wide and its impact on the public substantial.

In the 1954 recession, General Motors announced that it was undertaking a one-billion-dollar expansion program. The public relations tone surrounding the announcement suggested that it was purposely timed and framed as a stimulus to the economy. Whether so intended or not, it was widely heralded as an act of economic statesmanship. The beneficial impact of such an announcement may have been considerable, particularly if it really is true that businessmen act positively to calls for 'confidence', but in the case of General Motors there is no statistical evidence on how much other firms invested, or how many investments were saved from cancellation, by this particular announcement. If this was economic statesmanship, it was also evidence of something not so widely boasted of in the business and financial press: economic power. Consider the alternative possibility. What if General Motors had announced cancellation or postponement of a billion dollars of planned investment? Then the power implication would become a public issue, because the decision of one firm could be seen as a further depressant to a weak economy. When this power is exercised beneficially, no one calls it into question. If it can equally well have a harmful effect, and it can, should not the public be alarmed over its exercise by persons unaccountable to the affected public?

Presumably the auto maker's management saw that such expansion was necessary to insure its future profits. But a company's planning for market conditions a decade hence is not automatically determined by the market. It is a matter of policy and choice made possible by the tremendous size and concentration of economic power in the hands of a single firm. In 1953, according to Morton S. Baratz's computations, 12 per cent of total private investment was accounted for by only twelve firms, the three largest in four basic industries: steel, autos, chemicals and oil. This is a significant share of investment in the simple sense that its presence or absence could tip the scales toward inflation, recession or 'balanced growth'. This fact immediately affects government's economic responsibilities, for, if these few firms substantially cut their investment, then the government might have to engage in countervailing pump-priming actions. These firms have great power without corresponding accountability.

Consider briefly the impact of one industry's price policy upon national price levels. Otto Eckstein has estimated that the wholesale price index would have risen by 52 per cent less than it did in the 1953-9 period if it were not for the 'extraordinary' behavior of steel prices. Of course there was an equally extraordinary rise in wages, but the industry would not have been as willing to grant that increase if it were not for the strong market power of the steel companies. Thus the power of management in relation to the market is more basic than the pressure from the unions. It is also true that without unions the corporation would have less incentive or excuse to raise prices. The unions are not a negligible factor, even though they are a secondary factor, in power analysis. Even in time of slackening demand there is little pressure on firms in heavy industry to reduce prices – or at least not raise them – as a gesture toward economic stabilization. The reason is that such firms are now so situated that they can return a handsome profit while operating far below capacity. In the steel industry, for example, the break-even point – the point at which expenses are paid and profit begins – was calculated at 76 per cent of capacity in 1937-8. By 1950 the break-even point had been reduced to 50 per cent of capacity, and by 1958 to 41 per cent. Given these conditions, the classic force of change in demand as a determinant of price is greatly dissipated.

A second area of corporate decision-making which has significant impact on the public is that of income distribution. Except for diehard Spencerians, we long ago recognized that the community's notions of social justice are not automatically registered in the market distribution of rewards. Legal support for collective bargaining rests, for example, on recognition that unequal bargaining power between individual employees and the concentrated financial power exercised by the employer often resulted in a mockery of 'freedom of contract'. Minimum-wage laws are another effort to bring market results into line with the value placed by the community upon human dignity. Yet there remains an area of income-distributing power in which the values of management determine unilaterally the rewards going to themselves and to other participants in the productive process. Recently the most conspicuous example of this power has been provided by executive stock-option plans. If the stock rises in value, the executive exercises the option and sells the stock he has received from the company at the higher price; if it drops, he does nothing. He cannot lose; he can win tremendously. The corporation is deprived of the larger sum which could have been obtained by selling the shares publicly at the higher price. The rise in value will presumably be the consequence of improved corporate performance, which means that, of all employees, only the privileged few share in the reward.

When such other favored devices as delayed compensation, bonuses voted by the directors (often without relation to corporate performance), and the use of various company-provided facilities for transportation and recreation are added to stock options, it is clear that the ability of management to determine its own compensation becomes another significant impact of economic power. It is even possible that the amounts involved in a few corporations are large enough to have an inflationary impact. For example, Walter Reuther of the United Automobile Workers union claimed that executive bonuses at Ford Motor Company in 1960 totalled an amount that would have been considered excessive and inflation-inducing if it had been paid to the workers as a wage increase. And James Carey of the United Electrical Workers fears that the added inducement to raise profits so as to raise stock prices provided by stock options will mean additional management opposition to rank-and-file income increases.

The market power of large firms in concentrated industries affects income distribution in more subtle ways, too. The companies will insist that they pay reasonable prices to suppliers (and while the suppliers may disagree, they may be too dependent on their largest customers to say or do anything about it) and set reasonable prices on their products. But the comment of an economist, John B. Sheahan, on the 1961 price-fixing case is irrefutable:

The difficulty is that justice on the other side of the fence is decidedly hard to evaluate from the seller's own position. Slightly higher prices than necessary on sales of equipment to electric utilities simply result in slightly higher schedules of electricity rates. It is probably a matter of a few dollars less left over for groceries in the case of most families, and a few hundred dollars a year added costs for other firms. It is simply a small tax, taken by the seller out of everyone else's incomes in order to support the concrete and worthy objectives of the selling firm. On sales of electrical equipment to government agencies, the point is even clearer. Government expenditure is a little higher than it otherwise would be, and everyone's taxes are raised a trifle. No wonder that General Electric finds it necessary to campaign actively for economy in government.

Dividend policy also illustrated managerial power over income distribution. The after-tax profits 'belong' to the stockholders. On the average, they receive about 50 per cent of the pie, with the other 50 per cent going for internal financing of expansion. Maybe the stockholders would want to allocate their income to further investment, but the choice is not theirs to make; it is management's. If all of a corporation's net profit, or, say, 90 per cent of it, were given to stockholders, then they would really be free agents in the allocation of their income.

Another important area of impact consists of the patterns of consumption, both private and public. Economics starts with the pattern of consumer preferences and concerns itself with analysing the process by which those preferences are expressed in demand for goods and in the production of the desired products in the desired quantities. But as our economy moves further away from 'natural' commodities – food, basic clothing, basic shelter – into the era of invented commodities – TV sets, skiing equipment, power lawnmowers – consumer preferences themselves come to be an element in corporate calculations. The advertising industry, with expenditures amounting to twelve billion dollars per year and currently increasing at the rate of about one billion dollars annually, testifies to the effort made by business firms to mold consumer preferences, not just respond to them. The writings of Galbraith, Vance Packard and Martin Mayer give details of the manipulative process and assess its significance. That there are limits to this malleability of the consumer's tastes no one would deny: the fate of Ford's Edsel car is a classic example of advertising failure. But that the limits are broad and permit considerable latitude is also undeniable: witness the Davy Crockett fad for coonskin hats, the rise of the tail fin on automobiles, and the impact of certain now defunct television quiz shows on the earnings of their sponsors. The larger the proportion of goods and services people were unaware of or did not know they wanted until advertising told them they did, the greater the manipulative power of the large corporations maintaining the most expansive research and development units. Conversely, many large firms with heavy investments in existing processes have not always been quick to introduce a new product or process that would hurt their existing investment, even though these innovations already existed on the drawing boards and could easily be put into production.

Our industrial economy is heavily dependent upon basic materials for the fabricating of finished products. The basic materials are in the hands of large, oligopolistic firms: in oil, chemicals, steel, copper and aluminum, among other industries. Fabricators and processors are at the mercy of the allocations made by such firms when shortages occur. And there have been many shortages in the past few years. The power involved here is power to determine which goods are produced and which goods are not, by determining which manufacturers do and which do not receive the supplies. A recurring suspicion exists that independent fabricators get less than a pro-rata share of scarce materials, while fabricators subsidiary to basic commodity producers receive more.

By the kinds of decisions cited in the paragraphs above, corporate executives are not just setting 'administered prices'; they are, as Edwin G. Nourse has said, administering the nation's resources. And their managerial discretion is not confined to the area of private consumption: their private decisions have considerable consequences for the public sector, too.

The most apparent influence occurs when developments in the private sector of the economy compel complementary expenditures in the public sector. This symbiotic relationship goes a considerable distance, in fact, toward explaining the growth of government in this century. The growth of the automobile industry is the classic example, in its requirements of roads, parking facilities, policemen, courts, traffic engineers and so forth.

There is no question that the public costs necessitated by this private invention have been worthwhile and productive for the economy, but there are some particular decisions made by the Big Three automobile companies in Detroit that one may not be so happy about. To quote Nourse: 'Was it responsible administration from the standpoint of the economy to load nickel and chrome and other materials still in scarce supply and lavish labor on ever larger and more luxurious cars, of excessive power and gas consumption, which made obsolete our private garages and city parking meters, and required heavy municipal expense for street widening whilst extension of water and sewer lines lagged, slum clearance was deferred, and taxes soared?' Granting that the public did buy the outsized cars until Volkswagen and George Romney's Rambler reversed the trend, it is at least an open question whether the public would have done so if it had been aware of the costs cited by Nourse and if it had had a say in the matter once it was aware of the facts about the big-car development. But we were not aware of the costs, or that a choice existed. We were presented with a *fait accompli*.

This is just one instance of the social costs of private enterprise. Social costs are those burdens thrown on a community by one company's activity which are not paid for by that company or the purchasers of its product. A factory that creates a smoke nuisance and throws soot down on neighboring houses so that homeowners must paint more frequently is creating social costs in the private sector. A factory that pollutes a stream so that a community must install water-purifying devices is creating social costs in the public sector. In either case, the activity of one party is effectively influencing the allocation of resources employed by other parties.

More subtle than these types of allocation is the influence of advertising upon the balance between individual and community goods, meaning between those goods which are privately purchased and individually consumed and those which are purchased collectively for the use of all members of a community. Since this question of social balance is the theme of Galbraith's stimulating book, *The Affluent Society*, I will not dwell on it here. But Galbraith's thesis is pertinent: virtually all the weight of advertising – and twelve billion dollars a year amounts to a considerable weight – is devoted to pushing private sector products, while those public services which also contribute to the American standard of living, such as education, health services and recreational facilities, go largely unadvertised. It is not possible to measure the impact of this imbalance in promotional endeavor upon the taxpayer-consumer as he weighs choices between what he can buy personally and what his tax dollar can buy for him (such as whether to buy an air-conditioner or vote for a bond issue for a new school), but the burden of proof must surely be on anyone who would deny that it gives an advantage to the private sector.

A touch of irony will complete the picture. Having made private decisions that cause a need for larger public outlays (such as wider cars requiring re-spacing of parking meters), some business firms then go on to spend the consumer's money in lobbying against the increase in governmental revenues that their actions have made necessary. Thus pulp and paper manufacturers, whose industrial processes are a prime source of stream pollution, lobbied vigorously against a national grant-in-aid program designed to help municipalities build sewage plants. What is the connection? Simply this: if human waste as a cause of water pollution is eliminated, the continued pollution will point the finger directly at another primary source: pulp and paper firms. Then they might themselves have to absorb some of this cost of production that they now throw onto the community and downstream property owners.

Impact on society

Among the more subtle types of business influence is the role business firms and businessmen play in shaping the directions taken by non-business institutions. Schools and colleges, churches, and charitable, cultural, and civic organizations are all expressions of various strands in the complex of values that gives our society its specific tone. In a free society, the independent existence of diverse value-forming institutions is an essential bulwark against totalitarianism, defined as unchallenged dominance over all areas of life by a single institution. And governments are not the only potential totalitarians. The situation in the US is not totalitarian, yet one becomes concerned about the potential when one looks at the attempts of business to mold other institutions and general social values in its own image, and at the financial advantages supporting its incursions.

In education, for example, trustees of private colleges and universities are predominantly chosen from among men of wealth and high social status, business leaders and their attorneys prominent among them. Conscious of great financial need and desiring to avoid 'federal control' through federal aid, trustees increasingly seek business support, as individual contributions are quite insufficient to pay a college's costs these days. At the least, there must exist an expectation that the size of corporate donations will vary with the college's reputation in the business community. How many deans, presidents, and trustees, then, will knowingly take on controversial faculty members? How many of them will as vigorously seek out community contacts with labor leaders or religious and social service leaders as with businessmen? Hard facts are very difficult to come by in this area, but the relative absence of extremes of opinion on our campuses today is apparent to any faculty member, and the heads of most of our institutions of higher learning were notably quiet on civil liberties during the McCarthy period. The problem is not eased when college presidents become members of corporation boards, as some do.

A more apparent business influence upon higher education is seen in the shaping of curricula to fit occupational criteria rather than the criteria of a liberal arts education. Take, for example, the great rise in the number of undergraduate majors in the field of business administration. While most Ivy League colleges and other well-endowed liberal arts colleges have avoided succumbing to the marketplace in their undergraduate curricula, the less affluent colleges have made their appeal for students fairly frankly in terms of offering them courses that promise an immediate occupational reward.

This kind of influence on curriculum is indirect. A direct impact on educational institutions is made by restricted donations, that is, money given only for a specific purpose. General Electric, for example, apparently knows what education needs: a couple of years ago it offered grants to small liberal arts colleges to encourage instruction in industrial accounting. Some aircraft producers offer scholarships and/or money to colleges to be spent only on engineering programs. Again, the strongest institutions may sometimes forego such aid, unless it fits in with plans they have made themselves. The weaker institutions will take what they can get, and the humanities that form the backbone of western culture suffer in the process.

The type of business influence on education just cited at least has the merit of being fairly straightforward: the corporations say to the schools, you provide training in the skills we need and we will help finance you. But corporate funds are used in more devious attempts to stifle criticism of corporate power and practices which might normally be expected to come from institutions of learning. Thus the oil industry, which spends vast sums of money to influence the political atmosphere of the nation, has been able in a number of states to link severance taxes (those paid per barrel of oil extracted from the earth) to the financing of public education. Parents, teachers and legislators thus come to have a specific, dramatic vested interest in the fortunes of the oil companies and understandably may become reluctant to 'bite the hand that feeds them'. A number of corporations have tried to influence their potential critics by inviting groups of teachers to visit their plants and attend lectures on the benefits the company is providing for the community. To inform teachers about the workings of industry is of course unobjectionable; but the line between informing and propagandizing is easily – and, one gathers, frequently – crossed in these programs. Business organizations, using tax-deductible corporate contributions, engage in widespread efforts to put their message across to teachers through special-audience publications. The NAM, for example, issues a publication called *Dateline* directed at teachers and church leaders. Seen simply as part of a free and equal competition in ideas, these efforts would be unobjectionable. What is objectionable is the financial advantage that business possesses in this regard. The opinion-forming activities of business are financed by consumer and taxpayer, while the competing efforts of other groups are sharply limited by the size of the personal funds of their members.

In an effort to be the good neighbor in the communities where its operations are located, a company is often blatantly paternalistic in regard to the cultural, charitable and civic activities of those communities. Whether a community needs a new boys' club, a hospital or a higher tax rate to finance its school building program is a matter concerning all residents of the community, for the character and values of community life are involved. When a corporation (often a national firm whose home offices are elsewhere) gives the community a boys' club, it is exercising power over the community and establishing a base for influence on other occasions. The firm is imposing the values of its decision-makers upon the community – values that may or may not accord with the consensus of the community. And it is purchasing prestige and gratitude which it may well use to oppose the needed tax increase, even though the tax-increase issue bears no relationship to the act of generosity. Thus a contribution may have seemingly irrelevant but lasting secondary effects.

'We want people to like us and the free economy of which we are a part,' says an oil company public relations manual. 'Then the public will buy our products and take [our] side on controversial issues.' In using its powers of persuasion, a company may often win people over to its side on an issue, not because its arguments are rationally convincing but because it has prestige purchased with other people's money.

Public acceptance of business criteria and business definitions of public issues is a fundamental support for business influence. Closely related to this is the utilization of the communications media by business to help create this public acceptance.

The importance to democracy of the market place of ideas cannot be over-emphasized. A century ago, Abraham Lincoln saw the relationship of opinion formation to democratic government and expressed it as well as, or better than, any modern pollster:

Public sentiment is everything. With public sentiment nothing can fail. Without it, nothing can suceed. Consequently, he who molds public sentiment goes deeper than he who enacts statutes or pronounces decisions. He makes statutes and decisions possible or impossible to be executed.

Three twentieth-century developments have increased the

importance of public opinion: the extension of the electorate; the rise of national mass media; and the development of mass-persuasion techniques into quasi-scientific tools. Attempts to sway the public are not new, but in former times the scope of persuasion was limited by the slowness and limited circulation of the communications media employed. Today, the wire services, syndicated columnist, national magazines and radio and television networks have all vastly increased the ease with which those who have access to these media can reach a substantial portion of the public.

Today no group which desires political action confines itself to direct lobbying in the old-fashioned sense; they all use the mass media. If access to the media is unequal, political influence is unequally distributed, even though there is still the fact of one man, one vote, at the polling booth. How, then, does business obtain access to the communications media? And how extensive is the business influence upon the ideas transmitted by these media?

Probably the least important part of the relationship is the ownership of media by firms that are not primarily engaged in communications. Avco Corporation, for example, owns a few television and radio stations since its acquisition of Crosley Corporation; Minnesota Mining and Manufacturing has a controlling interest, it has been reported, in the Mutual Network, and General Tire and Rubber purchased station WOR, New York, a few years ago. I am not aware of any direct exploitation of such ownership to affect the general substance of programming or the specific substance of political affairs broadcasting; yet I think it also reasonable to assume that no direct pressure would be needed to ensure that the managers of a radio station owned by General Tire would not devote much broadcast time to airing, say, details of an anti-trust indictment of the owning firm, or to general discussions of problems of business power. If there is any direct exploitation, it has not come to light; until and unless it does, we should assume that it does not exist.

Of considerably greater importance is the coincidence of viewpoint between media businessmen and non-media businessmen. One evidence of this is the pattern of political endorsements by newspapers; endorsements of presidential candidates has run

65 to 85 per cent Republican over the past thirty years, or about the same proportion as that of business executives voting Republican. It is true that newspaper editorials are largely unread, and it is also true that Democratic candidates have not fared too badly at the polls, but still the political orientation of publishers is clearly the same as that of other businessmen. And the orientation may influence what is in the news columns as well as what is on the editorial page.

Perhaps the most striking evidence that the political preferences of publishers affect the news pages lies in the differential treatment of business and labor and business and government in newspapers and news magazines. Compare in almost any paper the attention given to investigations of labor racketeering with that given to the electrical equipment price-fixing case, for example, or to handling of strikes. Or the attention given a governmental error in comparison with that given to a business blunder of equivalent proportions, such as the Edsel fiasco. Or the economic and governmental content of articles in the *Reader's Digest*. Although it is only recently that the *Digest* has contained advertising, it has for many years serviced the business viewpoint. One recent example concerns the magazine's support of private utilities against public power. Addressing the Edison Electric Institute, the general manager of the *Reader's Digest* explained how several editors were going to write articles to explain 'the advantages of private enterprise to our millions of readers', in the hope that the people will not 'have to secure their electric service from any government'.

Greatest of all the overt influences of business on the communications media, however, are those derived from direct use of corporate money for advertisements and to determine the program content of broadcasting. General Electric informs us on television that progress is its most important product. US Steel 'educates' us through television to an understanding of its justification for higher profits. Du Pont explains to us through television all the advantages of giantism in business. General Motors, licking its wounds after Senate hearings on dealer relationships, has published a series of full-page advertisements extolling the aid it gives to small business and then reprinted the ads in a booklet to mail to social science teachers across the country. Electric utilities extol the virtues of 'investor-owned' power over public power in millions of dollars of advertising paid out of funds derived from consumer electric rates.

Much of this advertising – an increasing proportion in the past few years – is directly political and indirectly partisan. That is, it expresses corporate views on legislative issues and, while it never mentions one political party or the other, the stand taken is almost invariably the one favored by the Republican party. Some of it is only indirectly political: it seeks to build a framework of opinion that would support the corporation if certain matters which are not yet legislative issues were to become so.

The impact of such advertising is impossible to assess accurately because it cannot be isolated from all the other factors in opinion formation. But one aspect is so plain as not to require precise measurement: the dominance of the corporate viewpoint in all advertising. Unions advertise on occasion – most frequently in connection with a strike, ongoing or imminent – but only on occasion, because the cost of advertising with the same frequency and breadth of coverage as business would very quickly exhaust their financial resources. Membership dues are harder to obtain than consumers' hidden taxes. Consumer organizations are invariably penurious; they do little or no advertising. Thus, while there does exist today a liberal–labor ideology, it has not the financial access to the media that the business creed enjoys. Business tells its side of the story and, naturally enough, avoids calling public attention to issues and criticisms that might prove embarrassing to it. Thus, the presentation of business and the related issues of bigness, of what constitutes progress, and of the social responsibility of corporations is almost entirely one-sided.

Covertly, corporate advertising may have other effects on the media. Dependent as they are on business advertising, newspapers, magazines and broadcasting stations are notably reluctant to publish criticism of business. This is in good part, as noted above, because of the natural affinity of the owners of these media with business; the publications are businesses, too. But it is also in part due to fear of loss of patronage if they do otherwise – a fear that some advertisers are not bashful about exploiting explicitly.

The printed media have a tradition of separation of advertising from editorial content, a tradition honored at least by the stronger publications. But in broadcasting the dominant tradition has been to tie the two together under sponsor control. A magazine, say *Harper's*, would not dream of allowing an advertiser to buy pages twelve and twenty, say, and as part of his purchase tell the editor what subject and viewpoint were to be placed on the pages between 'his' pages. Yet this is exactly the way much television time has been handled: the sponsor buys the time, brings his package to the station or network, and the station or network only functions as a transmitting facility. Programs originated by the network, with some honorable exceptions in the public affairs category, are designed to attract sponsors, of course, and this means they are designed to please, not to offend, a potential sponsor. [. . .]

Since the political objectives of business are more frequently negative than positive, which means maintaining the *status quo*, business's own cause is aided substantially by broadcasting's failure to handle social problems. The corporations thus benefit doubly: their advertising creates sales, and the innocuous content of the programs they sponsor helps to forestall social criticism and governmental programs to deal with national problems.

It could be said that the fault here lies with the broadcasters, especially the networks, rather than with the sponsors. Legally, it is true, the responsibility for programming lies with the station owners. But the power of sponsors over networks, and of networks over individual stations, makes this a fiction. The fault of the broadcasting industry, then, lies in succumbing initially to the business pressures that debased this effective medium of communication. It need not have been so. When broadcasting began, it was assumed that financial support would be obtained through sale of sets. The first commercial stations were, accordingly, established by radio manufacturers. Program sponsorship and commercials were not used. But the pressure to transform a public medium into a private salesroom was too much for the broadcasters. Hence the present 'vast wasteland'. The criteria used to determine the content spread over the public airwaves is summarized in the bureaucratic prose of a 1960 FCC report:

All in all, the factors which go into the judgement of the advertisers and their agents as to the selection of a program, while they differ in emphasis and degree from advertiser to advertiser and agency to agency, are bottomed in the effort to attract an audience which will consist of potential customers for the product; to please that audience with the type of show that is appealing to it; to avoid 'offending' any considerable segment of audience; and to continue the show on the network only so long as it retains its appeal and is, in fact, 'doing the job' of selling the sponsor's product or service. A certain degree of diversity in programming results from the differences in objective and purpose of the advertisers, but that diversity remains within prescribed limits and will not include many program types and formats which are not of proven appeal to the audience. The reason for this is again tied to the 'commercial considerations' of the advertiser.

It is for such reasons that, as these pages were being written, the press reported that Howard K. Smith's outstanding, prize-winning program of news analysis was to be dropped from the network schedule.

The problem of business dominance is thus greatest in the electronic media because sins of commission through private censorship are added to sins of omission, and the net effect is that virtually all opinion that might question the business view is absent from the airwaves.

8 D. Lynch

Economic Power and Political Pressure

Excerpt from D. Lynch, *The Concentration of Economic Power*,
Columbia University Press, 1946, chapter 10, pp. 293–300.

The success of democratic institutions depends upon the ability
of voters to choose legislators who will exercise their judgement
to promote the welfare of all the people. Likewise, it depends
upon the responsiveness of legislators to the popular will and the
ability of the people to recall from office representatives who fail
to fulfill these responsibilities. But the rise of the great corporations and the concentration of economic power within these
agencies has facilitated the mobilization of financial resources
and of the instruments for controlling public opinion, with the
result that pressures may be put upon the elected representatives
to obtain legislation favoring those who control the corporations.
So well organized are the methods of 'reaching' the legislature
and so easily are the desired responses obtained that businessmen often look upon this method as the normal, legitimate and
expected mode of governmental performance. Without compre-
hending that they do so, frequently they look upon the legislature
as their legislature whose function is to serve their interest.
Popular government becomes government by pressure groups,
and legislation tends to serve special interests rather than the
common good.

This mode of behavior on the part of business is illustrated by
the activities of the Association of Life Insurance Presidents. The
methods used by this organization in surveillance of and lobbying
before state legislatures demonstrate how difficult it is to obtain
legislation for the general welfare if perchance some powerful
interest is mobilized to defeat it and, equally, how difficult it is
to defeat legislation sponsored by special interest groups, inasmuch as public opinion is not so readily mobilized and the
necessary funds with which to do so are seldom available.

Lobbying activities by the large insurance companies are not new; in 1906 the famous Armstrong Investigation exposed and denounced such practices.

Nothing disclosed by the investigation[1] deserves more serious attention than the systematic efforts of the large insurance companies to control a large part of the legislation of the State. They have been organized into an offensive and defensive alliance to procure or to prevent the passage of laws affecting not only insurance, but a great variety of important interests to which, through subsidiary companies or through the connections of their officers, they have become related. . . . Enormous sums have been expended in a surreptitious manner. Irregular accounts have been kept to conceal the payments for which proper vouchers have not been required. This course of conduct has created a widespread conviction that large portions of this money have been dishonestly used. [. . .]

The pernicious activities of corporate agents in matters of legislation demand that the present freedom of lobbying should be restricted. They have brought suspicion upon important proceedings of the Legislature, and have exposed its members to consequent assault. The Legislature owes it to itself, so far as possible to stop the practice of the lavish expenditure of moneys ostensibly for services in connection with the support of or opposition to bills, and generally believed to be used for corrupt purposes. The Legislature should free itself from the stigma which now attaches to the progress of measures affecting important interests. The laws against bribery and corruption, offenses which are difficult of proof, are sufficiently stringent, but an effort should be made to strike at the root of the evil by requiring under proper penalties full publicity with regard to moneys expended in connection with matters before the Legislature. Corporations should be required to keep accounts and vouchers in which all such payments should be fully detailed and receipted for, and an adequate statement regarding them should form a part of such reports as may be required (part 10, pp. 4802–3).

Apparently, the Association of Life Insurance Presidents maintained a 'watch dog' over each state legislature (pp. 4396–4405). The task of this representative was to keep the industry informed of measures which, if enacted into law, might affect life insurance. The lobby manager for the industry in Georgia

1. The investigation carried out by the Temporary National Economic Committee (TNEC). All references in this Reading are to the *Hearings before the Temporary National Economic Committee*.

frankly told the TNEC that his effectiveness was increased if his operations were clandestine.

I am a marked man, [he said]. I have the privilege of the floor and I have been down to the legislature several times, possibly a dozen or more. The speaker of the house has made the public statement that he does not wish any member to accept any invitation given by any person who has any interest in legislation before the house (p. 4405).

Consequently it became necessary for him to appoint an emissary who would operate in disguise; this was done by inducing a newspaper man to do the undercover work. This man had 'access to the floor of the house and a partner, so to speak, on the floor of the senate'. Thus, he was able to ferret out important information to enable the life insurance interests to anticipate measures which were about to be introduced in the legislative chambers. Members of the legislature and their sentiments toward the industry were kept under constant surveillance.

Once it becomes apparent that a measure is to be introduced which the industry does not want, there are several ways by which it may be opposed. The most effective, according to the testimony, is to destroy it before it materializes. Pressures are brought to bear.

We try to get hold of the man to introduce it and argue the question on its merits and get him to withdraw it. I might say to you, sir, if you will let me diverge a minute, we rather believe in that, like the dutch man at the boarding house where there were tough roosters. He said he ate them when they were eggs.

Since the description given here is that of an interested witness, one suspects that there have been many occasions when the owner of a 'tough rooster' has been able to tell of methods employed to kill a bill by means other than 'on its merits'. Should this strategy fail, the next attempt made is to kill the bill in the committee.

We make an effort in advance . . . to have friends on the committee and to have the meetings at the proper time and under favorable environment. This has frequently worked out.

Failing this, the next most effective method is organized obstructionism.

If we do not succeed in getting a bill adversed, we try to introduce another bill, hoping the whole thing will wind up in a row, to be plain about it. If a bill passes either house and goes to the other house, we try to repeat the above tactics (p. 4399).

But the task of controlling state legislation has just begun with these stratagems. The legislators themselves, compositely and individually, are subject to minute observance to discover, if possible, how their actions may be influenced. In 1935 a card index of the members of the Florida legislature was compiled; a careful itemization was made covering personal data for each, indicating the approaches which might prove effective. It was considered best that some of the personal data thus collected should not be entered on the card index, but should be kept on separate memoranda, suggesting a willingness on the part of the lobbyists to employ almost any method to obtain their ends.

Another course was to establish legislative contacts; these seemed to range from working through interested parties who knew the legislators to entertaining them personally. Entertainment may take place at the time important legislation is under consideration or it may pay larger dividends when done currently, regardless of the imminence of any particular measure.

We might mention in passing that we believe in killing a bill before it gets on the floor, or before a committee, if possible. It is much easier to handle one man or two men alone than it is to argue with a whole committee and it is impossible to argue with the whole house. This money has been spent in invitations to those of whom we wished to make friends, and seeing that their wives and daughters were looked after properly and courteously; and a large portion of it in giving a dinner after the session was over to all of those who were good enough to favor us. We have been told that one reason we are kindly received is that we do not forget favors after we get them (p. 4401).

There are various ways of bringing pressure to bear upon legislators to restrain them from voting as their judgement and their conscience might dictate. One way is to deluge them with calls, letters and telegrams from a presumably aroused public to obtain the defeat of a given bill. This may easily be accomplished, since life insurance companies are conveniently organized to mobilize the 'opinion' of their policyholders. There are many agents in the field, and if each agent solicits 'ten letters from policyholders', legislators quickly feel the pressure. The Association of Life Insurance Presidents employed such a procedure in Florida in a successful attempt to control legislation in that state; letters, telegrams and phone calls were inspired and, in fact, paid for to arouse this 'spontaneous' expression of public opinion (pp. 4385–6).

It is thought wise that there should be as many telegrams and telephone calls as possible to reach these members from their respective home communities. This, of course, is a matter with which you are thoroughly familiar. Furthermore, it is advisable to have as many communications as possible from policyholders. These, of course, are details concerning which you will use your own judgement (p. 4385).

An effective method such as this is not likely to be neglected. The same technique was used in Pennsylvania to defeat a bill which would have authorized savings bank life insurance:

I am pleased to inform you that the Wilkes-Barre Association of Life Underwriters, which represents all the 'old line' companies, and which are approximately 500 in number, were very much in accord with your letter, and immediately contacted all State senators, and each member of the house of representatives, including the chairman of the insurance committee, and protested strongly against House Bill No. 883.

Undoubtedly, such an avalanche of telegrams and personal calls has never before been received by these individuals. We have had definite assurance from them that the bill will be strongly opposed (p. 4427).

Another type of duress is to work through certain financial interests; industrialists, bankers and contractors often are in a position to influence the lives of state legislators, and their wishes are not to be lightly ignored. Oftimes the quiet word of these key citizens will carry a stronger influence than obviously inspired letters. The life insurance company presidents found this device useful and effective, as is illustrated in certain self-explanatory letters written during a successful attempt to influence the Georgia legislature:

The easiest way to handle this bill is to kill it. I think that has been done. The First National Bank, of Valdosta, Ga., is the financial backer of the Honourable Nelson, who introduced the bill. I hand you a copy of a telegram that was sent to Senator Nelson yesterday by this bank, at the instance of one of our agents. . . . I have an idea that the bill will now be withdrawn (p. 4414).

Please let me write you in a personal way. Last week I went to Rome, Ga., and invited to lunch twenty men, who I happen to know, large policyholders. Every one of them in our company, and, of course, with other companies, too, some of them. The twenty men carry a million and a half of life insurance.

I talked to them some about the taxation of premiums, as I am sure we are going to have a world of trouble with the next legislature. We have laid some foundation, I think, on which to build, to stall this. But what I want to say is, that I asked these men (and repeat, in a most personal way, they understanding that no company had anything whatever to do with it, but that I was inviting them and meeting them as a fellow policyholder) what they would do if it were indicated that this, that, or the other man would vote to increase the tax on their premiums. Their response was, to name the man who would do that and they would do the best they could to keep him from going to the legislature again. This is a straw (p. 4407).

But often control by means of lobbying and pressure upon individual legislators is too cumbersome, too obvious and perhaps too expensive. More efficient ways are available. Human nature is the same in legislatures as on the school playground; a few leaders often are influential enough to determine what is to be done and the manner in which it is to be done. The life insurance companies were realistic enough to recognize this fact and to capitalize upon it; key men, policy-determining men, were reached wherever possible. Influential men, men who possessed talent of leadership or a voice of authority, were sought out and put under obligation to the companies. Later, when their turn came to vote, knowing 'on what side their bread was buttered' or, perhaps more accurately, having acquired certain predilections and convictions, their weight was placed where the companies wished it to be. The following instructions by the vice-president of one large company to the effect that certain legal fees be channeled to a key legislator illustrates this type of approach.

He is one of two men to whom the legislature listens with the greatest respect, and has been on the law committee at every session that he has attended. We are going to need him in the legislature to cover the constitutionality of an act of depriving municipalities of the right to levy taxes, and that is the principal reason why I would like to see him in this *Lannie Thompson case*, aside from the fact that, as I said in my letter of 1 March, I believe that the respect in which he is held will be a material factor in securing a change in the point of view of our apellate court, one of whose judges did me the honor to discuss that situation academically yesterday (p. 4411).

Representatives of the insurance companies apparently saw nothing reprehensible in this method of influencing legislation (p. 4414). It was part of the code – the folkways of business. Sometimes, too, it was found effective to place the people's representatives under obligation to the trade – favors extended, even at financial cost, may return handsome dividends, even though the legislator finds it unnecessary to make any outlay in repaying his debt. Upon the advice of a willing accomplice in the office of the state insurance commissioner of Georgia, the lobbyist for the companies paid the occupational tax of an insurance agent who, hardly by coincidence, was also chairman of the committee on insurance, appointed at the 'instance' of the companies. That these favors were extended with the expectation of reciprocity is obvious from a letter presented in testimony.

A few days ago I had a call from Mr Harold Dobbins, who seems to have an agency contract with you and who is very much concerned about the payment of his occupational tax, although it had been my previous understanding that the company takes care of such matters for its agents. In any event, Mr Dobbins gave me the impression that he was called on to pay this tax and that by reason of his inability so far to close some business, although he said he had some under way which he expected to close if he could hang on, he found himself unable at this time to pay the tax levied against him, and asked whether or not it could be allowed to run along for a little while unpaid.

My plan was rather to take it up with you, in the thought that under all of the circumstances you might feel that it would be a good 'investment' for the company to meet this expense, at least for the time being, in view of the fact that Mr Dobbins is again scheduled, I understand, for the chairmanship of the insurance committee and his good will might be worth keeping.

Think it over, and destroy this letter when you have its contents in mind (p. 4415).

Another illustration of this policy of placing important committee members under obligation to the industry concerns the chairman of the controlling committee on life insurance in the Rhode Island legislature, who owed fealty to the industry as it was organized. As in the instance of the commissioner already referred to, commissioners of other states have served as plenipotentiaries of the companies rather than as tribunes of the public. In Rhode Island the Governor's report affecting an important issue was even written for him, through this channel, by the insurance companies. 'Pressure was brought upon our Governor for favorable action on the savings bank life insurance legislation, and he naturally turned to the chief of the division of banking and insurance for information.' (p. 4430.) The result was quite as TNEC member Henderson summarized it:

MR HENDERSON. Mr Crane sent some material to Mr White, of the Puritan Life. Mr White gave it to Mr Cummings, who had requested it, I gather. Mr Cummings then made a report to the Governor, as chief of the division of banking and insurance. Then he gave a copy of that to Mr White, and then he sent it to the various insurance commissioners. . . . So in effect this has been a sort of an adaptation of your idea . . . and it goes out now under the imprimatur of the chief of the division of banking (p. 4432).

If lobbying by life insurance companies is looked upon as a case example, representative of what businessmen have come to consider a customary, natural and approved method of procedure, it reflects truly a divergent course in the evolution of the free enterprise system and of representative government as these institutions were conceived of in the nineteenth century. Such practices, indeed, may be so out of harmony with both free enterprise and free institutions that they become the fruit which destroys the tree. We now have the phenomena of corporations that have little or no responsibility to the states wherein they are most active (having received their charters – often ultra-liberal charters – from foreign states) and show little evidence of responsibility to their stockholders so mobilizing their resources of finance, of legal talent and of publicity as to determine the action of the elected representatives of the people. When substantially all the pressure, suasion, duress and publicity is in one direction, legislators often willingly or unwillingly yield, and consciously or unconsciously alter representative government to a system of control by the dominant pressure groups. It appears that a pattern is being established; few businessmen seem to challenge it from an ethical standpoint or to have thought it out to its ultimate impact upon free institutions. No doubt many would brand as subversive anyone who might have the temerity even to raise the issue.

Part Four Managers and Technostructure

While there is little doubt that the emergence of big business created a power problem, there is less agreement about the locus of that power. Ever since Berle and Means published their famous *The Modern Corporation and Private Property* (1932) it has been no secret that the influence of the owner as such – the single shareholder in the big corporation – is minimal. Managers, officials of associations, lobbies have a decisive say in matters of far-reaching importance.

But the fact that such a 'managerial revolution' (Burnham) has occurred does not necessarily mean that power has passed from owners into the hands of paid officials. Managers are often shareholders, big shareholders tend to take up managerial positions, and, at any rate, managers will normally have every reason to satisfy the big shareholders who have appointed them. Thus while real conflicts of interest may exist in minor affairs – for example on dividend policy, scale of operations etc. – there is little reason to expect any serious differences between owners and managers on the fundamental question of strengthening and exercising big business power.

But the discussion on the shifts and extent of big business power continues and will continue, because reality also changes. The four Readings in this section all have a bearing on this question. Brady, in his study of pre-war industrial capitalism, deals with the tendency of big business and managers to create powerful associations ('Spitzenverbände') which take a decisive part in exercising power and influence for big business in general. The trends which he distilled from pre-war developments have not all continued, but the basic tendencies are unchanged.

Galbraith advances the thesis that the locus of economic power is very largely dependent on relative scarcities. Thus land provided the basis for power in pre-industrial times and lost it to capital with the advance of industry. In the present era, with capital becoming more plentiful, scarcity moves increasingly to highly qualified managers, technicians and scientists – the 'technostructure' – and this will lead to corresponding shifts in power. In the third Reading Pen presents some thoughts on the arguments and facts concerning the power of managers. (The Reading by Ulmer in the following section also contains reflections on this subject.)

Part of the power of managers *and* owners stems less from the extent of property over which they exercise control but rests on the social cohesion of leading circles in business and politics. Family relations, a similar educational and social background, parallel interests, etc. ease the access to better information and to the core of decision-making. The article by Wilson and Lupton, which took its inspiration from evidence given in the Bank Rate Tribunal,[1] offers interesting background material on this aspect of managerial power.

1. See Parker Tribunal (1957).

References

BERLE, A. A., and MEANS, G. C. (1932), *The Modern Corporation and Private Property*, Macmillan.
PARKER TRIBUNAL (1957), *Proceedings of the Tribunal Appointed to Inquire into allegations that Information about the Raising of Bank Rate was Improperly Disclosed*, HMSO.

9 R. A. Brady

The Power Hierarchy of Big Business

Excerpts from R. A. Brady, *Business as a System of Power*, Columbia University Press, 1943, chapter 9, pp. 294–320.

'The animosity of German capitalism against the state,' wrote Professor Bonn on the eve of the Nazi coup d'état, 'does not rest upon fundamental theoretical foundations, but upon purely opportunistic considerations. It is opposed to the state when state control is in the hands of a political majority whose permanent good will it doubts. German capitalism, which would like to be freed of the power of the state, and which seeks to push back state intervention as far as possible, is constructed exclusively upon the most thorough intervention of the state' (1931, pp. 95–6, 98). A correct generalization this, but one which might have been as readily applied to monopolistically-oriented business in any other major or minor capitalistic country. For the confessed objectives of German business which filled Bonn with gloomy foreboding – the drive for a well-nigh all-inclusive system of tariff protection, ever more elaborate subsidies and subventions, more and more governmental aid in the control over competition – were at that same time coming swiftly to dominate the programs of organized business all over the world.

German levels of organization were at that time doubtless somewhat higher than those obtaining abroad, the clarity of her business leaders less confused by serious factional cross-currents, and the attitude of the government in general was far more lenient. But the patterns of thought, the modes of procedure, the forms of organization, and the principles at stake were shared by companion interests in England, France, the United States and elsewhere. There was nothing in principle to distinguish the programs of the Reichsverband der deutschen Industrie from that of the National Association of Manufacturers in the United States or the Confédération Générale de la Production Française, nor of the immense and rapidly proliferating meshwork of trade-associations, cartels, syndicates, chambers and business institutes brought together in these general purpose peak associations, or *Spitzenverbände*. Nor, least of all, was there anything to distinguish the trend of economic thinking, social outlook and political interests of the huge combinations which had come increasingly to dominate the inner councils of their respective central associations in the capitalistic countries. [. . .]

Now, in appraising the significance of this morganatic alliance of private economic power and government it is important to remember, that the former derives from a system of monopoly, or of interlocking monopoly-minded groups, and that the institutional umbilicus of this monopoly-orientation feeds upon the sanctions of private property. It is, of course, a truism that even in its germinal form private property is far more than a mere economic category; that it is equally a 'political' institution. Through ownership of productive means, the individual is, under capitalism, vested with a bundle of definitive rights and prerogatives. Under these sanctions he is granted narrowly defined but inherently exclusive power to manipulate people in an environment of rigorously interdependent human relations. Whether, as Spencer once wrote in a scorching passage, 'the original deeds were written with the sword', it is nevertheless true that with and through such possessions one can coerce, bend others to one's will, withhold, restrain, settle the fate and alter the fortunes of growing numbers of non-owners without, and increasingly against, their consent. The natural frame of reference of ownership is, and has been from the beginning, as clearly political as economic, as obviously 'Machiavellian' as 'Ricardian'.

Fee simple is related to private monopoly as youth is to age, as acorn to oak. It is the miniscular shape, the germinal form, the archetypal pattern for the proliferating giants which have sprung from its institutional loins. If private ownership of the means of production prevails throughout an economic system and is largely unimpaired by hostile countervailing forces, then, sooner or later monopoly in all its manifold expressions must appear on the scene. For property is power, and collusion is as 'natural' as competition – a fact which the great Adam Smith was quick to recognize.[1] Because this is true, growth of such possessions expresses power cumulatively; left to itself this power is additive, unidirectional, without internal restraints and external limits. Its higher economic form of expression is monopoly, and monopoly prerogatives are to power as fulcrum is to lever.

Power is compulsive, and when distributed unequally between bargaining groups is irreconcilable with 'free contract'. Fee simple distributes power unevenly between the 'haves' and the 'have-nots'; monopoly heightens and complicates the disproportionalities in the graduated ranks of both. Law and the courts as frequently underline as correct the resultant distortion. It is this configuration of coercive forces, disproportionately matched, which accounts for the usual and inherently lop-sided 'contract', and not the nature of the 'rights' of bargaining groups. Power, in private hands, comes up against such claims as water comes to a wall, taking advantage of every crevice, depression, resource or structural weakness. The proper expression is not 'expansion of power' from these property nuclei, but cumulative permeation of power, as the history of the unfolding controls of all the great combines, cartels, trade associations and *Spitzenverbände* abundantly shows.

Now it is a common characteristic of all monopoly-oriented groupings, major and minor, that each newly acquired leverage is typically employed for further collusive, rather than for competitive, efforts. Not 'monopolistic competition' but 'monopolistic

1. The passages are well known: 'Masters are always and everywhere in a sort of tacit, but constant and uniform combination, not to raise the wages of labour above their actual rate. To violate this combination is everywhere a most unpopular action [today it would be known as an "unfair trade practice"!], and a sort of reproach to a master among his neighbours and equals. We seldom, indeed, hear of this combination because it is the usual, and one may say, the natural state of things which nobody ever hears of.' Again, 'People of the same trade seldom meet together, even for merriment and diversion, but the conversation ends in a conspiracy against the public, or in some contrivance to raise prices. It is impossible indeed to prevent such meetings, by any law which either could be executed, or would be consistent with liberty and justice. *But though the law cannot hinder people of the same trade from sometimes assembling together, it ought to do nothing to facilitate such assemblies; much less to render them necessary.*' Smith (1776). [Italics mine.]

collusion' paces the gathering up and centralization of power to determine business policies over ever widening areas.[2] In plans lying behind the strategies of price fixation such things as production control, market allocations, and similar economic programs become increasingly the vehicles for strengthening tactical position in the pressure politics of collusive *Realpolitik*; they are not ends in themselves as so many recent economic theorists have mistakenly assumed.[3] But more than that, as struggle for strategic position broadens out over wider and wider areas, both ends and means become increasingly enmeshed in more or less distinctly and canonically social and political issues – issues which, to employ the language of Karl Mannheim, reach to the 'roots of domination' and thus become 'vested with a public interest' in a new and revolutionary sense of the term.

Why this is so may be read directly from the record by the more astute who have steeped themselves in the raw materials of the combination and business organization movements. But there is a certain 'internal logic' to these transmutations of monopoly-minded policy which may be thrown into fluoroscopic

2. See Callman (1934, 1935); Lucas (1937) for the British story; and the various reports of the LaFollette Committee, the Temporary National Economic Committee, and the indictments of the Anti-Trust Division of the Department of Justice and the Federal Commission.

3. For example, and most notoriously, Chamberlin (1933) and Robinson (1933). (Not, however, Keynes, though many of his proposals in this connection appear as the product of 'split-personality'.) Chamberlin by implication (Appendix E, 'Some Arguments in Favor of Trade-Mark Infringement and "Unfair Trading"') and Mrs Robinson explicitly recognize as much when they admit that their examinations of monopolistic practices assume the absence of collusive intent or strategies reaching beyond the end of maximum gains. But it will no longer do to insist that an economist *qua* economist can only remain true to himself when he acts naïvely towards half to two-thirds of his problem, or, becoming sophisticated, insists on throwing the baby out with the bathwater simply because in his family tree such a baby must surely be illegitimate. The earlier economists, as well as the earlier political theorists (e.g. Machiavelli, Bodin, Hobbes, Filmer, Locke, Bentham, Burke) made no such mistake. For the orthodox tradition, after the lame synthesis of John Stuart Mill, the separation of economics and politics became an issue as important as the separation of church and state, but at a time when, in contrast with the latter, the real historical interdependence between the two was growing ever closer and more rigorous with the passage of time.

relief by a less direct and time-consuming method. Consider first the nature of the new business self-bureaucratization.

The nature of business bureaucratization

To say that business enterprise in all major capitalistic countries is becoming bureaucratic is to add nothing new. It is so well accepted in the technical literature as to no longer require proof.[4] Obviously the vast control apparatus and the elaborate organizational machinery of large-scale enterprises, of cartels and trade associations, and of their various peak associations call for functional division of duties, for circumscription of tasks and fixation of special responsibilities, for hierarchies of command and subordination, for special systems of recruitment and training of personnel at different levels of competence. Obviously the growth in size and complexity of the individual business enterprise, the spread of ever more inclusive cartel and trade association networks, the gathering up and centralizing of policies in series of interlocking *Spitzenverbände*, the formalization of relationships not only amongst these various business groupings but *vis-à-vis* the ever widening system of governmental regulation (whether friendly or hostile to business) and the ever greater attention paid to expert staff counsel, not to mention the science of management and administration itself – obviously these mean steady and cumulative bureaucratization of business. On present showing it is possible to predict that in the normal course of events the time will shortly arrive when all business activity, big and little, and from center to circumference, will be enmeshed in bureaucratic machinery, will conduct its activities in terms of bureaucratic dicta, following bureaucratic procedures, and complying with bureaucratic criteria.

Business, that is to say, is becoming organized; that organization is becoming large scale, highly centralized, and complex; and such centralization and complexity define the area of bureaucratic control. But there are many types of bureaucracies, good and bad. The question is not, 'Is business being bureaucratized?'

4. See, in particular, Mooney and Reiley (1931), Marshall Dimock and Howard K. Hyde, and the various summary volumes of the huge German *Enqueteausschuss*, in particular the *Gesamtbericht*. See also, Louis D. Brandeis's provocative volume (1936).

but rather, 'What type of bureaucracy is coming to dominate in business circles?'

There are three clues which merit especially close and careful inspection. First is the system of recruitment and training. The more one pages through the literature and publicity of the giant corporations and the networks of business and employer organizations brought together under the central policy direction of the *Spitzenverbände* the more one is struck by the increasing attention devoted to this subject.

Trends here move on three closely related levels. Most common and perhaps best known are apprenticeship programs. One line of emphasis in these programs calls for systematic and far-reaching attempts to overhaul public-school educational programs on more purely vocational lines. This feature has been particularly marked in England and Germany. Under the Nazis, and to a lesser extent in Italy and Japan, the program of *Dinta* and other closely allied groups has been extended to cover all educational training in the country. The second line of emphasis calls for greatly extending formal company-controlled apprenticeship training systems throughout industry in general. More recently in the United States, governmentally sponsored, but privately directed, local, state and national apprenticeship training programs have been worked out on a basis sufficiently comprehensive to forecast the time when they will include all jobs requiring some degree of skill. The various *Spitzenverbände* have without exception shown a lively and sustained interest in these systems for sifting, shaping, guiding and controlling the lower levels of future labor ranks.

A parallel interest has led in the United States to 'foremanship training'. Both the National Association of Manufacturers and the United States Chamber of Commerce and their various subsidiary and member bodies have paid much attention to this feature of recruitment, since it is recognized that the foreman is the 'front line representative of management'. Ideally, 'foremanship training' performs somewhat the same functions for the non-executive managerial ranks that apprenticeship and vocational education do for those who habitually handle the machines.

Within these two levels, training is in many instances almost entirely technical. But increasingly – notoriously in such cases as Ford, General Motors, Standard Oil of New Jersey, Mitsui, I. G. Farbenindustrie, Siemens and Halske, and particularly *Dinta* – there has been added schooling in economics, sociology, history and other subjects which may be manipulated to support the general social and philosophical point of view of management. It is probably safe to say that no large company, trade association, *Spitzenverband* or governmental employee-training program is now entirely free of this ideological coloring. In many cases, company propaganda plays a role as important or even more important than the formal technical training itself. This is particularly apt to be the case in company 'colleges', such as that of the Standard Oil Company of New Jersey.[5]

Through these methods business is attempting to create its own 'officialdom'[6] and its own 'civil service',[7] dedicated to business ends and loyal to business philosophies. However much the content of specific programs may vary in detail, the general tendency here is to evolve specialized training for specialized jobs, to delimit, define and circumscribe each and every specialized task, to define responsibilities and duties within each bracket of competence, to arrange these competencies in a rationally articulated hierarchy of command and subordination in which vertical movement is limited and defined by 'seniority', formal

5. See also literature of the Goodyear Tire and Rubber Co. on the 'Goodyear Industrial Union', which offers, amongst other courses, one on 'Business Science' dealing with 'The individual in self-analysis, his relation to others, his attitude towards his job and his understanding of the proper approach to the job'. (Circular of the Goodyear Tire and Rubber Co.) How many of these 'schools' and 'colleges' there may be, what ground they cover, what differences they show from one country to another, and to what uses they are being put nobody knows. A careful and critical study is much needed.

6. A particularly penetrating book was written by Kurt Wiedenfeld (one of the more acute German economists subsequently to enlist in the Nazi services) (1932). See also Dimock and Hyde (1940).

7. One of the common shortcomings of the more recent books on wage theory, as, e.g. Hicks (1932), is that employers are assumed to take a purely passive role *vis-à-vis* labor in that he is treated as a bargainer who does not really bargain since he is interested only in the wage-cost: labor-efficiency calculus, and whose only choices are (a) the sea in which he fishes, and (b) the bait he will use (bait is all of one sort; it varies only by more-or-less).

rules, and other formally graduated systems of employer-controlled rewards and punishments, and to direct the whole of these efforts along a more or less common ideological front.

Above foreman ranks, the story is somewhat different. A line somewhat similar to that found in governmental circles between 'civil service' and 'political appointees' seems to run between the two lower levels of business staff on the one hand and the directorial and upper managerial ranks on the other. Here, as has been pointed out, the evidence seems to show that 'position', 'pull', 'family', 'contacts', 'family wealth', 'nepotism', 'sinecure', 'indulgences' and the like are becoming increasingly important. These upper layers seem to be 'inbreeding' in business, just as the leading families of the upper wealth brackets from which they are mostly drawn intermarry within the charmed circles of the Social Register. There can be no question but that cooptation is the rule and not the exception throughout all business large and small, and that the practice holds as generally for the trade associations and their various *Spitzenverbände* as it does in principle for the more compact corporate set up. But more, that within the upper executive and directorial layers, co-optation is increasingly from socially acceptable ranks, and that the rules that guide selection come more and more to be woven of the same cloth as those which define the limits, the attitudes, the codes, and the social and political philosophies of self-conscious ruling-class status.

Before pursuing the implications of these developments a bit further, it will be useful to consider briefly the two other 'clues' to the nature of business bureaucracy hinted at above. The first of these relates to the fact that all attempts to rationalize business organization lead, under liberal-capitalistic political conditions, to dual, overlapping and, in part, 'competing', managements which become increasingly costly, inefficient, cumbersome and confusing with the passage of time, and which sooner or later require, by more or less common agreement, surgical treatment. It is a well-known fact that few efforts to coordinate, for example, private natural monopolies over territories coextensive with their natural potentialities have been successfully carried through without active governmental aid. The American Telephone and Telegraph Company is a partial exception, as are a few local tram and electric power systems. Railway unification, however, has nowhere been carried through except by government fiat. The Interstate Commerce Commission has striven for railway unification for years. The railway unification which led to the British 'Big 4' in the early twenties and the development of the unified rail networks of Germany and Japan were forced through on the initiative of their respective governments. The same holds for most electric power 'grid' schemes, unification of postal and telegraph systems, and most local and metropolitan transit networks.

The monopoly urge, in other words, seems to be typically stopped before monopoly has been really achieved. The results – the reasons why need not detain us at this point, for they require independent analysis, case by case and industry by industry [8] – however, belie at least in part the superficial impression. They seem to be about as follows:

1. Monopoly efforts are funneled increasingly through the machinery of trade association, Chamber of Commerce, and *Spitzenverband*.

2. Within these councils a broad line separates the inner governing cliques made up of the corporate giants and their medium and smaller satellite concerns.

3. The former divide markets, manipulate prices and production, and in general so direct affairs that, the total possible 'take' being treated as given, each of the former receives his due allotment where the gains are relatively speaking assured, and the latter are granted the more or less unprofitable fringes.

4. There is a cumulative pressure to 'settle into the allotted groove', and not to encroach upon 'most-favored company' territory, nor to push entirely out those whose existence on sufferance is deemed a continuous advantage for propaganda and other reasons.

5. Disputes concerning position are increasingly handled by the equivalent of negotiation, arbitration, 'treaty-making', special grant and privilege, etc.

8. Further combination may be stopped by fear of Anti-Trust prosecution, as in the United States.

6. Enterprise management is kept in a largely fractionalized state within each industry or trade, more or less irrespective of geographic, technological and other features.[9]

7. Increasingly, the leading functions of the trade association or *Spitzenverband* becomes the guidance and leadership on all social and political issues.

Finally, so long as either the internal coordinative functions or the external representative tasks of the central associations are pursued in the face of partially or largely antagonistic political authorities, the two facets will be dovetailed into a single program known as 'self-government in business'. [. . .]

Consequently, the more 'self-government in business' there is, the more governmental regulation there must be. There are some reasons for regarding the typical governmental regulatory body as organizationally superior to those evolved by the businesses they regulate, but that is quite another matter. Of key importance in the present connection are two by-products of the developments traced above. First, as pointed out above, there tends to be duplication all the way up and down the line between government and business administrative machines. And second, a large and increasing percentage of staff, and of the necessary facilities in terms of office space, office personnel, files and the paraphernalia for grinding out countless memoranda is taken up with the tactics of manoeuvre, concealment and uncovering of key information, legalistic haggling, enforcement and evasion, and so on, ad infinitum, brought about and dependent upon the conflicting interests expressed in such dual administrative control.

Facing this situation, what do the *Spitzenverbände* propose to do? First, they tend to duplicate in their own central headquarters

9. Patent pooling, standard grades and labels, simplification of types and varieties, cartel and syndicate practices, and the like, do not militate against this generalization, for these represent cost cutting, organization simplifying, and strategic manipulation factors. There is little or no evidence that they tend to 'rationalize' the industry either to the public good, or to cut down the plethora of separate managements. So far as the public good is concerned, these devices usually appear in combinations which retard the pace of change; they tend to slow down the weeding out which would occur under either 'normal' competitive or monopoly conditions.

the regulatory set-up[10] – thereby tending in many respects to further duplicate functions, staff and facilities – of their own membership. Not uncommonly, as an interesting by-play, they, or their member associations, or the strategically placed corporations which shape their leading policies attempt to entice governmental staff to join their own payrolls at higher salaries.[11] But most significantly, they seek direct representation on committees, commissions, advisory bodies and other governmental agencies which were either established at the outset for the specific purpose (or subsequently acquired the power) of determining in whole or in part the very policies which guide the administrative bodies themselves.

Thus the Federation of British Industries claimed before the outbreak of war to be directly represented on the Board of Trade Advisory Council and Council for Art and Industry, the War Office Technical Coordinating Committee on General Stores and Motor Transport Coordinating Committee, the Ministry of Health Joint Advisory Committee on River Pollution and the Town and Country Planning Advisory Committee, and the Ministry of Agriculture's Standing Committee on River Pollution. But this is only the beginning. It claimed that its representations before governmental bodies have resulted in adoption of its own plans for fiscal policy, tariff policy, imperial trade, commercial treaties.[12] There is scarcely a governmental committee or commission which affects its Members' interests at any given point upon which it did not claim membership or influence of decisive importance.

10. This is most readily shown in the departmentalization of the various *Spitzenverbände*; the range of the expanding committee and staff functions, the nature of the regional and functional groupings of membership, the content of regular reports to members in their official publications and annual congresses, etc. The same holds for many of their own member associations and certain of their larger member corporations.

11. Probably one-half of the leading figures amongst the directorial, executive and staff ranks of the leading *Spitzenverbände* have gone directly from governmental regulatory bodies to the firms and associations which they formerly regulated. Higher salaries are the common reason given. A careful study might reveal many others.

12. See, in particular, the NAM pamphlet 'Industry and Action'.

The British picture is not unusual but is typical for the liberal-capitalistic countries as a group. But it becomes quickly altered – in some respects drastically – the instant monopoly and business coordinative drives move from a 'liberal' to an 'authoritarian' environment. As evidenced in Germany and Italy, though by somewhat different routes, the inauguration of totalitarianism results in a general overhauling of business machinery along the following lines:

1. 'Streamlining', that is, a considerable mass of overlapping and duplicate trade association, regional and national, and peak association machinery is cut away.[13]

2. Correlatively, the combination and cartel movement is greatly strengthened; large and increasing numbers of small concerns are eliminated; compulsory association membership becomes the rule.

3. The relationships between governmental committees and commissions are altered in several ways, but in general these relationships become functional instead of 'fighting', coordinative instead of duplicating and overlapping, and 'self-government' follows lines of managerial decentralization rather than principles of checks and balances between governmental and private authorities. The basis of the 'efficiency' claims of all totalitarian systems is the cutting through and setting aside of conflicting machinery which has arisen (paradoxically, as a result of governmental 'interference') to coordinate and simplify business itself, or to prevent the inefficient disposal of social resources according to the common formulae of 'business as usual', or both.

4. Finally, the former 'self-governing' bodies are more or less formally vested with legal or quasilegal powers to formulate

13. This could readily be shown by following through in detail the change in any given line of industry or trade. But such 'streamlining', coupled with other changes indicated above, may well mean in many cases quite new and greatly elaborated machinery. For example, unorganized trades will now be organized; unfederated will now be federated; relationships between and amongst central associations and their various functional and regional divisions will be handled by various combinations of compacts, *ad hoc* and permanent committees, and so on.

policy within the larger 'totalitarian' directives, and to implement decisions with powers of enforcement.

Great and far-reaching as many of these changes may be in detail, they are, however, fully and without important exception in line with preceding trends. This could be shown in great detail by tracing through the successive changes, for example, which led to the formation in 1917 of the Reichsverband der deutschen Industrie out of two bodies representing respectively the heavy and light manufacturing industries, and the steps taken to transform the resultant body in 1933 into the Reichsgruppe Industrie. Or, again, by those whereby the former General Confederation of Italian Industry was made over into the Fascist Confederation of Industrialists. Another example is offered in the changes which signalized the pretty complete overhauling of the Confédération Générale de la Production Française, following the famous Matignon Agreement in 1936, into the Confédération Générale du Patronat Français. The formal dissolution in late 1940 of this latter body, which was modelled more or less directly after the Fascist pattern in Italy, seems to have been preparatory to remodelling along more distinctly Nazi lines. [. . .]

The 'slant' of the hierarchical or 'scalar' principle

So far as structure and control factors are concerned, trade associations and their *Spitzenverbände* tend to be modelled after the pattern of the typical large-scale corporation. The managerial hierarchy of command and subordination follows typically the 'line' or 'military' form of organization: any necessary breakdown in function and staff is so dovetailed into the 'line' of authority as to take maximum advantage of expert counsel and whatever principles of decentralization of management may be appropriate in each separate case. Policy-making power lies typically in the directorial and managerial ranks, and is not subject to check from below. So far as concerns the lower reaches of the hierarchy of command and the labor that performs the functions which management directs, the system is completely authoritarian (anti-democratic); all duties and responsibilities are fixed from above except when counter-organization of labor or other organized special interest groups may be able to force concessions via governmental or direct-action pressure.

More recently, as has been outlined in numerous places,[14] management has succeeded in largely freeing itself from owner or investor control. Conversely, labor is increasingly able to make its voice heard and its power felt only so far as it operates under the protection of government. The trade union may be the power that forces the government to act, but without government intervention the trade union finds itself increasingly unable effectively to make its influences felt or even to recruit its members. A first condition to trade union bargaining power is favorable law. That is to say, even in labor relations organized business finds itself facing the government.

Free in large part of direct investor control,[15] managements which for one reason or another are primarily interested in executive and not in larger policy matters, may be able greatly to rationalize productive operations where formerly such changes were inhibited by investor interest in higher returns. But even where this proves both possible and, from the point of view of management, desirable, management now largely swings free from all direct controls other than those which may be imposed upon it by governmental authority; this fact will and apparently does mean that the executive and managerial end will be handled by paid functionaries, the better to allow the leading figures within these ranks to focus the massed power of their pendulous corporations upon larger issues of policy. Business leadership not only acquires political interests, but it turns to the political arena already backed by enormous, fully mobilized, and easily focused power. There are but few good modern parallels for this situation in the field of internal-pressure politics. For most apt comparison one must turn to the massed and personally manipulable powers of ancient and tribal armies of legionaries and retainers, or to the medieval baronry of the crusading knights.

So far as this picture holds, the appropriate medium for

14. See the works of such authors as Berle, Means, Bonbright, Gordon and others (1933, 1932, 1938).

15. Here again government takes the place of the disenfranchised. Something the equivalent of the Securities and Exchange Commission is now to be found in most capitalist countries.

expressing, and the machinery for canalizing and focusing, the social and political power of management is the trade association and its *Spitzenverbände*. To the extent that paid functionaries in the hierarchy of management are enabled to handle matters on an authoritative but expert or 'civil service' basis (because they have been recruited from an especially trained and ideologically preconditioned corps), to that extent will policy matters be the more completely funnelled through supra-managerial apparatus organized for this specific purpose.

These trade associations and their *Spitzenverbände* are largely, if not in many cases exclusively, political-pressure bodies. This remains true even in those cases where trade associations act as coordinating bodies for cartels, or where they themselves have taken on cartel functions. The records are, of course, unsatisfactory, since here as elsewhere they leave next to no traces, such collusive practices as they may resort to proceeding by rules known from times immemorial within inner political party circles, and not by the etiquette of written statements and formal contracts.[16] Secrecy, long the essence of national diplomacy, becomes entirely natural and normal, as the *Spitzenverband* becomes a politically potent pressure group.

But the main concern of the supra-managerial business organizations is not, strictly speaking, economic. Even where it is so, the issues at stake are increasingly burdened with social, philosophical and political problems. That this is true can readily be substantiated by any reader who will take the trouble to leaf through a few thousand pages of trade-association literature, or who can find time to sit in on a few hundred of their congresses

16. Thus, when the author of the TNEC Monograph no. 18, *Trade Association Survey*, dealing with trade associations in the United States, finds little ground for the belief that trade associations have 'engaged in collusive restraints of trade,' he cites as proof not evidence, but the lack of it! Which is only to say that he has confused not only the nature of trade-association activity, but also the nature of such collusion and of its characteristic proofs. The evidence of NRA might have disabused the author, who was familiar with its practices, of this naïve interpretation. But if nothing else, he might have turned to a brief review of anti-trust indictments for proof that the very reverse was true. Political machines rarely keep vouchers or reduce understandings to the written form, as Lincoln Steffens was not the first to discover, nor Clarence Darrow (see his review of NRA) the last.

and conventions. What he will find is that the issues relate pre-dominately, at some remove or other, to known, felt, or feared challenges by labor or other groups – operating independently or through regular political channels – to the tenets underlying the capitalistic system as a whole.

As political-pressure bodies, the trade associations and their *Spitzenverbände* will be found responsible to their membership on the principle of representation, *de jure* or *de facto* according to property holdings and clique groupings. In practice, except perhaps for some of the associations representing smaller businesses, clearly most of them are as closely controlled by a few of the business giants as the bulk of their underlying corporate properties are controlled by a minor fraction of the managerial and directorial personnel. That is to say, where the structure of organization and methods of control recognized in constitution and by-laws do not permit – which typically they do – centralized, self-perpetuating control, the *Realpolitik* of power and clique effects a like result. This picture is so well accepted in association circles throughout the world and is so typical and general as to seem clearly beyond dispute in point of fact.

Both above and below the level of corporate managerial circles, the 'scalar chain' or principle of graduated hierarchical controls obtains. Leadership, so far as the respective underlying hierarchy of command and subordination is concerned, is typically self-appointed, self-perpetuating and autocratic. In the sub-managerial zones, this leadership impinges on the non-property interests of labor and the general public. But in the supra-managerial zones it bears largely, and in some respects exclusively, on business interests in general. Authority in both ranges from the top down, and responsibility from the bottom up. Below, authority coordinates the non- or but partially-property minded in an operative complex – policy being predetermined and given. Above, authority coordinates big and little business in a policy complex forged as a by-product of the *Realpolitik* practised by their own self-appointed general staffs. The same individuals, the same groups and cliques, the same interests dominate in each sphere; in each the principle of organization, relating as it does to policy issues, is that of an inherently undemocratic, authoritarian hierarchy. And in neither is it the property interest of the bulk of the corporate property holders which dominates the stage. Yet the issues are increasingly of a 'system-defending' or ideological character which reach to the 'roots of domination' in a capitalistically organized world.

The content of the new outlook

Contrary to certain implications of current usage, 'totalitarianism', like 'bureaucracy', is not necessarily undesirable if it is taken to mean a social-psychological outlook possessing at once a coherent unifying philosophy and a general program of action which comprehend the totality of organized social life. In this sense, even democracy, as a theoretically coherent web of postulates, freedoms, and qualified restraints, is 'totalitarian'. But the question naturally arises as to what the aim and content of a general doctrinal and programmatic position may be, when it appears that its formulators are responsible neither to the general public nor even to the property interests upon whose sanctions their authoritative powers rest. And how understand – how, indeed, even begin to formulate – a program when it seems impossible to define the interests to be promoted?

The difficulty, however, is more apparent than real. The leading managerial and directorial figures within the inner business sancta are real, not fictitious people, and they are drawn from, or have been absorbed into, the upper layers of wealth and income whose stakes it is their function to defend.[17] Under current conditions, they are called upon to defend these general interests in an environment wherein the issues are increasingly so drawn as to appear in some sense or other to jeopardize the whole system of evolving status and special-class privilege whose mobilized resources they have acquired 'emergency powers' to command. And for the opening struggle they have largely fought themselves free of the procedural and other forms of red tape imposed upon them by law – under the general business rule of 'live and let live' – in a vast political environment hostile to undue centralization of naked economic power. It cannot be forgotten that the world of relatively small-scale middle-class business of the not distant past,

17. It is at this point that Burnham (1940) flies off at a dangerous tangent and leads himself to an analysis as misleading as it is superficially plausible.

out of whose rich gleanings the great monopoly-oriented economic empires of the present gathered their first strengths, feared arbitrary political authority above all else. In limiting the state to *laissez-faire*, they were careful to see that its functions were so defined as to make the state the specialized guardian of its own duty not to interfere as the tool of any hostile interest.

The history of government regulation of business has been primarily the history of attempts of small business to employ government to defend their interests against the encroachments of business monopolies,[18] and of the latter to wrest the initiative from the small. The business giants, operating to an increasing extent in these matters through trade associations and their *Spitzenverbände*, seem to have found an effective means for neutralizing this opposition, and to be in a fair way to the achievement of a 'unified' and 'harmonious' outlook of the business world *vis-à-vis* labor and any other challenging interest.

Real conflicts of interests within the business world have not been eliminated by these means, but to some degree they have been coordinated. Such successes as the various *Spitzenverbände* seem to have achieved in their legislative and allied efforts in the several capitalistic countries seem to stem in large part from the fact that they have been able to act as though business were united in bringing their collective pressures to bear upon government. It holds as a corollary to this that the bitterest and most ruthless attacks will be made upon those businesses large or small which refuse to play the game according to the new rules.

There slowly emerges an apparent single view, a seeming common cause, and appearance of a general business 'harmony', the semblance of a certain common business social philosophy which takes on form and content step by step with the growth and expansion of the centralized influence of the great peak associations. And in proportion as this seeming internal unification takes place in organized business, one finds slowly being evolved

18. The vast and overwhelming bulk of complaints against the exercise of monopoly controls coming into the United States Department of Justice's Anti-Trust Division come, as Mr Arnold has frequently pointed out, from business circles. The pressure for enactment of state and federal anti-trust controls, as – for that matter – the bulk of the business regulatory machinery, emanates from similar circles.

parallel ideas *vis-à-vis* all other interests which, however and by whichever route they may come in conflict with any given business or aspect of business control, have no alternative but to appear to challenge the business world as a whole. Given comprehensive organization – the common ideal of the trade association all over the world – this posture of affairs appears inevitable in the very nature of the case. If conflicting interests, as, for example, in the case of labor, are organized on an equally comprehensive basis, the effect will be thrown in much sharper relief. And it is an effect that has gradually become universally evident throughout the capitalistic world of the last half century.

How do the trade, employer and business *Spitzenverbände* then proceed to meet challenges which they are led to interpret as in conflict with the tenets underlying the capitalistic world as such? By somewhat varying routes, organized business amongst the several capitalistic countries has arrived at pretty much a common set of solutions. For the sake of brevity these may be summarized as follows:

1. *Control over popular organizations*: the company union is father to the idea of universal, comprehensive, all-inclusive business-controlled joint labor-employer membership federations, of which the German Labor Front and the Italian General Confederation of Labor [19] are the highest development to date. Similar ideas have run through the literature of American, French and British business. An attempt was made to set up such a body in the United States in 1921; the Federation of British Industries was originally intended to include both labor and employers. The programs of De Mun, Harmel and the French Social Catholic movement evolved similar ideas before the turn of the twentieth century. The ideas and patterns of the company union are applied wherever any other form of popular organization – of farmers, consumers, little businessmen, professionals, women – has struck root. The idea is everywhere and in all countries the same: mass organization centered around the ideologies of the upper business and social hierarchies and controlled by the self-appointed and self-perpetuating 'natural' leaders from those ranks.

19. See Salvemini (1936, ch. 7).

2. *The militarization of employer-employee relations*: by a re-assertion of authority in the hands of the employer similar to that which obtains in the army. This can be read from all complaints in the literature of the *Spitzenverbande* and their subsidiary bodies when faced with effective labor protest, as in the events centered around the British General Strike in 1926, the movements of the French Popular Front centered in the Matignon Agreement of June, 1936, the rise of the CIO in the United States and complaints demanding modification of the National Labor Relations Board, and in the successes of German, Italian and Japanese employers, scored on the initiation of Fascist-type systems. The regimen of the 'unorganized' industrial plant such as that of Ford is here prototypal of objectives seen as desirable by spokesmen who may have power to suggest or act in the larger sphere.

3. *The evolution of a 'harmony-of-all-interests' propaganda in which the employer appears as benevolent pater familias*: such was the blending which underlay the social legislation of Bismarck, the programs of De Mun and Du Pin in the French Social Catholic movement, the Papal Encyclicals of *Rerum Novarum* in 1891 and *Quadragesimo Anno* in 1931, the 'Clerical Fascism' of Dollfuss and Schuschnigg in Austria and of Franco in Spain, the NRA and some of the American New Deal Legislation, the Japanese National Harmonizing Movement, and, of course, the whole of 'welfare capitalism'. The employer as 'patron' or 'trustee' becomes the *beau idéal* of the business world. Correlatively the trustee concept still is applied in all other relationships of real or potential conflict between organized business and the general public. The parallel to 'industrial relations' is 'public relations', and this latter is growing by every known criterion of relative importance in a sort of geometric ratio to all other corporate publicity interests, both in the United States and abroad. 'Public relations' advances the concept of a natural 'harmony' of interest between business and the public, business and the consumer, business and social and economic progress. The relationship is that of 'trustee of the people's property and welfare'.[20]

20. See Batchelor, (1938). The Nazi motto, *Gemeinnutz geht vor Eigennutz*, carries the precise equivalent for German businessmen for the dictum, 'A

4. *The 'educational emphasis' looks two ways*: towards 'neutralizing' the hostile amongst adults, while engraining 'loyal' staff and especially the younger generation 'through the doctrine of the organization itself'. 'Neutralization' involves recognition, wherever the *Realpolitik* of strategy may determine, of trade unions and similar organizations; emphasis upon 'cooperation' by promotion of labor-employment community activities; regional decentralization of plants; legal restraints upon the 'abuse' of labor power; use of police power, strike breakers, espionage at need; the mobilization of the middle and professional classes into patriotic and other federations; attacks on opposition leadership under the guise of attacking 'racketeering'; encouragement of fear of 'aliens', 'fifth-columnists' and other menaces which encourage in turn emphasis upon group loyalties, patriotic sentiments; especial types of interest programs and propaganda for women, children and the aged, etc. Conversely, education of the young calls for control over apprenticeship training; purge of school textbooks; vocational emphasis with belief in an eventual occupational stratification in which there is a one-to-one correspondence between economic station and presumptive IQ; evolution of a system of rewards and punishments which turn on the axis of loyalty to the concern; the substitution of non-commercial for commercial incentives; of group and 'social' for individual and personal incentives.

5. *The key to control is political*: executive authority and policy-forming power are concentrated in the same cooptatively renewed ranks, and these recognize that the key to power is twofold; (1) consolidation of all the 'ins' in a solid, interest-conscious bloc; (2) a popular following, the key to which is alliance with any faction, movement or party which has or may acquire popular following without disturbing the general social structure of command and subordination. This means compromise with the *nouveau puissant* as they are coopted into the movement on all matters relating to 'the take' – an old practice in relationships

---

widespread, favorable attitude of mind is a first essential to effective trusteeship in big business. People must expect and assume that managers will look out for interests other than their own. Managers in turn will then attempt to live up to expectations.' TNEC Monograph no. 11, p. 130.

between political rings and powerful vested interests all over the world, but now generalized to entire national economies, and rationalized with an eye to sterilization of 'take' knowledge and demand for participation below the upper ranks. And for these lower reaches, the evolving programs of the organized business world look to well-ordered, and especially trained and loyal cadres of hierarchically controlled employees over whom as 'leaders' they have complete charge – as Gignoux of the Confédération Générale du Patronat Français expressed the matter – 'not only of men but of souls'.

6. *The new power complexes are inherently expansive*: two things are united in this reaching for political power. One is the tendency of all democratically irresponsible power aggregations to expand without limit. And the other is the fact that the 'life styles' of the units which form the cells of the new power pyramids have each and all been dominated by a tendency to expand without limit – a fact with which all great business leaders have been thoroughly familiar and which has been traced at great length by Sombart and others. Given control or power decisively to influence the national state, imperial expansion is inevitable. The more or less rational combination of fully articulated systems of protection and privilege combined with imperial expansion, on the one hand, and the integrative pressures of a rationally articulated industrial technology, on the other, lead logically to the concept of the next largest politically omnicompetent and coherently organized imperial area, 'great-space economics' (*Grossraumwirtschaften*). [. . .]

References

BATCHELOR, B. (1938), *Profitable Public Relations*, Harper & Row.
BERLE, A. A., and MEANS, G. C. (1933), *The Modern Corporation and Private Property*, Commerce Clearing House.
BONBRIGHT, J. C., and MEANS, G. C. (1932), *The Holding Company*, McGraw-Hill.
BONN, M. J. (1931), *Das Schicksal des deutschen Kapitalismus*, Berlin.
BRANDEIS, L. D. (1936), *The Curse of Bigness*, Kennikat.
BURNHAM, J. (1940), *Managerial Revolution*, Indiana University Press.
CALLMAN, R. (1934), *Das deutsche Kartellrecht*, Berlin.
CALLMAN, R. (1935), *Unlauterer Wettbewerb*, Mannheim.
CHAMBERLIN, E. (1933), *The Theory of Monopolistic Competition*, Oxford University Press.

DIMOCK, M., and HYDE, H. K. (1940), 'Bureaucracy and trusteeship', *Temporary National Economic Committee Monograph*, no. 11.

GORDON, R. A. (1938), 'Ownership by management and control groups in the large corporation', *Q.J. Econ.*, vol. 52, no. 3, pp. 367–400.

HICKS, J. R. (1932), *The Theory of Wages*, Macmillan.

LUCAS, A. F. (1937), *Industrial Reconstruction and the Control of Competition*, Longmans.

MOONEY, J. D., and REILEY, A. C. (1931), *Onward Industry*, Harper & Row.

NATIONAL ASSOCIATION OF MANUFACTURERS, *Industry and Action*, undated pamphlet of the National Association of Manufacturers.

ROBINSON, J. (1933), *The Economics of Imperfect Competition*, Macmillan.

SALVEMINI, G. (1936), *Under The Axe of Fascism*, Fertig.

SMITH, A. (1776), *The Wealth of Nations* (ed. E. Cannan), Methuen.

WIEDENFELD, K. (1932), *Kapitalismus und Beamtentum: Produzententum und Konsumententum in der Weltmarkt-Wirtschaft*, Berlin.

10 J. K. Galbraith

Capital, Technostructure and Power

Excerpt from J. K. Galbraith, *The New Industrial State*, Hamish Hamilton, 1967, chapter 5, pp. 46–59.

No subject has been more faithfully explored by economists than the relation between what anciently have been called the factors of production – land, labor, capital and the entrepreneurial talent which brings these together and manages their employment. Until recently, the problem of efficiency in production – that of getting the most from the available productive resources – was envisaged, almost entirely, as one of winning the best combination of these agents. The elucidation by means of diagrams of the arcane problems inherent in factor combination remains one of the prime pedagogical rites of economics.[1]

1. Changing technology, it is conceded, alters progressively and radically what can be obtained from any given supply of factors. But there is no way by which this intelligence can be developed at length in a textbook. So economic instruction concedes the important and then discusses the unimportant. Thus Professor Samuelson, rightly the most noted of contemporary economists, who more than anyone else has instructed adult Americans in the subject, observes that the output that can be obtained from a given stock of factors 'depends on the state of technology'. He then adds: '*But at any time, there will be a maximum obtainable amount of product for any given amounts of factor inputs.*' Samuelson (1964, p. 516). [Emphasis his.] The problem of factor allocation is the subject on which there is an available doctrine. So having given it such importance as italics provide, this is the subject he discusses. Were this all, he would not be especially open to criticism. Much economic instruction, and notably so in such fields as advanced theory, foreign trade and monetary policy, depends not on the relevance of the subject matter but on the existence of an intellectually preoccupying theory. In this case, however, there is a conflict between the technological development, to which Professor Samuelson properly accords the primary role in increasing productivity, and the factor allocation which provides his pedagogical exercise. Technological development involves heavy commitment of capital and time which is safeguarded by planning and companion control over costs, prices and demand. But the approved pedagogical exercise leads to the conclusion that optimal allocation of factors is obtained by the minimum of such interference with the market.

Economists have been equally concerned with the way in which the prices of the factors of production – rents, wages, interest and profits – are determined. Indeed, in the classical tradition, the subject was thought of as falling in two parts: the problem of value having to do with the determination of the prices of goods and the problem of distribution or how the resulting income was divided between landlords, workers, capitalists and entrepreneurs.

One aspect of the relationships between the factors of production has, however, been less examined. That is why power is associated with some factors and not with others. Why did ownership of land once convey plenary power over the dominant form of productive enterprise and, therewith, in the community at large? Why under other circumstances has it been assumed that such authority, both over the enterprise and in the society at large, should lie with the owner of capital? Under what circumstances might such power pass to labor?

It is a puzzling neglect. On coming on any form of organized activity – a church, platoon, government bureau, congressional committee, a house of casual pleasure – our first instinct is to inquire who is in charge. Then we inquire as to the qualifications or credentials which accord such command. Organization almost invariably invites two questions: Who is the head? How did he get there?

One reason the question was slighted was that for a long time, in formal economic inquiry, no one associated with economic activity was thought to have any worthwhile exercise of power. In the classical economic tradition – that of Adam Smith, David Ricardo, Thomas Malthus, J. S. Mill and Alfred Marshall – and increasingly as concepts were better defined, the business enterprise (like the Wisconsin dairy farm today) was assumed to be small in relation to the market supplied. The price it received was impersonally and competitively determined by the market. So were the prices paid to suppliers. Wages were also set by the market. So was the interest on borrowed funds. Profits reduced themselves to a competitive level. Technology was assumed to be stable. Under these circumstances the ideal volume of production for the firm was externally established by the relation of costs to the market price at various levels of output. If the man in

J. K. Galbraith   193

charge of the firm has no power to influence prices, costs, wages or interest, and if even his best output is externally determined and his profits are subject to the leveling effect of competition, one can rightly be unconcerned about his power. He has none. Until well into the present century the economics of the textbooks assumed a world of such small and competitive firms. The counterpart neglect of the problem of power was both plausible and inevitable. Other traditions of thought, however, were less handicapped.

In particular there was Marx. In the middle of the last century he brought the subject of power into economic discussion with a vehemence which the world has not yet quite ceased to deplore. The notion of a system of competitive and hence passive business firms he dismissed as an exercise in vulgar apologetics. Production is dominated by those who control and supply capital – by a 'constantly diminishing number of the magnates of capital who usurp and monopolize all advantages of this process of transformation . . .' (1867, ch. 32, p. 836). Their authority in the enterprise is complete. Prices and wages are set in their collective interest. They dominate the society and set its moral tone. They also control the state which becomes an executive committee serving the will and interest of the capitalist class. There is no question of power being associated with any other factor of production. At this stage in historical development it belongs unequivocally and totally with capital.

In the classical tradition there was eventually a measure of agreement with Marx. The notion of the competitive market receded; it survives today in the textbooks as an exceptional case. The business enterprise is routinely assumed to have control over its prices and output – to have the power that is associated with one seller or monopoly, a few sellers or oligopoly, or with some unique feature of its product or service which accords it protection from competition. Only professional defenders of the free enterprise system, members of a lowly and poorly paid craft, still argue for the rule of competition, this being the test their clients are best calculated to fail.[2] There is general agreement

2. 'To the extent that a price is reached by means that are *not* impersonal – to the extent that either the buyer or the seller can dictate or influence the setting of the price – to that extent our system of controlling the use of

that 'market power which large absolute and relative size gives to the giant corporation is the basis not only of economic power but also of considerable political and social power . . .' (Kaysen, 1959, p. 99).

And the companion point of Marx is assumed. Such power as may be available naturally and inevitably belongs to capital. Its exercise is the prerogative of ownership. The claims of the other factors of production are inherently subordinate. In the assumption that power belongs as a matter of course to capital, all economists are Marxians.

Beyond this, the problem of power is still not much discussed. Prices and wages are fixed, investment determined, dividends declared, production decided by the owners of capital within the margin of discretion allowed by the market. Influence by business on the state is deemed irregular and illegitimate; such as is nonetheless exercised is by or in the interest of the owners of the enterprise. Alternatives as to the exercise of power by capital are not seriously considered.

In the last three decades there has been steady accumulation of evidence on the shift of power from owners to managers within the modern large corporation. The power of the stockholders, as noted, has seemed increasingly tenuous. A small proportion of the stock is represented at stockholders' meetings for a ceremony in which banality is varied chiefly by irrelevance. The rest is voted by proxy for the directors who have been selected by the management. The latter, though their ownership is normally negligible, are solidly in control of the enterprise. By all visible evidence the power is theirs. Yet there has been great reluctance to admit of a significant and enduring shift of power from the owners of capital. Some observers have sought to maintain the myth of stockholder power. As in foreign policy it is hoped that incantation may save what the reality denies.[3]

resources is not working properly' (US Department of Commerce, 1965, p. 13). This pamphlet was commissioned by John T. Connor while Secretary of Commerce, to promote understanding of (and indicate sympathy for) American business. By the test of the pamphlet all large business would fail.

3. 'When, for example, John purchased a new issue of stock from the Keim Corporation last year . . . [it gave] him a voice in the decision of "his" firm's management when he meets with other stockholders at annual meetings.' (US Department of Commerce, 1965, pp. 17–18).

Others, including all Marxians, argue that the change is superficial, that capital retains a deeper and more functional control. Only the naïve react to the obvious. Some have conceded a change but have deferred judgement as to its significance.[4] Yet others have seen a possibly dangerous usurpation of the legitimate power of capital that should, if possible, be reversed (Berle, 1959, p. 98). Comparatively few have questioned the credentials of capital, where direction of the enterprise is concerned, or suggested that it might be durably in eclipse.

Yet, over a longer range of time, power over the productive enterprise – and by derivation in the society at large – has shifted radically between the factors of production. The eminence of capital is a relatively recent matter; until about two centuries ago no perceptive man would have doubted that power was decisively associated with land. The comparative wealth, esteem, military position and the sanguinary authority over the lives of the populace that went with land ownership assured its possessor of a position of eminence in his community and power in the state. These perquisites of land ownership also gave a strong and even controlling direction to history. For two centuries, until about two hundred years before the discovery of America, it helped inspire the recurrent military campaigns to the East which are called the Crusades. Succor for Byzantium, which was beset by the infidels, and redemption of Jerusalem, which had been lost to them, served, without doubt, as a stimulant to ardor. But not exclusively. Relations between the eastern and western Christians were marked by profound mistrust. Jerusalem had been under Islam for 450 years; its redemption had not previously been considered of breathtaking urgency. The younger sons of the Frankish nobility, like the hungry peasants who followed Peter the Hermit, wanted land. Beneath the mantled cross beat hearts soundly attuned to the value of real estate. Baldwin, younger

4. See Mason (1958) and Haley (1952, pp. 221–2). It is Professor Mason's view that, while the capitalist entrepreneur has lost his power in the modern large corporation, there is no serviceable view of what has taken his place. Accordingly, one can still do best by assuming the entrepreneur and the traditional motivations.' [I] must confess a lack of confidence in the marked superiority *for purposes of economic analysis*, of this newer concept of the firm, over the older conception of the entrepreneur.'

brother of Godfrey of Bouillon, found himself faced on the way to the Holy City with the taxing decision as to whether to continue with the redeeming armies or take up an attractive piece of property at Edessa. He unhesitatingly opted for the latter and, only on the death of his brother, did he leave his fief to become the first King of Jerusalem.[5]

For three and a half centuries after the discovery of America, appreciation of the strategic role of land gave it an even greater role in history. The Americas were populated as also the Steppes and the habitable parts of the Antipodes. Once again, religion went hand in hand with real property conveyancing, somewhat disguising the role of the latter. Spaniards considered themselves commissioned by God to win the souls of Indians; Puritans believed themselves primarily under obligation to find a favorable environment for their own. For Catholics and Cavaliers the Lord was believed to favor rather large acreages with the opportunity these accorded for the spiritual custody of aborigines and, as these gave out, of Africans. For Puritans and Protestants spiritual merit lay with the homestead and family farm. But these were details. In the New World, as in the Old, it was assumed that power belonged, as a right, to men who owned land. Democracy, in its modern meaning, began as a system which gave the suffrage to those who had proved their worth by acquiring real property and to no others.

This eminence of land, and the incentive to acquire it, were firmly grounded in economics. Until comparatively modern times, agricultural production – the provision of food and fiber – accounted for a large share of all production as it still accounts for 70 to 80 per cent of all output in such economically poor countries as modern India. Ownership or control of land thus accorded one a position in the dominant form of economic activity; to be landless was to be crowded into what was left.

Meanwhile other factors of production had a much less strategic role. Agricultural technology was stable and uncomplicated; accordingly, slaves apart, it offered small scope for capital and, as a broad rule, slaves could only be used in conjunction with land. Non-agricultural activity being relatively

5. 'The opportunity of combining Christian duty with the acquisition of land in a southern climate was very attractive' Runciman (1954, p. 92).

unimportant, its demand for capital was small and limited further by simple and stable technology. So – a somewhat neglected point – until two hundred years ago a meager supply of capital was matched by an equally meager opportunity for its use. If a man had land in England or Western Europe he could get the modest supply of capital he needed to till it. Possession of this capital was no guarantee that he could get the land.

Nor was labor difficult to come by. Its well-established tendency was to keep itself in a state of great abundance. David Ricardo, having regard for experience to that time, could hold in 1817 that 'no point is better established than that the supply of labourers will always ultimately be in proportion to the means of supporting them' (1951, p. 292). That was to say that, given a little time, an unlimited supply would be forthcoming at, or about, a subsistence wage. Enough labor would be used so that, through diminishing returns, the contribution of the marginal worker would be about equal to his subsistence. If he gave up this narrow contest with privation he could easily be replaced. If a man adds little and can easily be replaced, he has small power and small bargaining power.

But no one could doubt the advantage of laying one's hands on an acre, or a hundred acres, or a thousand acres of fertile land. Nor could one doubt the deadly consequences of losing like amounts. This meant that possession of land was strategic and not even the philosophers whose ideas ushered in the Industrial Revolution could quite envisage a society where this was otherwise. Adam Smith, though he was at odds on most points with his Physiocratic precursors in France who had made land the ultimate source of all wealth, attributed a special bounty to real property which was returned, as a special mark of grace, to those who owned it (1776).[6] Forty years later, following the Napoleonic Wars, Ricardo and Malthus made ownership of land even more crucial. Population would grow in accordance with a biological dynamic of its own. This would make an ever more urgent claim on a much more slowly increasing food supply. In consequence the relative price of food and the share of income going to landlords would increase insouciantly and

6. See Gray (1931, p. 137).

without limit. The decisive factor was the scarcity of land. 'The labour of nature is paid, not because she does much, but because she does little. In proportion as she becomes niggardly in her gifts, she exacts a greater price for her work. Where she is munificently beneficent, she always works gratis.'[7] Not surprisingly, those who owned this rare resource would exercise full authority in the dominant agricultural economy and be men of prestige and power in the community at large.

Ricardo wrote at a moment in history when land was being dethroned. That was partly because the scarcity to which he attributed such importance had set in motion a phenomenal search for a new supply. And the two Americas, South Africa and Australia were all found to have large, unused and highly usable amounts. New land could be obtained or lost land could be replaced by going to the frontier. The need now was for capital to pay the passage for seed, livestock and equipment and to tide a man over until the first harvest. And if a varlet could, on occasion, get more acreage in the New World than the most majestic aristocrat owned in the Old, land was no longer a secure source of distinction.

Meanwhile, mechanical inventions and the growth of metallurgical and engineering knowledge were prodigiously expanding opportunities for the employment of capital. From this greater use of capital in more advanced technology came greater production. From that production came greater income and more saving. It is not clear that in the last century the demand for capital grew more rapidly than the supply. In the new countries, including the United States, capital was usually scarce and the cost was high. But in England, over most of the century, rates of return were low and Englishmen were under strong compulsion to find more profitable employments for their savings in distant lands. But there coal, iron and steel, railways, locomotives, ships, textile machinery, buildings and bridges were commanding an

7. Ricardo (1951, p. 76). Ricardo is here taking issue with Adam Smith's suggestion that the return to land was payment for nature's bounty. The point is of no importance here. For both, nature, by way of land, played a large part in determining incomes.

increasing share of the national product. For producing these, capital was what counted. Agriculture, with its peculiar dependence on land, contributed a diminishing share of total product. The man who owned or controlled capital could now command the needed labor and land. Control of labor or land accorded no reciprocal power to command capital.

So power over the enterprise passed to capital. And so did prestige in the community and authority in the state. At the beginning of the nineteenth century the British Parliament was still dominated by the great landed families. By the middle of the century they were acceding to industrial pressure to lower the price of food, and therewith the level of factory wages, at the expense of their rents. By the end of the century the premier figure in British politics was the great Birmingham industrialist and pioneer screw manufacturer, Joseph Chamberlain. At the beginning of the century, the United States government was dominated by landed and slave-owning gentlemen of Virginia; by the end of the century by common agreement power had passed, depending on point of view, to the men of enterprise or the malefactors of great wealth. The Senate had become a club of rich businessmen.

The change, a point of much importance for what follows, did not seem natural. George Washington, Thomas Jefferson and James Madison seemed far more appropriate to positions of public power than Collis P. Huntington, J. P. Morgan or Andrew Mellon. They were credited with capacity for action apart from their own interests as the capitalists were not. And action in their own interest – the defense, for example, of slavery – seemed more gentlemanly, reasonable and legitimate than action by the capitalists in their own behalf. This contrasting impression still survives in public attitudes and the elementary history books. We may lay it down as a rule that the older the exercise of any power the more benign it will appear and the more recent its assumption the more unnatural and even dangerous it will seem.

It will now be clear what accords power to a factor of production or to those who own or control it. Power goes to the factor which is hardest to obtain or hardest to replace. In precise language it adheres to the one that has the greatest inelasticity of supply at the margin. This inelasticity may be the result of a natural shortage, or an effective control over supply by some human agency, or both.[8]

In its age, if one had land then labor and capital (in the meager amounts required) could be readily obtained. But to have labor and operating capital did not so readily insure that a man could get land. There was an admixture, here, of cause and effect. Because land provided special access to economic and larger power, steps were taken, as through the laws of entail, to confine possession to the privileged or noble caste. And this, in turn, limited the opportunities for acquiring it and further increased the economic power and social authority which, from one generation to the next, land conferred on its owner.

In the age of capital, land was readily available in the minor amounts required for industrial enterprise and increasingly so for agriculture. Labor continued to be plentiful. Now possession of land and labor did not allow one to command capital; but with capital, land and labor could easily be obtained. Capital now accorded power in the enterprise and in consequence in the society.

Should it happen that capital were to become abundant, or redundant, and thus be readily increased or replaced, the power it confers, both in the enterprise and in the society, would be expected to suffer. This would seem especially probable if, at the same time, some other factor of production should prove increasingly difficult to add or replace.

In the modern industrial system, while capital is used in large amounts, it is, at least in peace-time, even more abundantly supplied. The tendency to an excess of savings, and the need for an offsetting strategy by the state, is an established and well-recognized feature of the Keynesian economy. And savings, we have seen, are supplied by the industrial enterprise to itself as

8. Thus a union, which accords considerable power to labor in relation to such specific decisions as those affecting wages and working conditions, involves full control of supply. (In a successful strike the supply price of labor on the plant side of the picket line is infinitely high.) The union power is increased if the supply of labor is not too abundant.

part of its planning. There is high certainty as to their availability, for this is the purpose of the planning.

At the same time the requirements of technology and planning have greatly increased the need of the industrial enterprise for specialized talent and for its organization. The industrial system must rely, in the main, on external sources for this talent. Unlike capital it is not something that the firm can supply to itself. To be effective this talent must also be brought into effective association with itself. It must be in an organization. Given a competent business organization, capital is now ordinarily available. But the mere possession of capital is now no guarantee that the requisite talent can be obtained and organized. One should expect, from past experience, to find a new shift of power in the industrial enterprise, this one from capital to organized intelligence. And one would expect that this shift would be reflected in the deployment of power in the society at large.

This has, indeed, occurred. It is a shift of power as between the factors of production which matches that which occurred from land to capital in the advanced countries beginning two centuries ago. It is an occurrence of the last fifty years and is still going on. A dozen matters of commonplace observation – the loss of power by stockholders in the modern corporation, the impregnable position of the successful corporate management, the dwindling social magnetism of the banker, the air of quaintness that attaches to the suggestion that the United States is run from Wall Street, the increasingly energetic search for industrial talent, the new prestige of education and educators – all attest the point.

This shift of power has been disguised because, as was once true of land, the position of capital is imagined to be immutable. That power should be elsewhere seems unnatural and those who so argue seem to be in search of frivolous novelty. And it has been disguised because power has not gone to another of the established factors as they are celebrated in conventional economic pedagogy. It has not passed to labor. Labor has won limited authority over its pay and working conditions but none over the enterprise. And it still tends to abundance. If overly abundant savings are not used, the first effect is unemployment; if savings are used one consequence is a substitution of machine processes for unskilled labor and standard skills. Thus unskilled labor and workers with conventional skills suffer, along with the capitalist, from an abundance of capital.

Nor has power passed to the classical entrepreneur – the individual who once used his access to capital to bring it into combination with the other factors of production. He is a diminishing figure in the industrial system. Apart from access to capital, his principal qualifications were imagination, capacity for decision and courage in risking money including, not infrequently, his own. None of these qualifications are especially important for organizing intelligence or effective in competing with it.

Power has, in fact, passed to what anyone in search of novelty might be justified in calling a new factor of production. This is the association of men of diverse technical knowledge, experience or other talent which modern industrial technology and planning require. It extends from the leadership of the modern industrial enterprise down to just short of the labor force and embraces a large number of people and a large variety of talent. It is on the effectiveness of this organization, as most business doctrine now implicitly agrees, that the success of the modern business enterprise now depends. Were this organization dismembered or otherwise lost, there is no certainty that it could be put together again. To enlarge it to undertake new tasks is an expensive and sometimes uncertain undertaking. Here one now finds the problem of an uncertainly high supply price at the margin. And here one finds the accompanying power.

References

BERLE, A. A. (1959), *Power without Property*, Harcourt, Brace & World.

GRAY, A. (1931), *The Development of Economic Doctrine*, Longmans.

HALEY, B. F. (ed.) (1952), 'Comment', *A Survey of Contemporary Economics*, vol. 2, Irwin.

KAYSEN, C. (1959), *The Corporation in Modern Society* (ed. E. S. Mason), Harvard University Press.

MARX, K. (1867), *Capital*, Modern Library.

MASON, E. S. (1958), 'The apologetics of managerialism' *J. Bus. Univ. of Chicago*, vol. 31, no. 1.

RICARDO, D. (1951), *Works and Correspondence of David Ricardo* (ed. Piero Sraffa), vol. 1, Cambridge University Press.

RUNCIMAN, S. (1954), *A History of the Crusades*, vol 1, Cambridge
University Press.

SAMUELSON, P. A. (1964), *Economics*, McGraw-Hill, 6th edn.

SMITH, A. (1776), 'Of the rent of land', *Wealth of Nations*, Bk 1,
Methuen.

US DEPARTMENT OF COMMERCE (1965). 'Do you know your
economic ABCs? Profits in the American Economy'.

11 J. Pen

What about the Managers?

J. Pen, *Harmony and Conflict in Modern Society*, McGraw-Hill, 1966, chapter 21, pp. 247–59.

We are governed by a minority – an unavoidable situation, if only for reasons of efficiency. But sometimes we distrust the High and the Mighty; we begin to regard them as a close-knit club with its own ideology, which imposes its will on the masses. These masses will not benefit by this; perhaps they are too dumb to notice, but occasionally the conflict is sensed by some intelligent individual or the other. His awareness and frustration give birth to the theory of the ruling class. It reappears again and again in the history of ideas, and sometimes rightly: dramatic conspiracies against the interests of the common man have been not infrequent. The recent European past offers unpleasant instances, and the present is by no means free of them. For this reason it can never be correct to reject the sombre theories of the ruling class entirely – one can at most demonstrate that they do not apply in some situations.

The most influential theoretician of the ruling class was G. Mosca *Elementi di Scienze Politica* (1895). This title was translated into English as *The Ruling Class*, though Mosca himself speaks of the political class. It appoints itself, monopolizes power and reaps the reward of the domination of the people. The masses are dominated by force, and also by means of the 'formula': a fine-sounding justification appealing to lofty ideas (what Sorel later calls the 'myth'). At first Mosca saw only one class with beneath it the amorphous masses. In later editions of his book (1922 and 1938) he introduced other strata beneath the small, tough political class: loyal puppets of the régime who propagate the 'formula' and help to manipulate the masses. But they are not among the rulers.

Mosca's set-up forms the classic picture of the theory. Later writers have given us other variants, in which in particular the 'sub-strata' interposed by Mosca offer much food for further speculation. (In fact Mosca has introduced a Trojan horse into the simple construction: if the top rulers do not watch out they can have all kinds of trouble with these substrata. The power of the political class and the consistency of the theory can go to the dogs hand in hand.) In these variants the terminology may change – for instance the word *élite* became fashionable after Pareto – but they still maintain the idea that there is a small, solid clique whose interests are opposed to those of the common man. It may be that this conspiracy is not particularly malevolent, but it remains an iron oligarchy. Democracy does not escape the laws of the élite – not even in Schumpeter, who bluntly states: 'Democracy is the rule of the politician' (1947, p. 285).[1] According to this pessimistic theory, the America of today forms no exception to the iron law: it is subjugated to the power élite. This new term comes from C. Wright Mills, whose book of the same name (1956) contains the most impressive condemnation of the present-day social and political structure. The high and the mighty who form this group are themselves barely aware of their power and their role in society, and they do not consciously conspire together, but according to Mills they have a joint ideology which is structurally founded in the interests of these people. The power élite consists of three interlocking groups: 'the political directorate, the corporate rich and the high military.' Or, to use the popular term which has been put into circulation by Burnham in particular, they are the managers (1940).[2] They exercise power without being effectively supervised by others. They pull the levers, and this usually bodes ill for us.

It is not my intention to discuss the political side of these élite

1. However, Schumpeter uses this statement as a stepping stone to explain why 'politicians so often fail to serve the interest of their class'; this brings him into an entirely different world from that of Mosca and Mills.

2. One could philosophize at length about these terms. Mills rejects the term 'ruling class' because in his opinion 'ruling' has a political content and 'class' an economic one. Burnham has used the expression 'managers' rather elastically; at first he tries to demonstrate that top business executives possess power, and calls them 'managers', but gradually he gives the name of manager to everyone who exercises factual power.

theories. They have been repeatedly attacked, especially from the following points of view: in a democracy the rulers do not appoint themselves; they do not really form a close-knit class; nor can they follow a policy diametrically opposed to the people; the pluralistic society abounds with more or less powerful groups: political parties, unions, the agricultural front, the churches, professional associations of doctors and lawyers together with other bodies as numerous as the grains of sand on the seashore; the powerful group is heterogeneous and has differing interests and ideologies; press, radio and televison are by no means in the hands of the rulers but play an independent role of their own; political authorities are closely watched and blocked by veto groups (David Riesman); they are also subject to laws which they did not make themselves; the élite is above all subject to its own ethics: that of a reasonable, balanced society (Mannheim). I may further refer the reader to the fascinating essay by Meisel on the theories of the élite (élitism), in which they are described as myths (1958).[3]

Now if we want to form an opinion on the debate between élitists and pluralists we cannot confine ourselves to speculation, however deep this may be; we shall have to examine concrete balances of power, and we shall have to try *in politicis* what this essay is endeavouring to do *in economicis*. This is what Mills has done, and in grandiose fashion, although his argument has turned out to be one-sided. But anyone who calls power diffuse may not ignore the fact that one group has more political influence than the other; in specific situations important decisions may be in the hands of the very few. Diffuse power is not in itself a balance of power. Even in a democracy, in particular in the field of international politics, small committees can present us with the most radical *faits accomplis*; decisions on war and peace are taken by a small group. And outside the field of international politics, too, democracy can be frustrated and weakened. As always, 'it can't happen here' is not a sensible attitude to take. But the political side of the élite theory would require a book to itself. The point that interests us here is whether

3. The foreword that Meisel wrote for the paperback edition in 1962 is particularly delightful.

those who run business wield power of frightening proportions. This is alleged by Burnham and Mills – is it true for Western Europe and the United States?

Now there is no doubt that the managers of large corporations are real commanders. Inside their organizations they can direct, promote or demote people. Outside, their decisions affect consumption, prices, employment. They may ruthlessly close down redundant plant. It is also undeniable that industrial managers have considerable latitude in their policy towards other groups. Their independence of the scattered shareholders had already been established in 1932 by Berle and Means, and at the time this created a considerable stir, especially in combination with the concentration of power in the 200 largest corporations. A new ideology has sprung up, which depicts the top executive as a mere employee, with great power but without capital; but as a fact most top people are shareholders as well, and this of course strengthens their position. Mills has pointed out that the power élite and the key shareholders are often the same people or maintain close relations with each other; he does not really believe in the separation of capital and management, and he is doubtless right to the extent that the corporate top executives are rich.

Besides the legal structure other somewhat less familiar trends operate in the same direction of the independent top executive. For modern technology is engaged in further weakening the control of the anonymous shareholder. It has gradually changed the nature of companies' assets: they have become less tangible. Take as an extreme instance the steam engine: a solid piece of equipment, which was born of some teaspoonfuls of concentrated intellect and a large volume of material and labour. This machine has to last a long time. It appears on the balance sheet at a recognizable value, which admittedly is too low as a rule, but the hidden reserve is nevertheless relatively discernible. The same applies to buildings, stocks and traditional machinery. Compare this with the equipment of a hypermodern automated factory. The machines consist of nine parts of intellect and one of material. They wear out quickly, not physically but economically. Tomorrow there will be a new product, a new machine and a new technology. As a result the economic strength of many modern industries lies not so much in the tangible machinery as in the capacity to think up new products, processes and equipment and put them to use. This capacity does not appear on the balance sheet. Nobody knows the exact extent of this hidden reserve; the managers do not, and the shareholders certainly do not. But it is the managers who at least have an impression of it and who have to actualize this technological potential. This increases their power in relation to that of the shareholders.

Similar forces lie in the plane of the organization. The large modern corporation is being increasingly institutionalized; it has become an independent entity with a life of its own. Financing is becoming more and more detached from the willingness of old and new shareholders; 80–90 per cent of gross investments are paid out of retained profits. The holding company is an artful device for strengthening the position of people behind the screens. A beautiful example is the Belgian Société Générale, which controls many Belgian industries; a good deal of its shares is scattered, but a decisive majority is owned by a couple of insurance companies, which happen to be controlled by the Société itself. It is clear that all this gives the managers once again a greater freedom of action.

And then it is often said that their group is relatively self-contained. They appoint one another, without supervision from outsiders. Only fragmentary figures are available on their origin. It is difficult to form an opinion on this, and the data are contradictory. Lipset and Bendix (1959) have investigated where the top American executives come from. They found that 69 per cent are sons of businessmen and another 5 per cent of gentry farmers. The liberal professions supplied 11 per cent, manual workers only 3 per cent and the farmers 4 per cent. These percentages indicate that the social groups from which managers are recruited are limited. Workers' children here play an even smaller role than in higher education. Moreover, who are the 3 per cent who are the sons of workers? It seems probable that these newcomers are selected on their readiness to embrace the ideology of the managers.

However, there are other results of empirical research. Warner and Abegglen (1955) found that 8 per cent of the top American executives are the sons of owners of big businesses; 15 per cent of major executives; 18 per cent of small businessmen; 15 per cent of workers, 3 per cent of foremen and 8 per cent from the white-collar group. This gives the impression of a self-recruiting percentage of at most 25, and entry from the lower status groups is likewise 25 per cent. This is quite another view from that of Lipset and Bendix; the picture is not clear. For Britain, too, similar conclusions have been reached. Clements (1958) found that one in five of company directors and more than a third of the top managers started life as a clerk or a manual worker. This points to open competition.

Furthermore, the picture differs from country to country. In France the top managers in business come from the *Grandes Ecoles* (above all the *Ecole Polytechnique*), they have received a civil service training (*Inspecteur des Finances*), or they are members of the owner's family. Cultural criteria are important in the selection process. The same is, of course, true of Britain, where it is a definite advantage to start one's career at Eton.

Family relationships certainly give one a fine start. According to G. H. Copeman, no less than 60 per cent of British directors of public companies have business connections in the family, but the advantage is greater in moderate-sized companies than in the big ones (1958). A survey from the Netherlands by Vinke shows even more striking results (1961). It relates to the origin of 600 managers and directors of Dutch companies. In over two-thirds of the public companies one or more directors and top managers are related to the founders; in the private companies this figure is even three-quarters! Almost half of the boardroom élite are related to other top businessmen! Inbreeding in the group seems to be greater than that on remote islands. Admittedly, these figures relate to a small country.

Vinke's work brings something else to the fore: the interlocking directorates. This is a familiar phenomenon, but one which has assumed enormous proportions in the Netherlands (it is not discouraged by law there, as it is in the United States). Some managers hold down ten, twenty, thirty, forty or fifty jobs at once in various companies. Almost 15 per cent of the managers have more than five jobs, and almost 25 per cent of the directors. Some large concerns are simultaneously interlaced by various persons. Such a picture encourages the most pessimistic theory of the power élite. (The figures which Mills gives – p. 384 of his book – are more moderate. Of the 556 directorships in the twenty-five largest corporations in the United States, over one hundred were in the hands of forty-eight men in 1950. One had four director-ships and seven had three. But in the United States legal limits are set to interlocking.)

Let us, for the sake of discussion, assume that there is a more or less self-contained and cohesive group of industrial managers though this is by no means sure. It is the most unfavourable hypothesis; it serves to accentuate the question: at what is the power of these people *in economicis* directed? Are the interests of this group in conflict with those of the majority? Or do they more particularly oppress small minorities?

The managers can harm the consumer by high prices – that is inflation. This requires an interplay of monetary factors, but the pressure group of the rich can encourage this as well (unintention-ally) by turning against the Exchequer and urging tax cuts, even if the latter should lead to national overspending. (But does the big businessman play a worse political role in inflation than the large group of small ones? I doubt it!) High taxes are partially shifted on to the consumer, but that would also happen if there were less interlocking and more mobility into managerial ranks. The managers can harm the workers by low wages, but that does not tally with their enlightened self-interest, nor with the wage inflation to be observed everywhere. The managers can mislead the public with advertising, but this is a game of only limited scope. If they want to, they can hold up technical progress, but as a rule this is not to their advantage. A more real, but not very frightening, conflict is that they can harm the shareholders' interests by embellishing their offices in exaggerated fashion, by surrounding themselves with a personal retinue, by increasing their expense accounts and entertaining lavishly. And there exists a new and rather fashionable suspicion: managers are dangerous because they try to humanize their concerns. The criticism sounds all the more sophisticated because it has such a paradoxical ring to it. The old reproach levelled against capital-ism is that it creates conditions unworthy of human beings in dark, barbarous factories – something that in the nineteenth century was, of course, the order of the day, and which has not yet disappeared in smaller firms; the big corporations are showing the way to improvement in this respect. The twentieth-century businessman is now accused of the opposite: whereas old-style capitalism bought human labour and human sweat and for the rest let the worker go to the devil, the modern concern has come to interest itself in his personality, his happiness and his family; the complaint is heard: business wants the worker's soul.

The great inspirer of the human-relations approach was Mayo. In 1927 the effect of lighting on labour productivity was studied in a factory at Hawthorne; the effect proved inconsiderable, but the cooperation of the workers which had been enlisted proved all the more important. The experiment made those workers into a tightly knit group, and that gave an impetus to their productivity. The Hawthorne Experiment was the starting point for a new philosophy: the worker wants to feel secure and at home among his comrades. His happiness lies in his work, not so much in the creation of a result as in working together with others. Money does not bring happiness, but a sense of solidarity does. This community of labour existed in the Middle Ages; the industrial revolution and economic liberalism disturbed it. It has to be rebuilt, for the good of the concern and the individual alike, according to Mayo.

His words did not fall on deaf ears. The unions were against it, but the large corporations saw a great deal in the new doctrine. 'Belongingness' became the motto of a new personnel policy. Individual conflicts between employer and employee, which according to Mayo are based on misunderstandings and a lack of communication, are remedied by cosy relations on the shop floor and, if necessary, by a good cry on the shoulders of the father confessors of the personnel department. So readjustment is accomplished. The concern prefers well-rounded employees, well-adjusted persons with a pleasant home, a loving wife interested in helping her husband along the road to success and two children, who are almost the children of the firm as well.

The consequences of this social ethic have been described by Whyte in *The Organization Man* (1956). In all its documented matter-of-factness it is a compelling book which, without any pretentious scholarship or inflated prophecy, investigates the rapid spread of a human type. Whyte is particularly concerned with the middle ranks of business executives; they are the modest, kindly heroes of modern times. Not the managers themselves, although the latter are linked by fatherly ties to the big family. The group within the corporation dominates the life of the organization men, even outside working hours. Concern with human relations extends to the new districts where they live. Life in suburbia, where the bungalows (there are differences in these houses, just as there is a hierarchy in the corporation) stand in neat rows, is entirely regulated in conformity with group life in production. A difficult or solitary nature, individuality, quarrelsomeness, genius – these are all deplorable phenomena which are eliminated collectively. The group is right, the group brings happiness, the group is life itself. That is the direction in which the managers are driving us.

Whyte is not happy about this collectivization. But he suggests to us no 1984, no exaggerated disasters, no secret terror. These organization men have a pleasant life, and they think so themselves, although they may grumble under their breath at times about the rat race. But all the same they accept the urgent advice: 'love that system'. The managers, who have arranged things like this, are no wily inquisitors but cordial and fatherly figures. They try to make a well-oiled organization of their corporation, in which not only technical but also a kind of social progress is furthered. What they in fact want is a first-rate business measured by 'human standards' and not solely by maximum profit, although they hope that profit will be served by the social ethic. It really resembles harmony more than conflict.

Whyte's objections to this set-up are, of course, much more subtle than Marx's violent criticism of exploitation, Veblen's sarcasm about his sabotaging and robbing captains of industry or the doom of the managerial revolution suggested by Burnham and Mills. Whyte finds that there is too little individualism in American society as it is; the social ethic of the large organizations must not discourage it still further. The search for common values leads to a pressure to uniformity. Minor variations become blatant deviations. The 'quest for normalcy' may lead to neuroses. Conformity, elevated to an ideal, becomes a strange affair as soon as it is not certain precisely to what one has to conform. And then the organization and the group surpass the individual; in the event of a conflict the individual goes to the wall. It is true that Whyte sees a number of ways of improvement; his views are not deterministic. The above trends need not inevitably continue in business, and the individual can ultimately wrest himself from the grasp of the group if only he wants to.

The Procrustean bed of the organization seems to me personally to be not quite as bad as it is painted. Collective enforcement of social values is as old as society; it is certainly less in a large corporation than in a farming village, and perhaps less than in a small university town, where the tea-cosy of bourgeois and religious rightmindedness gradually smothers undesirable patterns of behaviour. Small business was never indifferent to the morals and the behaviour of its employees. The new American suburbs may, after the *kibbutz*, be the most communal places this side of the Iron Curtain, but at the same time a good deal of emancipation prevails, which preserves the residents from obstructed breathing.

In my opinion Whyte's book belongs in the same category as Packard's *The Hidden Persuaders* (1960), although it is written in a more balanced and scientific vein. It moralizes about the signs of the times, but it does not describe a clear conflict. It criticizes a culture and a system of values rather than the power relations in present-day society. Both the advertising and the philosophy of the big corporations set their stamp on society, just as the cinema, and the press, and literature, and the churches and schools do. I can hardly regard it as an indictment of managers, and *The Organization Man* does not disturb me so greatly. An overdose of togetherness is not the worst of my worries. But this is, of course, a matter of personal taste.

However, there is a final and very obvious objection to the power élite. The managers are able to fix their personal incomes. The share that they take of the corporation's total income can be varied within wide limits. The market mechanism does not operate here; the income is not reduced by the entry of newcomers. The rules of the game form the principal limits, but the managers make these rules themselves. True, a constraint is formed by the desire not to upset shareholders and others too greatly. But the ploughing back of profits into the firm leads in the long run to high dividends; the management's share of profits is tied to this percentage, and that keeps them very happy.

Incomes of half a million dollars are not impossible, and then there are generous fringe benefits as regards housing (holiday homes, hunting cabins where business associates are received), transport (a private plane), expense accounts, the stock option and the like. These high incomes reflect the manager's economic power, and the savings that accumulate from the incomes, and the capital gains that accrue to the savings, increase that power. The onesidedness of the personal distribution of income and wealth proves to be deeply rooted in the present organization of society.

There is, of course, an apologetic theory possible that explains these high incomes by the managers' productivity, their experience and their knowledge; these arguments aim at eliminating this conflict too. And in fact that is not entirely nonsense; after all, big business must be led, and the difference between good and bad leadership is worth millions to the firm and to society. But, to put it mildly, it is rather questionable whether these expensive people are all so especially expert and experienced. The figures produced by Copeman, Vinke and others on family connections are somewhat at variance with the theory of excellent personal qualities, unless one were to sustain the daring thesis that managerial ability runs in families. The productivity of a manager is in fact based more on his knowing the right people or belonging to the right circles (if necessary via his uncle or his wife). In the capital goods industry in particular it may be of vital importance for a firm to have flourishing personal contacts with its customers. Interlocking and the Old Boy network do not form a chance circumstance; it is the manager's function to ensure this oligarchical connection. If he does this well, he is more than worth his income (to the firm, but not to society); he can even claim that he is being exploited in the Marxist sense, and he sometimes does. Some managers like to view themselves masochistically as the modern victims of industrial society.

Yet the incomes thus obtained obviously entail a conflict. For they are secured without an adequate social *quid pro quo*. The economic contribution may even be a negative one: harm to productivity through favouritism, through restriction of competition and through organizational slack. In the overall growth of the national income these negative factors are probably limited, although they may count in special sectors. The question that remains is: who foots the bill for the managers' high incomes?

In the first instance it is the shareholders; managerial shares in the profits are charged primarily against dividends. It may be that the shareholders do not form the group whose interests are a subject of concern for the majority of readers of these lines. And I should like further to restrict this concern by pointing out that the shareholders, as a collective body, themselves help to determine the return from their investments via share prices. The low returns which we now see everywhere and which sometimes assume the form of a virtual absence of return are not the result of large shares in profits by management, but of the high level of share prices. Reflection on this tends to evaporate economic conflicts between the managers and any special group. But what is left is the inequality in the distribution of income and wealth and social stratification: the fact that an élite exerts great economic and financial power. These are fundamental defects of our society. As stated, they are not the product of chance, but are the result of the particular organization of production.

To the follower of C. Wright Mills all the above is faint-hearted and hardly relevant. He falls back on what for him is the heart of the matter: the political influence of industrial managers via their grip on the political machine, on the mass media, on all that is for sale in a venal society. As I have said, a real discussion of this problem would require a book to itself.[4] Still, I should like to

4. Like Sampson's *Anatomy of Britain* (1962). But in this extremely informative book the question 'Who Runs Britain?' . . . 'soon seemed to be ground to dust in the machinery of committees. . .' (p. 627). On the one hand the author says: 'the rulers are not at all close-knit or united. They are not so much in the centre of the solar system, as in a cluster of interlocking circles . . . touching only at the edges. . . . The frictions and balances between the different circles are the supreme safeguard of democracy. . .' (p. 624). He also concludes: ' . . . brooding over all these self-contained circles, sitting in every committee, is the ubiquitous figure of Muddle, for whose power and influence I have developed a growing respect' (p. 626). But on the other hand Sampson feels that 'despite the managerial revolution, a great deal still depends on two hundred men. . . . In spite of the age of the common man, and the webs of committees and statistics, much of the history of our time has been forged by a handful of men, as different as Reith, Heyworth, Cousins and Norman Collins' (p. 628). These conclusions contain a good deal of anti-élitism, but they offer by no means a clear-cut picture.

make it clear with a few remarks why I am sceptical about Mills's impressive generalizations. The basic reason lies in the pluralism which has already been briefly discussed above: power is more diffuse and consequently the political arm of the managers does not reach as far as *The Power Elite* suggests. The proof of this pudding is in the eating. If a small élite determines policy, pessimistic theories only have any point if this forms a reactionary factor – otherwise we might just as well save ourselves the worry. But if the power élite follows a conservative policy, where does the gradual expansion of socially oriented government expenditure come from? How did progression ever get into the tax system? How did the extension of social security become possible? In short, how is the Welfare State, incomplete and unwieldy as it still is, reconcilable with the all-prevailing influence of the corporate rich and their political allies? How did the decrease in the income share of the top 7 per cent come about? In fact these things are irreconcilable unless it were to be asserted that the system of social provisions is a new form of opium for the people which serves to conceal the real situation. This is so mystical a point of view that it is incontrovertible.

In fact I believe that, though some managers play a conservative role, would like to reduce the progression in taxation, perpetuate the loopholes in the tax system, resist the taxation of capital gains, find social security nonsense, consider medical provisions for all undesirable, and hamper a Keynesian policy in public finance, this factor is not as predominant as Mills suggests. In the socio-economic force field the conservative part of the power élite forms a group which is pulled and pushed in a direction which it does not choose to take itself rather than a group at the switchboard. In spite of its enormous financial power it retards development but it does not govern it.

Now such a picture of the politics of the rearguard has been painted by Mills himself, but with reference to the middle classes (1951). In his view it is the white-collar groups that follow uncertainly, without clear aim or political cohesion. The melancholy descriptions which Mills gives of the political role of the middle classes in my opinion apply with slight changes to the reactionary section of the rich managers. It should also be borne in mind that another section of the executives are not at all conservative; they can afford to live and let live. And it is not a wild guess that most business managers are far too busy with their own job to devote time and energy to politics, and that they share the popular opinion that political decisions are taken somewhere else.

This criticism of Mills's view does not mean that we need not be alive to the political influence of groups of industrial managers. This influence does exist; the problem remains: how far is it permissible? A factor that must definitely be taken into account is that it is greater under conservative than under progressive governments. And there is always the danger that industrial magnates, after having first withdrawn from supervision by society, alienate themselves ideologically from that society, are frustrated in their pursuit of political power and adopt fascist methods. They may support Moral Rearmament, advocate a reckless policy in the cold war, favour segregation, back a new Hitler. But such political blood-poisoning is not inevitable; the prospect is not structurally anchored in economic conditions.[5] I do not even believe that the reactionary danger comes from big business; some small businessmen have more reasons for fear, worry and frustration. This holds true for such different countries as the United States, France and the Netherlands. However, it is true that an eye must be kept on the managers. For perhaps it is a wise policy to mistrust people with economic power, even if they do not give much cause.

5. As it would bring me into the strictly political field of the cold war, I am avoiding a ticklish problem here, viz. what is the influence of the economic pressure group on international politics? Is it true that the industrialists advocate a tough line because it is in their interests? Little is known about this, but there is food for thought in the fact that in his farewell speech President Eisenhower devoted quite alarming words to the 'undue influence' of the military/industrial complex.

References

BURNHAM, J. (1940), *The Managerial Revolution*, Indiana University Press.
CLEMENTS, R. V. (1958), *Managers: A Study of Their Careers in Industry*, Allen & Unwin.
COPEMAN, G. H. (1958), *Leaders of British Industry*, Gee.
LIPSET, S. M. and BENDIX, R. (1959), *Social Mobility in Industrial Society*, Cambridge University Press.
MEISEL, M. H. (1958), *The Myth of the Ruling Class*, Cresset.

MILLS, C. W. (1951), *White Collar: The American Middle Classes*,
Oxford University Press.

MILLS, C. W. (1956), *The Power Elite*, Oxford University Press.

MOSCA, G. (1895), *Elementi di Scienze Politica*; translated as *The
Ruling Class*, McGraw-Hill, 1960.

PACKARD, V. (1960), *The Hidden Persuaders*, Penguin Books.

SAMPSON, A. (1962), *Anatomy of Britain*, Hodder & Stoughton.

SCHUMPETER, J. (1947), *Socialism, Capitalism and Democracy*, rev. 2nd
edn, Allen & Unwin.

VINKE, P. (1961), De maatschappelijke plaats en herkomst der
directeuren en commissarissen van de open en daarmee vergelijkbare
besloten naamloze vennootschappen, Leiden.

WARNER, W. L. and ABEGGLEN, J. C. (1955), *Big Business Leaders in
America*, Atheneum.

WHYTE, W. H. (1956), *The Organization Man*, Simon & Schuster;
Penguin Books, 1960.

12 C. S. Wilson and T. Lupton

The Social Background and Connections of
Top Decision Makers

Abridged from C. S. Wilson and T. Lupton, 'The social background
and connections of "top decision makers"', *Manchester School of
Economic and Social Studies*, vol. 27, 1959, no. 1, pp. 30–51.

Our interests as sociologists have led us to make use of the Parker
Tribunal evidence as a convenient starting point for the analysis
of some social connections between persons prominent in banking,
insurance, politics and public administration. Our choice of
persons and categories was influenced by our starting point, and
our inquiries were limited by considerations of time and space,
and by gaps in the published sources of data. For these reasons our
results are not statistically significant. But they will be of interest
to sociologists, as representing the beginnings of an analysis of
the social origins and interconnections of what we shall call the
'top decision makers'[1] in British society. We think that economists and political scientists will also be interested. To our
knowledge, no such analysis has previously been made. [. . .]

In attempting to interpret the behaviour they observe, sociologists look first at personal 'networks' or relationships, and at the
kind of training people receive to occupy positions within them.
It seemed to us likely that there would be a 'structural' explanation
for some of the behaviour described by witnesses at the Tribunal.
This article is an attempt to map out some parts of the social
structure of 'top decision makers'. Bagehot wrote:

. . . all 'city' people make their money by investments, for which there are
often good argumentative reasons, but they would hardly ever be able, if
required before a Parliamentary committee, to state these reasons
(1892).

1. The term 'top decision makers' is used as a makeshift. We are aware
that not all the persons we consider are of equal prestige and authority.
There are difficult problems of definition raised by this kind of investigation
but we think it wise to postpone consideration of these. We shall presently
state whom we have included in the category of 'top decision makers' for
the purpose of this paper.

The statements from several witnesses at the Parker Tribunal justified this forecast. At one point, after varying attempts to explain how Lazard's came to a decision to sell gilt-edged securities, Lord Kindersley interrupted counsel to say:

I have had a feeling – I have been here listening to the evidence in the last day or two – that there is some lack of understanding as to the way my firm works (Parker Tribunal, 1957, p. 187).

The evidence of Lord Kindersley and others revealed that some important decisions were taken and others accepted because colleagues knew about, and relied upon, each other's beliefs and special aptitudes. Lengthy analyses were not a necessary prelude to decision making. This is not surprising. When decisions have to be made quickly most persons have to act according to precedent and 'hunch' and not in the light of detailed analysis of the current situation.[. . .]

In addition to the influence of custom and precedent in decision making, informality in relationships between decision makers came out clearly in the evidence. A good example of this came out during the examination of Lord Kindersley by the Attorney General. The Attorney General was asking Lord Kindersley why he, and not Mr Cobbold, had gone to see Lord Bicester about the possible effect of the Bank Rate rise on the Vickers issue and on relations between the 'City' and the Bank of England. Lord Kindersley replied:

I consider it perfectly natural that I should be allowed to go and talk to a colleague on the Bank of England. . . . I do not think that Lord Bicester would find it in the least surprising that I should come to him and say to him: 'Look here, Rufie, is it too late to stop this business or not?'

and:

I have discussed this with Jim – with the Governor and I am coming on to see you (Parker Tribunal, 1957, p. 191).

The same kind of informality was seen in the activities of directors of some City merchant houses as described before the Tribunal.[2]

The basis of informality in social relationships is often a shared

2. See, for example, the evidence of the Keswick brothers (Parker Tribunal, 1957, pp. 94, 100, 103, 108).

social background, which promotes shared beliefs and confidence in customary procedures. It was this evidence of informality and custom which led us to look for common social background, and links between persons other than those arising from the formal needs of business life. There were pointers in the evidence itself and elsewhere that we might find connections of kinship and of affinity.[3] Ties of friendship and common interest were revealed by the description of a shooting party at which members of the Keswick family were joined by Mr Nigel Birch and others; and by the meetings of Messrs J. M. Stevens and D. McLachlan.[4]

Since it was clear that many of the 'top decision makers' whom the evidence mentions were interlinked in sets of relationships other than those directly arising out of business arrangements, we wondered whether the same kind of affiliations would be found in a wider sample of such persons, i.e. whether such affiliations tended to be typical of the social milieu of this particular set of 'top decision makers'. Our choice of a wider sample was influenced by our starting point, and the reader will find that it is biased. But we have included enough persons to make our findings of some sociological, if not statistical, significance.

The following are the six categories of 'top decision makers' we have chosen to study:

A. Cabinet Ministers and other Ministers of the Crown.
B. Senior Civil Servants.
C. Directors of the Bank of England.
D. Directors of the 'Big Five' banks.
E. Directors of 'City' firms.
F. Directors of insurance companies.

Category A includes all the persons named.[5] Category B includes the twelve senior members of the Treasury staff and the permanent secretaries and their immediate deputies of twenty-one other ministries. Category C includes all directors of the Bank of

3. Intermarriage amongst banking families has often been referred to. See for example: Presswell (1956); Truptil (1936); Clay (1957); Adlard (1947).
4. See the evidence of Mr J. M. Stevens (Parker Tribunal, 1957, p. 222) and Mr D. McLachlan (pp. 16, 17).
5. *Her Majesty's Ministers and Heads of Public Departments* (1958).

England (as listed by Mr Cobbold before the Tribunal). Category D comprises all directors of the 'Big Five'. Category E includes the directors of fourteen merchant banks or discount houses, several of which were mentioned before the Tribunal. Some of these are private banks, others public companies, but all have an authorized capital of two million pounds or more. We have taken the directors of only eight insurance companies, all with an authorized capital of over three million pounds, to make up category F. The selection of these eight out of all insurance companies with authorized capital of over three million pounds was not entirely random (Stock Exchange Yearbook, 1958). We made sure that the two large companies mentioned in the evidence were included. The analysis of the education, club membership, and connections of kinship and affinity, is based entirely on published data.[6]

Table 1 summarizes the data on schools attended by members of the six categories. We have lumped together under the heading of 'other public and grammar schools' a large number of schools of diverse size and character. No single one of them had educated enough of the persons in our categories to justify being named separately. The Table shows that between one-quarter and one-third of the persons in each category except category B went to Eton College. Two-thirds of the Bank of England directors and a half of the ministers went to the six named public schools, and in all categories except B nearly half were educated at these schools. Only three persons from all categories attended state elementary school only. The data on school education shows that the majority of persons in all categories shared the same kind of school education, with the exception of category B.[7] We have not attempted to make anything of the totals in the right-hand column since they are distorted by the fact that many persons are members of more than one category and this applies especially to categories C, D, E and F. We have 529 names, but not 529 persons.

This last remark applies also to Table 2 which summarizes the

6. *Who's Who*, 1958; *Burke's Landed Gentry*, 1952; *Burke's Peerage, Baronetage and Knightage*, 1956; *Debrett's Peerage, Baronetage, Knightage and Companionage*, 1957.

7. It is interesting that category B is the only one of the six to which entrance is by competitive examination.

Table 1 Schools

			Category				
	A	B	C	D	E	F	Total
Eton	11	3	6	44	35	46	145
as percentage	32·4	4·1	33·3	29·7	32·7	30·9	
Winchester	3	3	2	9	4	7	28
Harrow	1	1	0	8	4	7	21
Rugby	0	5	2	3	2	4	16
Charterhouse	0	1	0	4	0	6	11
Marlborough	2	1	2	3	1	0	9
Total	17	14	12	71	46	70	230
Total as percentage	50	19·2	66·6	48	43	47	
Other public and grammar schools	15	54	4	53	13	26	165
State elementary school only	1	0	1	1	0	0	3
No data	1	5	1	23	48	53	131
Total	34	73	18	148	107	149	529

information on College and University education. A feature of Table 2 is the predominance of Oxford and Cambridge. Over 70 per cent of all ministers went either to Oxford or Cambridge, and nearly 70 per cent of all senior civil servants, 50 per cent of Bank of England directors, 50 per cent of directors of the 'Big Five'. The financial categories C, D, E and F show the greatest proportion of persons with no university education.[8] It will be noted that in Table 2, as in Table 1, large numbers of category D, E and F members are to be found under 'no data'. If our information were complete the picture might possibly be significantly different. Like Table 1, Table 2 shows that, for those persons in our six categories for which we have data, the majority shared the same kind of post-school education, although there are some

8. Reflecting perhaps a tendency for persons to enter banking and finance as young men, and to forgo a university education.

differences in this regard between the first three and the last three categories. Similarity of educational background forms a link between many members of our six categories both within categories and across their boundaries. And there are also many shared directorships in the last four categories.

Table 2 College and university

| | Category | | | | | | |
	A	B	C	D	E	F	Total
Oxford	18	30	2	46	24	30	150
Cambridge	7	20	7	28	13	27	102
Total	25	50	9	74	37	57	252
Total as percentage	71·5	68·5	50	50	34·6	38·3	
London	2	5	0	1	1	2	11
Other universities	1	10	2	10	2	8	33
Sandhurst	1	0	1	5	3	6	16
Dartmouth	1	0	0	1	1	5	8
Woolwich	0	0	0	1	1	1	3
None	4	9	7	36	13	21	90
No data	1	3	1	23	51	55	134
Total	35	77	20	151	109	155	547
Number in category	34	73	18	148	107	149	529

The only systematic information we have been able to collect about the leisure time activities of members of this sample concerned club affiliations. This is summarized in Table 3. Table 3 is less complete than Tables 1 and 2 because club membership was not always listed in the references we used. But many persons are members of more than one club. The totals at the bottom of the Table represent a count of all the clubs listed in published sources. Below this is given the number of persons for whom information was available, and the number of persons in the category. The clubs named in the list are those most frequently mentioned. Others have been counted under headings such as 'sports clubs (various)' which includes polo, fishing and golf clubs. Yacht clubs, have been named separately, and also the MCC. The various university clubs have been collected under one heading, and so have the various services clubs, with the exception of the Guards and Cavalry clubs; these are separately named. A striking feature of the Table is that the civil servants'

Table 3 Club membership

	A	B	C	D	E	F
Athenaeum	4	8	2	14	4	8
Bath	0	2	1	11	4	6
Beefsteak	2	0	1	3	5	8
Boodle's	0	2	1	4	2	8
Brooks's	4	4	2	24	11	20
Buck's	2	0	0	3	3	8
Carlton	18	0	1	23	8	16
Cavalry	0	0	1	5	4	4
City of London	0	0	1	13	8	5
Guards	0	0	1	5	1	3
MCC	2	1	1	8	5	20
New (Edinburgh)	2	1	0	4	3	3
Oriental	0	0	1	6	3	2
Pratt's	5	1	0	7	4	5
Reform	1	15	0	6	0	2
Services (various)	2	1	0	5	3	5
Sports (various)	1	4	0	11	1	18
St James's	0	3	1	5	0	4
Traveller's	0	3	0	7	2	8
Turf	5	1	2	6	7	11
University (various)	0	15	2	6	0	3
White's	6	0	2	13	13	23
Yacht clubs	3	2	1	20	5	8
Other clubs	11	22	3	67	5	28
Total clubs	68	85	24	276	101	226
Number for whom data was collected	31	63	14	119	53	90
Number in category	34	73	18	148	107	149

club membership is confined largely to the Reform Club and to University clubs. There are few members of the other categories in these clubs. Amongst the other categories the clubs most frequently represented are the Carlton, Brooks's, White's and the Athenaeum. The information we have shows that none of the senior civil servants in category B belong to the Carlton club or White's.[9] Again, in Table 3, a good number of the members of our six categories are shown to be linked by the sharing of a common activity, in this case club membership.

The evidence we shall assemble in this section is of a different order to that we have so far studied, and we shall say something to introduce it. It might occur to some readers that the most important feature of the diagrams we present below is the recurrence of certain long established family names, and they might wish to read significance into this in the light of other knowledge and interests, or of preconceived ideas. Others might argue that the diagrams mean nothing because they do not include certain prominent families, or because they are incomplete and biased; and so on. That is why we want to make it clear at the outset that, for this analysis, the diagrams are only intended to show the connections of kinship and affinity of some persons who are members of our six categories of decision makers. We used the following procedure: we began by taking persons who were prominent in the Tribunal proceedings, for example Lord Kindersley and Mr Cameron Cobbold. We traced the names of parents, siblings, spouses and children, and constructed a small 'family tree'. By following up the names of paternal and maternal kin it often proved possible to join the 'family trees', together into a kinship diagram.[10]

9. We do not know how to assess the relative prestige or exclusiveness of the various clubs, but it is probable that the traditional impartiality of the Civil Service precludes its members from joining the Carlton, a club so clearly associated with one political party. Petrie says: '. . the great names in the Tory hierarchy down the centuries have always been found, and are still to be found, in the list of members of the Carlton.' (1955, p. 15).

10. Properly speaking, a diagram of both kinship and affinity. Triangles represent males and circles females. Unshaded signs represent living people. The equals sign signifies a marriage connection and the asterisk, a former marriage connection.

We have not been able to trace the kinship connections of all persons in the six categories; and it is only possible to present a limited amount of the material so far gathered. To include all connections of kinship and affinity for even a few dozen people would clearly require a great deal of space and demand greater resources of time and personnel than those available. There may be no kin connections between a great many of the people we have selected; and there are persons represented on the diagrams who belong to none of the six categories. This has partly arisen because we had already the kin and affinal connections of some people referred to at the Tribunal before we extended the scope of inquiry.

For ease of exposition the material is presented in a series of small abridged diagrams. The names of some persons who link one diagram with another are enclosed in heavy black rectangles with numbers of linked diagrams in small circles attached. Persons who are members of one or more of the six categories have the appropriate group letter or letters below their names.[11] The names of some persons who are directors of other concerns, industrial or financial and commercial, are indicated, where appropriate, with the letters 'G' and 'H' (Directory of Directors, 1958).

We now trace some of the connections illustrated, indicating links between diagrams, links which would make one chart in reality. It would take too long to trace every connection on all the diagrams; the reader is invited to complete this task for himself.

Figure 1 shows some of the connections of Mr C. F. Cobbold, Governor of the Bank of England and a member of a family of landed gentry. He is related on his father's side to the late Lt.-Col. John Cobbold, who married a daughter of the 9th Duke of Devonshire. Lt.-Col. Cobbold's sister married Sir Charles Hambro, a Director of the Bank of England. Lt.-Col. H. E. Hambro, married the widow of the 5th Earl of Cadogan, whose grandson married a daughter of Lt.-Col. Cobbold (see Figure 9).

Figure 2 traces links established by the marriage of Sir Everard Hambro with a relative of Lord Norman, who was formerly Governor of the Bank of England. A cousin of Lord Norman married an uncle of the present Home Secretary, the Rt Hon.

11. For reasons of space we have had to shorten some names and titles; we trust no one will take offence at this.

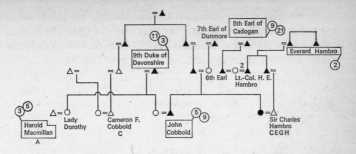

Figure 1

R. A. Butler. A daughter of this marriage married Sir George Abell, a Director of the Bank of England, whose brother-in-law, Mr Nicholas Norman Butler, married into the Hambro family.

Figure 3 illustrates the marriages of other daughters of the 9th Duke of Devonshire, among them that of Lady Dorothy, wife

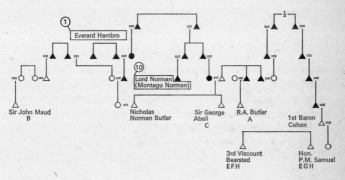

Figure 2

of the Prime Minister and sister-in-law to Lt.-Col. John Cobbold. One of her cousins (father's brother's daughter) married the 28th Earl of Crawford, whose son, Lord Balniel, is Parliamentary Private Secretary to the Minister of Housing and Local Government (late PPS to the Financial Secretary to the Treasury). The Earl is brother-in-law to the Attorney-General (see Figure 15), and also to the Marquess of Salisbury. This name takes us to

Figure 4 which shows marriages of sons of Lord Eustace Cecil. One son married a daughter of the 10th Duke of Leeds, father-in-law of Lord Chandos, Chairman of AEI (see Figure 12). Another son was Baron Rockley; his son, the present Baron, and Mr M. J. Babington Smith (a Director of the Bank of England and of AEI) married daughters of Admiral Hon. Sir Hubert Meade Fetherstonhaugh, who is connected by marriage to the Glyn banking family (see Figure 21).

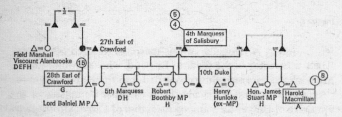

Figure 3

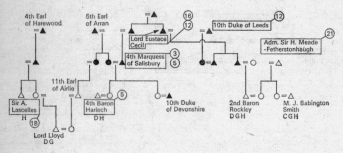

Figure 4

The 4th Marquess of Salisbury connects Figures 4 and 5. His daughter, sister of the present Marquess, married Baron Harlech, the father of the Minister of State for Foreign Affairs, and father-in-law of the Prime Minister's son. Figure 5 also connects with Figure 1, through the late Lt.-Col. John Cobbold; he was related on his mother's side to the 7th Earl of Dunmore, whose grand-daughter married Mr D. A. Stirling, a 'Big Five' director. Her brother, the late Viscount Fincastle, brings us to Figure 7. He married a daughter of the 2nd Baron Wyfold; another daughter is married to a son of Sir George Schuster, the brother-in-law of the Chairman of the Tribunal, Lord Chief Justice Parker.

Figure 6 traces some of the connections of the Prime Minister's nephew by marriage, the 11th Duke of Devonshire, a brother-in-law of the writer Nancy Mitford; she married a son of Lord

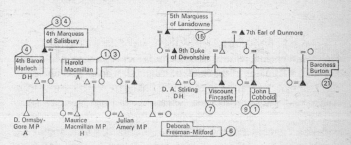

Figure 5

Rennell. Lord Rennell's wife is a sister of Lord Bicester, a senior director of Morgan Grenfell and Co. and a Director of the Bank of England. Lord Bicester, a witness at the Tribunal, was the 'Rufie' mentioned in the evidence. Lord Rennell links Figures 6 and 22, for one of Nancy Mitford's sisters was married to Lord Moyne, grandson of the 1st Earl of Iveagh. Figure 16 shows that Lord Rennell is also connected to the Keswick family by the marriage of his sister to a brother-in-law of J. H. Keswick. Mr W. J. Keswick, Director of the Bank of England, is related through his wife to Lord Lovat, brother-in-law of two Conservative Members of Parliament.

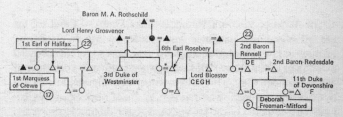

Figure 6

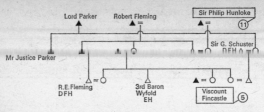

Figure 7

Figures 8 and 10 are joined by the name of the wife of Mr M. R. Hely-Hutchinson, whose brother is father-in-law to Mr J. M. Stevens, a Director of the Bank of England, who gave evidence at the Tribunal. Her father's family was linked by marriage to Baron Ashcombe, whose brother married a niece of Lord Norman. (Her later marriage is shown on Figure 19.) Baron Norman's brother's wife was a daughter of the 4th Earl of Bradford, whose grandson, the 6th Earl, is a Crown Estate Commissioner. Another daughter of the Earl of Bradford married the 7th Duke of Buccleuch, brother-in-law to the 3rd Viscount Hampden. Viscount Hampden's son (now the 4th Viscount), managing director of Lazard's, was also a witness at the Tribunal.

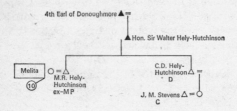

Figure 8

The name of Viscount Hampden links Figures 14 and 15, for the 1st Viscount's daughter was mother to Mr J. H. Bevan, brother-in-law of Earl Alexander of Tunis. Earl Alexander married a daughter of the 5th Earl of Lucan, whose wife was a daughter of Mr J. Spender Clay. This brings us back to Figures 11 and 12, by-passed in the previous paragraph. A son of Mr J. Spender Clay married a daughter of the 1st Viscount Astor. Figure 11 shows the Astor–Devonshire link; Figure 12 shows that the granddaughter

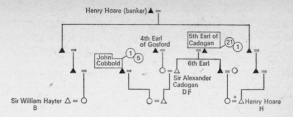

Figure 9

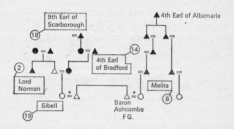

Figure 10

of Mr J. Spender Clay, married the Hon. David Bowes-Lyon, and traces some other marriage connections of members of his family. A daughter of the Hon. Malcolm Bowes-Lyon married a son of the 13th Duke of Hamilton; another son is First Lord of the Admiralty. The 14th Duke is Lord Steward of the Queen's Household.

Mr H. C. B. Mynors, Deputy Governor of the Bank of England and witness at the Tribunal, is descended on his mother's side

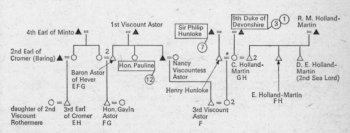

Figure 11

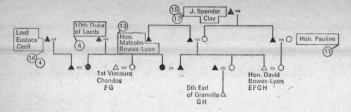

Figure 12

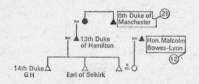

Figure 13

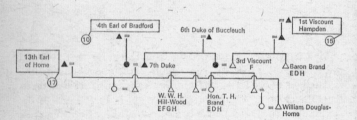

Figure 14

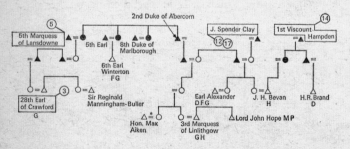

Figure 15

from a sister of Mr J. Spender Clay (see Figure 17). His brother, and the Earl of Home, Minister of State for Commonwealth Relations, married sisters, members of the Lyttleton family. The Earl's brother, William Douglas-Home, son-in-law of the 4th Viscount Hampden, links this Figure with Figure 14. Further

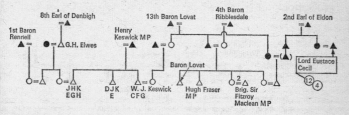

Figure 16

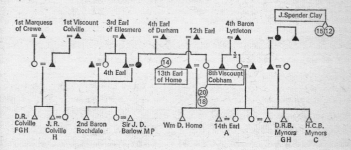

Figure 17

Lyttleton connections are shown on Figure 18. The son of Lord Chandos (Oliver Lyttleton) married a daughter of Sir Alan Lascelles (Figure 4), brother-in-law of the 1st Baron Lloyd. The first wife of Lord Chandos' father was a member of the Tennant family, also referred to in the last Figure. This repeats the name of the late Mr R. H. Benson. One of his sons married a daughter of the 2nd Earl of Dudley (Figure 21). The Earl's sister married the 4th Baron Wolverton and a daughter of this marriage became the wife of Mr Nigel Birch, MP. He was Economic Secretary to the Treasury at the time of the decision to raise the Bank Rate and also a member of the Keswick shooting party mentioned in the evidence, a party which also included a member of the Hambro Bank family. Figure 21 also shows two other members of the Government, the Secretary of State for Air, brother of the 3rd Earl of Dudley, and the Earl of Gosford, Parliamentary Under-Secretary of State to the Foreign Office. Their two families are linked by a marriage in the previous generation.

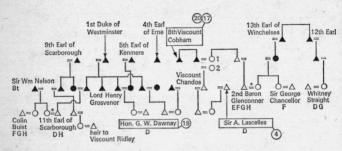

Figure 18

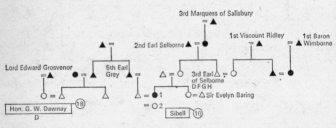

Figure 19

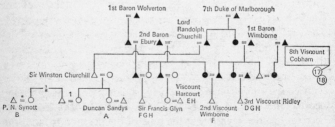

Figure 20

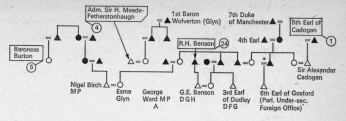

Figure 21

The next Figure (22) introduces Lord Kindersley, Director of the Bank of England and a prominent Tribunal witness. His brother married a niece of the 2nd Earl of Iveagh, father-in-law of the Rt Hon. Alan Lennox-Boyd, MP, Minister of State for Colonial Affairs. The Earl of Iveagh is father-in-law to a sister of another Conservative Minister, the Rt Hon. John Hare, MP, whose wife is sister to Viscount Cowdray, who was mentioned in evidence at the Tribunal in connection with the Pearson Group of

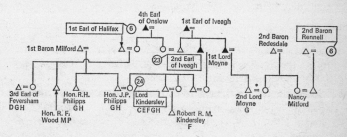

Figure 22

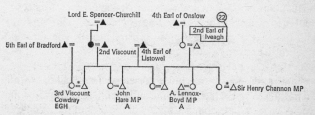

Figure 23

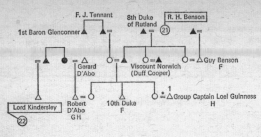

Figure 24

Companies. These connections are shown on Figure 23. The final Figure refers to some further connections of Lord Kindersley.

Seventy-three of the persons in the six categories appear in the kinship diagrams. We know that there could have been more had not the diagrams been abridged. Eight ministers are included in the diagrams; and three senior civil servants. For the other four categories there are more names than persons, since there are multiple directorships. Nine of the category C names appear, twenty-five of the category D names, twenty of the category E names, and thirty-two of the category F names. The only category to be markedly under-represented in the diagrams is category B (top civil servants) with only three included of a total of seventy-three in the category. This may arise partly from the method used in compiling the diagrams.

Some estimate of the extent of multiple directorships may be gained if the number of names on the diagrams in categories C, D, E and F is compared with the number of persons: eighty-six as compared with sixty-two. Finally, in comment on the diagrams, only about 18 per cent of all the names in the categories appear in the diagrams. On the hypothesis that all persons in the categories are linked by kinship or affinity (one to which we do not subscribe) it would take a great deal more research to include them in a series of diagrams.

So far in this article we have presented facts baldly without attempting to assess their meaning and significance. It would have been unwise to have done so in view of the bias of the sample and the incompleteness of the data. Our study must be regarded, then, mainly as a contribution to the 'ethnography' of finance, politics and administration. But we cannot conclude without attempting briefly to relate what we have said to one aspect of social structure which is of particular interest to us.

We have referred to the tradition of intermarriage between banking families. Also by tradition, some merchant bankers become directors of the Bank of England. It is not surprising then that the kinship diagrams show connections between directors of merchant banks, and between merchant banks and directors of the Bank of England. Nor is it surprising that we find that positions in certain firms are occupied by adjacent generations of the same family. The positions of chairman of Lazard Bros. and director of the Bank of England, for example, are now occupied by Lord Kindersley and were once occupied by his father.

What might seem surprising is that kinship connections of this kind have persisted through many changes in the scale and functions of banking, in the organization of industry, and in the complexity of politics. Weber has argued that bureaucratic, 'civil-service-type' structure, in which recruitment and promotion are based on specific technical qualifications, and in which authority vests in the office and not in the person, is the most appropriate to modern conditions, while traditional structures are unsuitable from the point of view of effectiveness. But Weber also argues that, for effectiveness' sake, decision making and execution ought to be separate. And he notes that: '. . . administrative structures based on different principles intersect with bureaucratic organization' (Gerth and Mills, 1947).

Some of the organizations to which we have referred seem to have the separation of decision making and executive functions to which Weber refers. Possibly they incorporate both traditionalistic and bureaucratic structure. They have both directors and the managers, generally different sets of persons, possibly of different social background and training. While there have been studies of the influence of kinship as a mode of succession amongst managers (Clements, 1958, Stewart, 1958), we are not aware of any study which has extended to boards of directors.

Weber's point about the intersection of different structural principles has not been followed up by empirical research in the area covered in this article. Gouldner's examination of some hypotheses derived from Weber in the light of facts about factory social structure could be taken as a model for such work (1955).

The intersection of different social principles has another, individual aspect, that of role conflict. Our evidence shows that many people occupy several social roles. For example, a person may have one role in a kinship system, be a member of one or more boards of directors, and a member of various clubs and associations. [. . .]

This raises a general problem of comparative social structure. The field we have ourselves surveyed provides extensive data relevant to this problem. These data suggest that 'top decision makers' as well as being linked by kinship, business interests and similar background, are also divided by competing, even conflicting interests. Indeed, kinship itself, in certain circumstances, may act as a divisive as well as a uniting force.

To carry out the research into the problems we have briefly outlined would require investigation of a wider field than we have surveyed, and the use of techniques other than those we have used. Interviews, direct observation of behaviour, complete quantitative analysis of such items as leisure time activities, as well as the construction of complete kinship diagrams would be necessary. This latter technique would close many gaps in knowledge of British social structure. Sociologists, including ourselves, have tended to concentrate on the study of working class groups or small local communities where there is much knowledge of the operation of kinship in social life. For our 'top decision makers' we have only biographical material, inspired comment, and little more. It is possible that sociologists have avoided the problem of kinship in 'higher circles' because of the formidable problems presented for empirical field research. We can see that there may be many problems of this kind but there is no reason why the published sources of data should not be fully used.

References

ADLARD, E. (ed.) (1947), *Robert Holland Martin*, Muller.
BAGEHOT, W. (1892), *Lombard Street*, Routledge & Kegan Paul.
Burke's Landed Gentry (1952), Burke's Peerage Ltd.
Burke's Peerage, Baronetage and Knightage (1956), Burke's Peerage Ltd.
CLAY, H. (1957), *Lord Norman*, Macmillan.

CLEMENTS, R. (1958), *Managers: A Study of Their Careers in Industry*, Allen & Unwin.

Debrett's Peerage, Baronetage, Knightage and Companionage (1957), Odhams.

Directory of Directors (1958), Skinner.

GERTH, H. M. and MILLS, C. W. (1947), *From Max Weber*, Routledge & Kegan Paul.

GOULDNER, A. W. (1955), *Patterns of Industrial Bureaucracy*, Routledge & Kegan Paul.

Her Majesty's Ministers and Heads of Public Departments (1958), HMSO.

PARKER TRIBUNAL (1957), *Proceedings of the Tribunal Appointed to Inquire into allegations that Information about the Raising of the Bank Rate was Improperly Disclosed*, HMSO.

PETRIE, C. (1955), *The Carlton Club*, Eyre & Spottiswoode.

PRESSWELL, L. W. (1956), *Country Banking in the Industrial Revolution*, Oxford University Press.

STEWART, R. (1958), *Management Succession*, Acton Society Trust.

Stock Exchange Yearbook (1958), vol. 1, Skinner.

TRUPTIL, R. J. (1936), *British Banks and the London Money Market*, Cape.

Who's Who (1958), Black.

Part Five **Countervailing Power?**

The competition model could neglect power because under a regime of perfect competition nobody seems to be able to yield power. There may, however, be another constellation, in which power, though its existence is recognized, is reduced in importance, because only minor effects are expected from it. If power positions reliably and regularly call forth counter-vailing action by groups of comparable influence, then the *effects* of power could be largely neutralized and its neglect would not matter so very much.

That such a general tendency towards countervailing power exists is the thesis of a well-known work by Galbraith (1957). The details of this theory need not detain us here.[1] What we have to ask is whether this idea makes the concern about power and its effects superfluous or not. The critical articles in this section throw doubt on the pervasiveness of countervailing power. Ulmer deals with general shortcomings in the theory of countervailing power, while Hunter finds little evidence for its operation in the British economy.

1. The essential ideas are contained in Hunter (1969) and Reading 7.

References

GALBRAITH, J. K. (1957), *American Capitalism*, Hamish Hamilton, rev. edn; 1st edn 1952; Penguin Books, 1962.
HUNTER, A. (ed.) (1969), *Monopoly and Competition*, Penguin Books.

13 M. J. Ulmer

Economic Power and Vested Interests

M. J. Ulmer , 'Some reflections on economic power and economic theory', *De Economist*, vol. 107, 1959, pp. 337–46.

Perhaps no subject in the entire range of the social sciences is more important, and at the same time so seriously neglected, as the role of power in economic life. No less than three significant aspects of the problem may be distinguished, only one of which has been given extended attention heretofore – at least in the austere pages of orthodox economists. The first is the direct influence of monopoly power on the volume of an industry's production and on the level of its prices. This, of course, is the traditional branch of the subject and has been studied at length, though not always, we must hasten to add, with unqualified success. The second aspect is the impact on economic behavior of power considered as a direct objective of economic activity. This topic has received mention but almost no analysis in the main stream of economic thinking. One difficulty has been that this approach threatens to interfere with one of our more precious assumptions: that is, the image of the economic man whose life and work begins and ends with the maximization of profits. The third aspect of our problem concerns the role of power as it is wielded in economic affairs by social groups, sometimes called vested interests. This topic has been given about the same joyous reception by orthodox economists as the United States Department of State would give to an ambassador from Communist China.

The fact is that neither of the last two aspects of the role of power has been given adequate attention in the main body of economic literature, and this neglect, I think, has been costly both from a scientific as well as from a social point of view.[1] I

1. Of course, I do not imply that the role of power has been given *no* attention in economic thought. A few of the outstanding treatments of the subject are mentioned or dealt with below. Nevertheless, with the partial

shall try to indicate the knowledge which may be won, and perhaps some of the social gains which may be achieved, by a more complete and systematic recognition of this branch of our subject.

Let us turn first to power as a goal of economic activity. It has long been conceded, even by orthodox economists, that economic activity is motivated by a variety of drives. In particular, it has been recognized that businessmen, and perhaps some others, seek not only maximum profits but power too. Perhaps the latter tendency, that is, the drive for power, has been intensified by the growth of the progressive income tax. For today, in most developed countries, there are practical limits to how wealthy a man may get; but there are no such practical limits to how much power he may acquire. In any event, orthodox economists have duly recognized these facts but have denied their importance, for they have always assumed that the surest way to achieve power in a capitalist society is to acquire wealth. More generally, when an individual maximizes the returns on the wealth at his command, he at the same time increases his power. And in the case of monopolies and oligopolies, the degree of power they exercise simply contributes to their profits. In all important cases, it would seem, at least outside of government, the goal of acquiring power goes hand in hand with the goal of maximizing profits. They are consistent with, and complementary to, one another. Hence, we may concentrate in our studies on the maximization of profits, and can legitimately ignore the role of power as such. So goes the argument that, I think, is at present generally accepted. It is an argument which I must seriously question.

Indeed, I suspect that we shall learn to doubt this argument the more closely and critically we examine it. Let me cite just one example of what I believe to be a real and, perhaps, profound difficulty. In the modern corporation, we know, there is a divorce between ownership and control. By and large, stockholders do

---

exception (to which we shall return) noted in the preceding paragraph, the notion of economic power has yet to be incorporated in a single generally accepted economic law or principle. It remains, so to speak, an annoying excrescence of social behavior, a bothersome qualification to the efficiency of our models, rather than an integral component in the structure of our thinking.

not run their corporations; elected corporation officials do. And the jobs of such officials, in practice, come to be self-perpetuating. I think I can safely say that in the United States this divorce between ownership and control is virtually complete, and the conclusion probably applies in considerable measure to other western democracies too. With rare exceptions such as Krupp in Germany, the bulk of all big business industry is run by paid managers, not by the owners, and big business typically accounts for the major part of all production.

Now the power and prestige of these paid managers rest to a considerable degree on the size of the corporations they command. The man who runs a two million-dollar concern is not in the same class with the august individual who runs a billion-dollar firm; still less does he rate with the financial emperor who sits atop one of the lofty giants of industry with assets ranging from five to twenty billion dollars, such as, in the United States, General Motors, American Telephone and Telegraph Company, Standard Oil or Du Pont. Furthermore, observation of personnel practice shows that there is very little turnover among top managers. Each official is married to his corporation, much as a labor leader is to his union, and in a connection at least as enduring and stead-fast as the average contract between man and wife. Hence, if a corporation president is to grow in prestige and power, his firm must grow too, and it must grow relatively to all others.

This is a consideration which places a premium on expansion, and it is a proposition, I think, that challenges one of the basic conclusions of presently accepted economic theory. Since David Ricardo economists have supposed that capital tends to flow to its more profitable uses. Combine this tendency with the law of diminishing returns and we have the resulting tendency, familiar in theory, for the profit rate to be equalized in all branches of industry – after allowance, of course, for differences in risk and in certain qualitative factors. To be sure, we concede that this wonderfully benign tendency is modified by monopolistic influences, and that it is obscured at all times by the presence of dynamic changes. But the tendency, we typically insist, is there nonetheless, and the fact that capital is attracted irresistibly to its more profitable uses is to this day considered one of the grand and inimitable merits of the free enterprise, capitalistic system.

This tendency, we say, is our insurance that resources are turned to their most economical and efficient use. It is the bulwark of our faith in the providential results of permitting individuals, within broad limits, to follow freely the dictates of their own self-interest. I would contend that this theory is a pathetically weak reed upon which to rest faith of any kind.

For consider once again our modern captain of industry. He has, to be sure, a profound interest in maximizing his corporation's profits. Why not? On the corporation's success hinges his own professional destiny. But does he have an equal interest in maximizing the returns on the total assets which legally accrue to stockholders? There is an important difference here, and a conflict of interests, which is easily illustrated by a specific example.

Suppose that Corporation A earns a profit which is equal to about 5 per cent of its assets. Now suppose that most other giant corporations at this time are doing relatively better than Corporation A, with profits ranging from 10 to 50 per cent, instead of just 5 per cent. If the managers of Corporation A were primarily interested in maximizing the returns of stockholders, they would pay out in the form of dividends every penny of the profit that their concern had earned. They might even pay out some sums ordinarily allocated to depreciation. This would provide stockholders with the opportunity for transferring their funds, that is, for investing their funds in other, more profitable, enterprises. And we might legitimately trust that stockholders would seek out the most profitable means for investing their funds. If things really operated in this fashion, our general theory of capital allocation might be at least roughly correct. But the facts, of course, show that corporation managers do not usually behave in this way, and the reason lies in the quest for power. Experience demonstrates that, on the average, corporation managers will pay out only half, or less, of the firm's profits in the form of dividends; they will plough back the rest in the construction of new plant and equipment. Not only are business managers loath to see their corporations contract, for this would mean, ultimately, the end of their own jobs; they will typically insist on further growth. And they will do this even though the marginal productivity of capital, even though profit opportunities, are greater elsewhere.

In short, capital does not flow, necessarily, into its most

profitable uses. The pattern of allocation may be as arbitrary as it would be under government direction, and may be more so. Now, of course, it is one thing to say that capital is not allocated in accord with present theory. It is quite another to construct a new theory which will explain its flow. To accomplish the latter something more than mere abstract speculation is required. Empirical studies are needed to describe the patterns and uniformities, if any, in corporation and financial policies. My own tentative researches in this field, and many more are needed, suggest that there are predictable patterns, and that the rate of a corporation's internal financing – that is, the rate of its retained profits – depends on a number of factors and only in small part on its profit rate. Among the other factors are, first, the size of the corporation in relation to the other corporations in its industry; second, the relative position of the corporation among all business concerns in the economy as a whole; third, the pattern of ownership of the corporation's securities, that is, whether widely dispersed or closely held; and fourth, the rate of growth of the industry in which the corporation does business. These are all factors which bear on the competitive race for power. And I would suggest that if power, not relative profits, governs the flow of capital, a strong case can be made for government intervention, in one form or another, in the direction of investment. Logically, such intervention could take the form of the system which has prevailed in recent years in the United Kingdom, or it could appear in the much milder form of a relatively high tax on retained profits, high enough to ensure that all, or nearly all, of a corporation's profits are paid out currently to stockholders.

But my principal purpose here has not been to diagnose social problems, and, still less, to prescribe their corrections, for there are many difficulties and value judgements which enter here that we cannot examine. I have been chiefly interested in suggesting how our knowledge may be extended by a consideration of the role of power in life, and I should like to turn now to the second relatively neglected aspect of this problem – the power wielded by social groups, or vested interests.

Perhaps the only attempt in modern times to grapple seriously with this problem is found in a book written a few years ago by John K. Galbraith, in which he develops his now well known theory of countervailing power. This theory has one important advantage over the usual approach to the analysis of industrial organization. It at least recognizes that the important economic decisions in modern society are made not only by individuals, as consumers, or as businessmen, but that they are also made by groups of individuals, as groups, or by individuals representing groups in society, in and out of government. This is an important contribution, obvious as it may seem to laymen, because in the main stream of economic thinking, omitting the heretics such as Karl Marx and Thorstein Veblen, such phenomena have been virtually unacknowledged. However, it cannot be said that Galbraith has presented us with a theory which all economists are compelled to support. Some have already expressed serious scepticism of its truth, and I must say that I share these doubts. Galbraith's story consists, essentially, of two propostions, and the big question is: are they consistent, in an objective and verifiable way, with the facts of group behavior as found, at least, in western democracies. I think that they are demonstrably inconsistent, and furthermore, that if believed and acted upon, they could prove to be a dangerous illusion.

Galbraith's first proposition is that for every center of power in the economy there is a tendency for an offsetting or countervailing center of power to develop. The second proposition is that one center of power tends to countervail another center of power in a way which functions in the public interest. In effect, Galbraith has drawn a portrait of Karl Marx with a ribbon in his hair – for conflicts of interest in modern capitalism, as Galbraith sees it, simply serve to promote the public welfare.

For example, Galbraith says that the development of a high degree of monopoly power in the meat packing industry in the United States led to the rise of monopolistic, or oligopolistic, chain stores in food retailing. The bargaining power of the great chain stores offsets the monopoly power of the meat packers, and hence prices are kept lower for the general public. Some have questioned the historical accuracy of this example, but since one illustration would not in any case prove a general theory I shall not pursue it. I use the illustration only to explain Galbraith's meaning.

The fact is that the implications of his theory would be profound, if valid. For Professor Galbraith has resurrected the unseen hand of Adam Smith, but with this difference. According to Smith, the uninhibited efforts of each individual to further his self-interest operate, through the mysteries of competition, to maximize the public welfare. According to Galbraith, the public welfare is also maximized, but in this case it is due to the un-inhibited efforts of each *group* in society to further its self-interest, operating through the mysteries of countervailing power. It would be a splendid, heavenly world if either theory worked out, and especially if it applied to international relations.

Unfortunately, both of Galbraith's main propositions seem highly questionable. First of all, it is demonstrable that there are many centers of power which are *not* matched by opposing or countervailing power concentrations. For example, in the petro-leum and steel industries in the United States, employers enjoyed monopolistic power for three-quarters of a century or more before unions were organized, or before any other serious off-setting power developed. In the construction industry today, the unions are powerful and well organized, but the employers con-sist of numerous relatively small concerns which are unorganized and as a group wield little influence. Many other examples might be cited in the United States and elsewhere. If there is really a tendency for one center of power to induce the development of another, therefore, it must be pitifully weak and uncertain, at best; for in many cases it does not operate at all and in others it functions with a lag long enough to span generations.

But the weakest element in Galbraith's theory is not this; it lies, instead, in his second proposition. When one center of power does 'countervail' the other, there is simply no evidence that the public welfare is the beneficiary. When farmers develop market power to offset that of the monopolistic food industry, the result most often is higher prices than otherwise would prevail, and also burdensome surpluses in warehouses and smaller supplies in the market. When strong labor unions face monopolistic industries, the result is often an inflationary spiral. It is a delusion, I think, to refer to such opposing powers as countervailing. If there is any outstanding characteristic of their relationships it is that they are mutually emulating, each contending against all others for a larger share of the fruits of the nation's economic activity.

It is important, though, before proceeding, to indicate more clearly than we have thus far, what is meant by a center of power. I refer by this phrase to any individual, organization or to any groups of individuals or organizations, the decisions of which, taken by themselves, may have an appreciable effect on the national economy. What particular centers of power we identify, how finely we break them down, depends essentially on the purpose of our analysis. For some objectives – for example, in explaining the formation of broad national economic policies – it may be necessary to recognize only three major power interests: big business, labor and agriculture. In the United States big business is by far the most important and leaves its imprint on nearly every aspect of our society, including even tastes of consumers, the attitude of workers toward work and leisure, and the attitude of women toward their homes. The tactics of big business, its needs and goals, together with those of agriculture and labor, with which they are often in conflict, influence the formation of practically every national economic decision. For example, without reference to these centers of power, and especially to that of big business, it would be impossible to explain the United States tariff policy, or the fiscal and monetary policy followed during the last year and one-half in the presence of 5 million unemployed, or our agricultural policy, or our official attitude toward labor-management relations. For on an objective or national basis, none of these policies is thoroughly rational; they are in considerable measure the outcome of an emulatory struggle of powers. I do not think that this situation differs materially in other western democracies except, perhaps, in degree, and in the particular distribution of influence among the major power groups.

But for many purposes it is necessary to study more specific vested interests. The petroleum and steel industries in the United States, for instance, are relevant as interests groups not only in explaining petroleum and steel prices but also in accounting for certain characteristics of our tax laws. The shift in emphasis in economic analysis that I am suggesting is from the individual firm to cohesive groups of firms, even in the study of price determination. As another example, the attitude of one of our great unions, the United Automobile Workers, toward its wage contract cannot be accounted for without realizing that this union competes, so to speak, not only with automobile manufacturers, but also with the United Mine Workers, the Steel Workers, the Amalgamated Clothing Workers and other unions, for in the quest for power, and in economic attainments, all are in mutual competition and their behavior is accordingly closely related. In the study of wage determination too, therefore, we need to attend to the relevant power relationships and not merely to the behavior of an individual firm or an individual trade union considered in the abstract. Though I have drawn in my examples from American experience, I do not think that such phenomena are entirely unknown in the United Kingdom, France, West Germany, Belgium or the Netherlands. And of course the activity of centers of power is not without influence in international relations, in and out of the new European Common Market.

Since it is the business of economists to explain economic behavior I suggest that these power relationships are worthy of study. But I think that there is a more practical reason, aside from the mere thirst for knowledge, for impelling our efforts in this direction. This reason follows from one of the broad conclusions which our analysis thus far suggests.

If the exercise of economic power is mutually emulatory rather than countervailing, as I have contended, then two possibilities arise; first, its impact may at times conflict with the public welfare; second, government itself may be used, at least in part, as a vehicle in the struggle for power, that is, as a medium for securing special privileges, advantages or benefits. Since the world we live in is far from the best of all possible worlds, we know that both possibilities have often materialized. As a corrective in democracies, there is available, I think, only what I would call the national consciousness. I would distinguish this influence sharply from gross nationalism. What I mean by national consciousness is a conscious awareness of the mutual interests of the people of a nation and along with this, an awareness of a standard of social morality by which those interests can be judged. A national consciousness of this kind can be used deliberately as a countervailing power, through government, to offset the thrusts of special interest groups or the rapacious onslaughts of one class or sector of society against others. One of the marks of the stability, maturity and progress of a democracy may be found in the degree to which this national consciousness is now developed, and among western democracies today the degrees differ rather widely.

As already suggested, the successful development of a national consciousness depends in part on the formation and acceptance of a standard of social morality by which conflicts of interest can be judged and adjudicated. It also depends on the development of a body of knowledge concerning those interests. If economics is an art as well as a science, and some think that it is, it can help in the creation of both of these prerequisites. It can build the body of knowledge and it can help to inculcate the ethical foundation upon which the public, in democratic countries, can act. For if we are to live in a progressive society, nationally as well as internationally, a countervailing power must be deliberately and consciously exercised by the people themselves, and this means by the institutions of government, at the very highest levels, by international government. The study of economic power, and the cultivation of the techniques and institutions by which it can be fruitfully controlled or channelled, is a task of economists in which all humanity has a stake.

14 A. Hunter

Countervailing Power?

A. Hunter, 'Notes on countervailing power', *Economic Journal*, vol. 68, 1958, pp. 89–103.

To begin with a broad and somewhat too dogmatically stated proposition, private economic power is held in check by the countervailing power of those who are subject to it. The first begets the second. The long trend towards concentration of individual enterprise in the hands of a relatively few firms has brought into existence not only strong sellers, as economists have supposed, but also strong buyers as they have failed to see. The two develop together, not in precise step but in such manner that there can be no doubt that the one is in response to the other (Galbraith, 1957).

Thus does Galbraith introduce the thesis that competition, the only 'autonomous regulator' of economic activity, has been superseded largely by what he calls the 'countervailing power' of large buyers. The comprehensiveness of the thesis extends far beyond the bounds of industrial enterprise and purports to explain also the structure of distribution, trade unions and agriculture and the changed nature of competition. Americana predominate in the institutional and factual material; but, by implication, the development of countervailing power, in one form or another, is typical of western industrial society (pp. 111–14, 126–7, 141). Perhaps the most important aspects of the new phenomenon are its beneficial welfare effects: it promotes, invariably, lower retail prices, greater efficiency, a more productive allocation of resources, a better distribution of income, etc. If even partially correct we have here an important contribution to market theory.

This article examines the concept of countervailing power mainly in a British context. Its incidence on the development and present structure of the distributive trades is assessed in Part 1; Part 2 examines the countervailing function and performance of the Cooperative Movement; and Part 3 surveys the position in manufacturing industry. Finally, Part 4 is devoted to a brief discussion of some of the logical difficulties presented by the theory.

The most crucial section of Galbraith's thesis is on distribution. This may be judged partly by the weight of material and example devoted to retailing; and partly because it is evidently expected that the 'mass retailers' will provide the most significant development to offset the market power of the industrial oligopolist. The forms of organization which, to Galbraith, are the vehicles of countervailing power in this sphere, are 'the food chains, the variety chains, the mail-order houses (now graduated into chain stores), the department store chains and the cooperative buying organizations of the surviving independent department and food stores' (p. 119). The British equivalents are the multiple stores, including the variety chain stores, the department stores and the consumer Cooperatives. It is to be noted that large-scale retailing is more developed in Britain than in the United States in the sense that multiples and Cooperatives account for a larger proportion of retail sales than do their American counterparts.[1] The question which now arises is whether the development of these large-scale retail outlets is a direct reaction to the market power of oligopolistic producers.

On examination it would appear not. We may take the assessment of J. B. Jefferys, perhaps our foremost authority on the development of the retail trades (1954). It seems that *multiples*, the most important of the large-scale retailers,[2] have developed mainly in order to exploit considerable economies of scale open to them through organizational and merchandizing techniques. Such economies do include special buying advantages, and there is therefore the beginnings of a case for the countervailing power thesis: the multiples can make large-scale purchases on behalf of all their branches, purchases which carry an appropriate discount; there are also discounts for cash trading not easily available to the

1. But not in the sense of 'average sales volume passing through individual retail outlets' Hall and Knapp (1955, p. 801).
2. See table on the proportion of total retail sales undertaken by different types of retailer (Jefferys, 1954, p. 73).

Type of organization	1900, %	1910, %	1920, %	1925, %
Cooperative societies	6·0–7·0	7·0–8·0	7·5–9·0	7·5–8·5
Department stores	1·0–2·0	1·5–3·0	3·0–4·0	3·0–4·0
Multiple retailers	3·0–4·5	6·0–7·5	7·0–10·0	9·5–11·5
Other retailers (by difference)	86·5–90·0	81·5–85·5	77·0–82·5	76·0–80·0

Type of organization	1930, %	1935, %	1939, %	1950, %
Cooperative societies	8·5–10·0	8·5–10·5	10·5–11·5	10·0–12·0
Department stores	3·5–5·0	4·0–5·5	4·5–5·5	4·5–6·0
Multiple retailers	12·0–14·0	14·0–17·0	18·0–19·5	18·0–20·5
Other retailers (by difference)	71·0–76·0	67·0–73·5	63·5–67·5	61·5–67·5

small retailer; and there are 'special discounts and allowances obtained by negotiation with producers including the right to sell some lines under "own brand" marks'. In this way 'a strong buyer in the market can influence the pricing decisions of the producer' (pp. 31–2, 68–9, appendix C). On the other hand, the major advantages of size appear to originate on the organizational side of the business and not as a function of market power; they follow quite conventionally from the scale of operations of the multiple stores. Following Jefferys's analysis there is, for example, the specialization of function and increased division of labour made possible by size and centralized control (in general administration, buying, advertising, stock control, shop lay-out and siting, transport, etc.). This is complemented by 'standardization of procedure, practice and method in all branches'. There are also advantages in integrating the wholesale and retail functions; lower inventory costs are obtained from a faster rate of stock-turn than is possible in a smaller organization; and there are the other incidental advantages of size, such as the spreading of risk over a large number of retail outlets, ready finance for hire-purchase credit, for spot purchases of useful shop-sites, etc.

In all this it is difficult to see the greater bargaining power of the multiple firm as anything other than one more by-product of size.

It certainly would strain the principles of inductive reasoning to interpret it as the prime object of the growth of the multiples (pp. 11 and 464).[3] A further point confirms: amalgamation, one of the main routes to large size among multiples (and currently much in operation) apparently takes place for such diverse reasons as an increased specialization of management functions, economies of buying and transport, an economic acquisition of a set of attractive shopping sites or for the purely financial gains involved in taking over another company's assets and recapitalizing the firm (pp. 73–6).

The *variety chain stores* (which, however, account for only 20 per cent of the sales of all multiples) appear to offer more scope for an exercise of countervailing power. A well-known feature of their policies is the establishment 'of close links with and the making of bulk purchases from producers'. Organizations like Marks and Spencers Ltd 'give assistance and advice to their suppliers even to the extent of helping the firms mechanize, lay out and extend their factories and purchase the raw and semi-finished materials used by their suppliers' (p. 71). And it is on record that the policies of the variety chain stores, on one occasion at least (and with the help of competition from Japanese imports), compelled one oligopolized industry to produce a specially branded, cheap commodity for exclusive retailing through these stores (Monopolies Commission, 1951, ch. 8). This looks promising. Unfortunately, Jefferys also states quite firmly that 'the success of this form of retailing was not dependent to any great extent upon the development of large-scale production . . . it was more the outcome of the application of large-scale retailing to the distribution of a wide range of physically small, low-priced, near-essential goods'. And he mentions the very large number of separate producers who supply goods to any one variety chain store (pp. 70–71). That is, merchandizing technique and not large-scale bargaining is the basis of this form of retail organization.

Finally, the development of *departmental stores* presents an

3. For countervailing power to be exercised the interests of the large-scale retailer must be distinct from those of the manufacturer. In fact, vertical integration is common among multiples in such important trades as men's clothing, footwear, confectionery, groceries and chemists' goods.

analogous picture. Briefly, this method of trading 'did not depend on the existence of large-scale methods of production; its success lay rather in the coordination of supplies from a large number of producers and provision of a much wider selection and range of goods, and more attractive shopping conditions, than could be offered by competitors' (pp. 32–4, 60, 87).

Evidently, great ingenuity would be required to fit the principal factors in the development of our large-scale retailers to the requirements of Galbraith's thesis. And it is significant that the possibility of growth for the sake of countervailing power has never occurred to Jefferys and other students who have given considerable attention to the minutiae of the distributive trades. But perhaps the most devastating weakness is yet to come. The other side of this model hardly exists: the oligopolists, in reaction to whom the large-scale retailer is supposed to evolve, are very thin on the ground. Mention has already been made of the large numbers of producers who supply department and variety chain stores; and an analysis of the individual trades in which large-scale retailers as a group have had most success demonstrates a similar pattern. These are the trades: the footwear trade (with 61 per cent of total national retail sales by 1939), the women's wear trade (47 per cent), grocery and provisions (47 per cent), the dairy trade (47 per cent), chemists' goods (42 per cent), men's clothing (42 per cent) and furniture and furnishings (39 per cent) (pp. 74–6). Now there is some concentration of production in the chemists' goods trade; otherwise, if we except certain individual items, such as cocoa, sugar, condensed milk and margarine, there is no significant concentration among the producers of this group of commodities.[4] Indeed, the production of footwear, clothing, furnishing and farm produce come close to being text-book examples of small-scale competitive industry. By contrast, 'large-scale retailing made relatively little headway in the trades where production was concentrated in the hands of a few firms or where the products were nationally advertised, branded and resale price maintained, for example, tobacco and cigarettes, chocolate and sugar confectionery, certain grocery goods and electrical goods of various descriptions' (p. 97). The thesis that the motive-force

4. See Leak and Maizels (1945, pts 1–2), and the *Census of Production 1951*.

behind the growth of large-scale retailing is the need to countervail the large-scale producer receives no support from British conditions.

Among large-scale retailers there is one more candidate for the role of countervailer – the Cooperatives. They deserve special attention: first, because Galbraith specifically observes of them that in Britain (and in Scandinavia) the consumers' Cooperative, rather than the chain-store, is 'the dominant instrument' of countervailing power in the consumers' goods market (Galbraith, 1957, p. 126). Secondly, because the Cooperative technique is different. The main countervailing effort is not made in negotiations with large-scale suppliers. Instead, the movement attempts to have an indirect effect on the market power of oligopolized private enterprise through an organization, owned and operated by consumers themselves, which competes by offering an alternative source of supply for most ranges of consumer goods, together with a separate system of retail outlets.[5]

One can appreciate that, theoretically, such a structure comes close to being an ideal for Galbraith's purposes. But close examination of practice reveals that the movement, rather than exploiting an advantageous position, has, on the contrary, neglected its opportunities for exercising countervailing power.

For example, although the Cooperatives initially had a resounding success by establishing themselves as suppliers of a high standard of quality in food and household stores, they failed to maintain the initiative as other classes of goods came within the reach of working-class incomes. The percentage share of the Cooperatives in total national retail sales rose from 6 per cent to 12 per cent over the period 1900–1950. But if we examine the structure of sales by 1950 we find that in only one commodity group do the Cooperatives secure a share higher than the 12 per cent for total sales: the *food and household stores* group accounts for 16–18 per cent of total national retail sales. In other commodity groups the shares are distinctly poorer: *clothing and footwear* 8·0–9·5 per cent; *reading and writing* and *confectionery goods* 5·0–

5. Carr-Saunders, Florence and Peers (1942), gives the most scholarly and impartial account of the British movement. See also Bailey (1960) and Digby (1960).

6·5 per cent; and *other goods* (a large and nowadays important group including chemists' goods, furniture and furnishings, electrical goods, bicycles, hardware, pottery, glass, etc.) runs at 4·0–5·0 per cent of total national retail sales (Jefferys, 1954, pp. 73–80). It seems that the Cooperatives, ensconced in the traditional grocery and food businesses, have found difficulty in entering the durable consumer-goods trades. Hence the rate of growth of the Cooperatives markedly decreases after 1920 and, significantly, compares badly with that of the rapidly expanding multiples.[6] Most commentators account for this phenomenon by pointing out strong conservative characteristics stemming from the egalitarian nature of the movement in this country (Carr-Saunders, Florence and Peers, 1942, chs. 20–29). Whatever the cause, it is clear that the Cooperatives, operating on this very restricted commodity base (three-quarters of the turn-over consists of food sales alone), cannot hope for an effective exercise of countervailing power. The concentration of production lies elsewhere (pp. 480–2; Bailey, 1960, p. 40).

Secondly, consider the movement as a price competitor. One would expect Cooperatives to play a leading part in introducing price-cutting – either in a general campaign or in selected ranges of goods – thus exerting pressure on private-enterprise markets on behalf of the consumer. With independent sources of manufacture and supply, as well as its own retail outlets, the organization is ideally equipped for this role. In practice, the Cooperative Societies, and the movement as a whole, almost unanimously avoid such a policy. They prefer to charge 'market-determined' prices (i.e. determined by private enterprise) and concentrate on paying the highest possible dividend (Carr-Saunders, Florence and Peers, 1942, chs. 5, 12, 27, 29; Jefferys, 1954, pp. 57–8). Evidently, they are firmly of the opinion that the dividend is the 'most important factor in maintaining the trade of customers' (Carr-Saunders, Florence and Peers, 1942, p. 478). And the movement is not prepared to abandon the certainty of one set of customers for the shifting loyalties of a competitive market. This attitude is persistently held, despite the fact that a 'fighting' policy offers the only method of maintaining a rate of expansion which will parallel the growth of the multiples. Where branded

6. See table above, p. 257.

and resale-price-maintained goods of outside manufacturers are sold through retail societies this attitude is repeated. The Cooperatives are prepared to sell such goods at the manufacturer's price even where, as in tobacco and chemists' goods, the resale prices are determined by a monopolistic group or a trade association enforcing a price-ring. The only objection the movement has felt compelled to make are in those cases where outside manufacturers withhold their goods on the grounds that the Cooperative dividend is a form of price-cutting; or where supplies are made available only on the condition that the dividend is withheld in respect of the price-maintained goods. This type of action is denounced as 'infringing Cooperative principle'. But on the practice of resale price maintenance itself the Cooperatives have never taken a stand on principle. Indeed, through a passive acceptance of the practice and some of its benefits, the Cooperatives may be said to have favoured it.[7] Altogether, the record shows a marked absence of positive action in the price-competition field.

Thirdly, the Cooperative movement can hardly commend itself to consumers as a militant 'trust-buster'. It is true that the major part of the Cooperative market for certain commodities is supplied by Cooperative factories (soap, preserves, margarine, footwear, cycles and men's clothing for example) or imported from Cooperative organizations abroad.[8] But in few industries is the share of the Cooperative plants very high; flour-milling, with a 25 per cent share, is exceptional. Exceptional also is the concern which Cooperative competition has caused, on occasion, in relatively concentrated industries such as soap and margarine (Wilson, 1954, vol. 1, pp. 118, 124, 278, 303, vol. 2, pp. 175, 291). This failure to press production in concentrated industries is the more surprising when it is noted that, as well as possessing their own retail outlets to guarantee disposal of goods, the wholesale societies invest as much as 75 per cent of their available capital

7. Yamey (1954, pp. 83–6). On the other hand, the Cooperatives do attempt to promote their own products as alternatives wherever possible.

8. About two-thirds of the supplies to retail societies have a Cooperative origin. On the other hand, it is calculated that allowing for the value of bought raw materials the 'value-added' element contributed by Cooperative production, British and foreign, is as low as 19·3 per cent (Carr-Saunders, Florence and Peers, 1942, pp. 409–11).

outside of the movement (Carr-Saunders, Florence and Peers, 1942, ch. 25) in securities and equities of various kinds. It is true that some considerable liquidity is desirable (customers' shares are withdrawable on demand), but this figure is, by most commercial and banking standards, incredibly conservative. If, as the Co-operative credo appears to imply, there is a special obligation on the movement to protect the consumer from 'monopolistic exploitation' the will to use these resources should be found. There are a number of industries which currently deserve the attention of militant cooperators – detergents, processed milk products, tobacco, sugar-refining, household electric goods, petroleum distribution, etc. – all of them well within the technical competence of the wholesale societies. But the gage is not taken up and is not likely to be. On the contrary, the wholesale societies, it appears, prefer to make life less arduous by finding some *modus vivendi* with monopolists and oligopolists (p. 494).

Thus, Galbraith's vision of an embattled movement fighting big business on behalf of the consuming public is, at best, a very small part of the truth.[9] The existence of a Cooperative movement does not, in itself, guarantee the exercise of countervailing power.[10]

The evidence for a development of countervailing power in the distributive trades in Britain is poor. However, where one does find examples of its exercise is in inter-industry and inter-firm transactions – mainly within manufacturing industry. Galbraith devotes only two paragraphs of his book to countervailing power in 'producers' goods' markets, preferring to highlight the more conspicuous cases of the consumers' goods markets. But he does provide in passing what is probably the correct explanation of the occurrence of the phenomenon: he notes that the manufacturer of producers' goods cannot count his customers in thousands but possibly, his important ones, only in dozens or less (p. 123). And it may happen that the firms of a concentrated

9. In particular, see the conclusions of Carr-Saunders, Florence and Peers (1942) on the performance of the movement in this respect, pp. 521–2.

10. Swedish experience has differed. The Kooperativa Forbundet developed in a more concentrated economy from a smaller number of consumer societies and was fortunate in finding a strong, imaginative leadership prepared to pursue the ideals of the movement (Hedberg, 1937); also Ames (n.d.).

industry find themselves in the position of selling a large part of their output, perhaps the main part of it, to the few members of an equally concentrated industry. In such circumstances the buyers can play off sellers one against the others. They can go 'from one manufacturer to another breaking down their prices. They may get a low price from one company short of work; the next company would be told that if they wanted a contract they must quote equally low or go without' (Monopolies Commission, 1957a, ch. 32, para. 716). For example, we find in the tyre industry that the prices of 'original equipment' tyres sold to the motor industry are decided in this way by the car manufacturers themselves, and not by the five main tyre manufacturers, who supply 95 per cent of this trade. Depending on the buying of the purchaser, discounts of anything from 40 to 60 per cent of the retail price are secured by individual car manufacturers. And the profit on this class of trade is small and often negative for the tyre firms.[11] In the electronic valve and tube industry, effectively concentrated in four firms, manufacturers are compelled to sell 'first equipment' radio valves and television tubes, with discounts ranging from 60 to 80 per cent, to the manufacturers of radio and television sets. The trade operates a price-fixing arrangement for the majority of its products, but 'the prices charged to the larger makers of equipment . . . cannot effectively be subjected to any price control': there is 'intense competition between the valve manufacturers for the business of the bigger set manufacturers'; consequently, 'prices offered are frequently insufficient to cover the costs of production and sale'.[12] And in the non-ferrous metals industry, which itself is only mildly concentrated, the trade association complains that the industry is subject to the pressure of 'powerful buying units in the electrical, motor and engineering industries and others grouped together into powerful buying organisations which negotiate terms collectively'; or it is subject to the potential competition of customers who have the technical

11. In contrast to the export and replacement trade which were price-fixed and otherwise controlled. Monopolies Commission (1956a, paras. 169–78, 463 and 193–200).

12. The profits of most firms are made on the sale of 'maintenance' valves to wholesalers and repairers. (Monopolies Commission, 1957b, paras. 118, 132 and 193–200).

competence and resources necessary for going into the manufacture of non-ferrous components for themselves (Monopolies Commission, 1956b, paras. 83–4, 268–9, 301–302).

Then, unexpectedly perhaps, the growth of nationalized industry and the development of certain government departments has centralized a number of purchasing interests, and thus extended the area of manufacturing industry in which countervailing power may be exercised. We know, for example, that in the domestic market of the heavy electrical industry the Central Electricity Authority buys 73 per cent of all mains cables, 78 per cent of heavy generating equipment and 60 per cent of heavy transformers; that the GPO buys 90 per cent of telephone and telegraph cable and (with the Admiralty and Cable and Wireless Ltd) 100 per cent of submarine cable; and that the Ministry of Health is now indirectly the main purchaser of the products of the pharmaceutical industry (Monopolies Commission 1952a, 1957a, 1952b). To these we must add the purchasing activities of nationalized gas, railways, the airways corporations, the Ministry of Supply and the Atomic Energy Authority, the Admiralty, etc.

Thus it appears that genuine cases of bilateral oligopoly do occur; and they seem, in most cases, to benefit the ultimate consumer by keeping down the level of price and stimulating the efficiency of the countervailed industry.[13] Further, if we can take the industry reports of the Monopolies Commission as representing a fair cross-section of manufacturing industry, cases occur frequently enough to merit special consideration. On the other

13. See the reports quoted on p. 270, n. 18. On consumer welfare there is one ambiguous point, however. Occasionally the countervailed industry compensates for the zero or negative profits on sales to strong buyers by fixing higher prices to other groups. Thus the customer has cheaper motor cars and television sets, but the *replacement* of tyres and electrical components, of electronic valves and cathode-ray tubes is maintained at much higher prices and margins. Whether the balance of the public interest lies in cheaper original prices, a faster turnover of goods and therefore a greater scale of output for the industry, or in cheaper replacement prices and therefore a longer life of the good, is not clear at this stage. Probably it depends on the precise circumstances. In practice, the Monopolies Commission prefers not to interfere in these commercial arrangements of the industry; except, of course, to recommend prohibition of any collective discrimination or enforcement against the weaker group of customers which may assist, indeed make possible, such price discrimination.

hand, it must be said firmly of these bilateral oligopoly situations that the countervailing powers of the buyers did *not* develop, à la Galbraith, in direct response to the concentrated market power of the suppliers. To look at our examples once again: the motor industry certainly is concentrated; but its concentration is adequately explained by the economies of scale which large size gives to an assembly industry of this character.[14] A set of tyres is, after all, only 3–5 per cent of the cost of even a moderately priced car. Similarly, the structure of the radio industry is defined by production possibilities rather than the need to bargain with the valve and tube manufacturers, even although valves are 15 per cent and tubes 35 per cent of the factory cost of radios and television sets.[15] And in the case of the non-ferrous metals industry it seems that the concentration of buying-power which it faced had *preceded* and gone farther than its own concentration – of selling power – a development which evidently gave rise to a sense of grievance, but which was clearly determined by the technology of its main customer-industries (Monopolies Commission, 1956b, ch. 10; Hunter, 1956). Finally, the centralization of buying power in the hands of the nationalized industries and government departments cannot really be classified except as one of the incidents of British political life.

One is forced to conclude that, however useful and desirable countervailing power may be, its incidence on manufacturing industry is, from the economic point of view, erratic and unpredictable.

14. The buying advantages of the motor industry, taken in the aggregate, for such components as radiators, electrical equipment, body assemblies etc. are not to be despised. Indeed, they have become essential to the industry; depending on the manufacturer, 56–78 per cent of the value of the finished vehicle consists of 'bought-out' components. But these advantages *follow* from the scale of operations rather than create them; and they are more likely to be directed against small-scale than large-scale industry (see Andrews and Brunner, 1955, pt 3, ch. 4; and PEP, 1957, chs. 2, 3, 10).

15. Indeed the valve industry is the more concentrated of the two. But in competing for the custom of the larger set makers the valve and tube manufacturers have become the victims of their own efficiency: low-cost production has become very closely geared to long runs of standardized work in this industry. Thus buying power is the outcome of a technological accident not industrial concentration (Monopolies Commission, 1957b, paras. 193–200 and 223–30).

It would appear that the theory of countervailing power obtains but thin empirical support from British conditions in the manufacturing and distributive trades.[16] And, lest this absence be considered a reflection of decadent British economic organization, it should be noted that serious deficiencies of a similar nature have been found in relation to United States conditions (Stigler, 1954; Miller 1954). Nevertheless, the idea that there is a tendency for concentrated market power to be countervailed by forces from the other side of the market succeeds in securing some support from common sense and experience; the thesis is put forward most plausibly by Professor Galbraith; and it would be surprising if a complete book had been written on a concept with no substance at all. But there is a lacuna somewhere between practice and theory; and to get at its nature a closer examination of the internal structure of Galbraith's model is required.

The essence of countervailing power is contained in the spontaneous and often inevitable concentration of weak buyers (or sellers) when confronted with the established, 'original', power of strong sellers (or buyers). This concentration may occur through the ordinary processes of growth and amalgamation until a roughly bilateral oligopolistic situation is developed. It is this theoretical situation that Galbraith, so far as one can tell, usually discusses (pp. 111, 137–8, chs. 1–8). But to judge from his examples, he also has in mind the growth of countervailing power in a much wider range of market situations and industrial structures. He mentions the unorganized bargaining power of the small-scale building industry *vis-à-vis* trade unions (pp. 124–5); the development, with or without government support, of trade unions to counter the bargaining power of employers; and the formation of consumer Cooperatives to by-pass, rather than bargain with,

16. Galbraith also places great emphasis on the role of countervailing power in stimulating trade-union organization. 'As a general rule there are strong unions only where markets are served by strong corporations' (1957, pp. 114–15). Even the most superficial knowledge of trade-union history fails to bear out this analysis. British trade unionism was originally craft unionism (engineering, shipbuilding, printing, e.g.); later spreading to coal-mining, metals, textiles and footwear. None of these were ever particularly concentrated industries. And eventually the most powerful unions came to be the engineering and 'general' unions, which secure their strength from a coverage of a variety of trades – not from organizing one particular industry.

large-scale suppliers (pp. 126–7). More unexpected still, we find direct intervention by the Government in agricultural markets to provide support prices for farmers; and state regulation of wages in those industries which have not succeeded in establishing satisfactory negotiating machinery. The spontaneity of counter-vailing power, it appears, is not necessarily a market phenomenon: political lobbies and the legislative process may also provide the means whereby 'disadvantaged' groups assert their economic interests against strong market positions (pp. 136, 152, ch. 10). Thus, stated in its most general form, countervailing power becomes *any* strengthening of weak-market positions in almost any circumstances.

One could argue simply that here we have a series of proposi-tions on such a level of generalization, and applied to such a mixture of situations, that they are not susceptible to a uniform analytic treatment and cannot yield precise results. That is, the concept is not operationally meaningful. But more concrete criticisms are available.

First, if our interpretation of the nature of countervailing power is correct, and it seems the most reasonable interpretation, then it can be shown that Galbraith arbitrarily ignores certain classes of countervailance. For the sake of completeness he should add to his examples the activities of certain manufacturers' and distri-butors' associations formed to improve the market position of their members, *vis-à-vis* other groups, by restricting competition. To take examples from British practice (and there are abundant American examples)[17] we have the London Building Conference, which organized a level-tendering arrangement mainly to eliminate 'excessive competition' and 'the domination of building owner and architect' in this market, and thus secure 'a reasonable return' to the trade. Then there is the British Non-Ferrous Metals Federa-tion, whose members organize extensive price-fixing arrangements for most groups of product in order (*inter alia*) to 'protect them-

17. See TNEC Monograph no. 21 (1941) for numerous cases of manu-facturers' and distributors' associations which enforced regulations and boycotts on one another to control margins, to assert the right to handle goods exclusively, to regulate the price paid for raw material or component supplies, etc. 'In all of these cases association members have employed the boycott as a means of enforcing outsiders to conform to programs which they have adopted in their own interests' (pp. 224–58).

selves against the pressure of powerful buyers' (Monopolies Commission, 1957b, paras. 266–71). And there are numerous distributive associations who operate 'exclusive buying' arrangements (agreements to buy only from named firms) 'as a protection for the small distributor against a large and powerful supplier or group of suppliers' or to negotiate favourable terms from a powerful manufacturers' association (White Paper, 1955, chs. 4, 6). Clearly, these activities constitute attempts of relatively weak buyers and sellers to improve their market positions. But it is a serious reflection on Galbraith's concept that they are also cases of restrictive practices; that the majority were found to operate against 'the public interest' by keeping prices and margins unnecessarily high, protecting inefficiency, etc.; and that all are now presumed illegal under the 1956 Restrictive Trade Practices Act.

Secondly, it is not clear, even in the most favourable cases, that the exercise of countervailing power will necessarily increase economic welfare. Take the emergence of bilateral oligopoly. Galbraith shows convincingly enough, what we have noted already, that an oligopsonist is in a position to drive down the oligopolists' prices (Galbraith, 1957, pp. 120–21). The difficulty is to see why the oligopsonist should pass on his gain to the ultimate consumer. This is crucial. On the basis of existing theory one would assume that bilateral oligopoly will do no more than redistribute gains between oligopolists and oligopsonists (Stigler, 1954, p. 9). Galbraith has two answers to this point. The first is that the mass buyers, chain stores, variety stores etc., are anxious to increase their volume of sales: profits are a function of output for them, and a low level of prices is regarded 'as the major device for obtaining and maintaining volume' (Galbraith, 1957, pp. 123–4). The second answer – an afterthought in response to criticisms of his book and incorporated in the revised edition – is that although the 'mass buyers' are oligopsonists on the buying side, they remain subject to intensive competition from other types of retailer on the selling side, and are therefore compelled to pass on their gains in the form of lower prices (Galbraith, 1954, pp. 3–4; 1957, pp. 117–18).

Unfortunately, no evidence is offered that either of these two effects operates generally. Conceivably, the output factor could have the effect Galbraith ascribes to it during periods when the size of the retail market is rapidly increasing. Equally conceivable is a static or contracting market, in which further economies of scale are not to be found and there is no incentive to pass on the gains in low prices. The second line of defence – that the oligopsonistic mass buyers are subject to intense competition on the sales side – Galbraith would have been wiser to omit. If accepted, it is only reasonable to suppose that the same competitors must also be encountered in buying activities. And this conclusion inevitably suggests that the large-scale retailers are never oligopsonists except perhaps in a few specialized lines of product; that they are not therefore in a position to control oligopolistic producers; and that their market power merely consists of the familiar advantages of large-scale buying (see p. 256) in a competitive market. In any event, these welfare arguments are developed only for the mass distributors in whom Galbraith places so much faith; it is not shown why the industrial oligopsonist must pass on his gains. In certain circumstances this effect will occur in manufacturing industry. For example, the motor industry appears to be oligopsonistic in character when buying one component of uniform quality – tyres – within the domestic market. It is undoubtedly a much more competitive industry when selling a variety of types and qualities – cars and light commercial vehicles – in what is an international market. Again, it can happen that the oligopsonist is a nationalized industry, and will therefore pass on the benefit of its bargaining power to the consumer.[18] But it is obvious that these examples are no more than the accidents of market and industrial structure; it cannot be shown that they are automatic in their appearance. And, to take the alternative, one can hardly base an important welfare theorem on the assumption that oligopsonists are altruistic.

Thirdly, it is a source of confusion for the reader of Galbraith's book that when countervailing power is exercised by what may

18. Galbraith would have been on more solid ground had he emphasized the greater efficiency generated in countervailing power situations. The oligopolists who are confronted by strong buyers now have the benefit of specialized production and long runs of work; also, they are likely to be subject to pressures to conform closely to quality and design specifications, to use up-to-date methods of production, to have their works costed by independent accountants to determine a fair basis for price negotiation, etc. (see Monopolies Commission reports, 1952a, 1957a, 1956b, 1957c).

be called general interest groups, it becomes a welfare principle that the gains are *retained* and not passed on to the ultimate consumer! The organization of trade unions to bargain with employers or the successful lobbying of farmers to raise agricultural prices are cases in point (pp. 115–16, 136–7, 152). This is a serious inconsistency. Even if we leave the inconsistency aside, it is difficult to see why this form of redistribution of income, in favour of particular interest groups, necessarily increases economic welfare. In a society which, broadly, favours a greater degree of equality of income the organization of groups 'disadvantaged' by weak market positions is likely to be acceptable. But one would hesitate to state a general theory along these lines. At what point in a series of successful operations does the 'disadvantaged' group pass into the ranks of the 'advantaged'? To be concrete, does the bargaining power of the National Union of Mineworkers always operate in the public interest? Are the successful lobbying activities of the National Farmers' Union or the British Medical Association always to be regarded as increasing economic welfare? Galbraith does not enlighten us on this point. Indeed, it is difficult to see that he could, since no existing welfare theory can demonstrate that the successes of one interest group operate to the general advantage. One is left with the impression that any form of institution or organization designed to strengthen weak market positions earns his uncritical approval. But it would be fallacious to suppose that comprehensive organization into economic interest groups is a universal panacea for inequality. In Stigler's trenchant phrase, 'we should encounter new inequities in income distribution which would affront our sensibilities quite as much as any we can find now' (p. 14).

It is becoming clear that most of these internal difficulties revolve around the welfare implications of the concept – what countervailing power is expected to do. *Prima facie*, Galbraith is concerned to demonstrate that the benefits of countervailing power are the orthodox welfare effects. It operates, he says, 'in the right direction' to reduce monopoly returns, to give lower prices, larger outputs and a more desirable use of resources (p. 170). More generally, it replaces competition as 'the autonomous regulator of economic activity' in a world of oligopolies and monopolies (p. 112). But a second reading of *American Capitalism* brings out the variety of situations, extending quite out of the market at times, which countervailing power encompasses; and a corresponding variety of 'welfare' effects many of which clearly do not fit into accepted welfare systems and which are mutually incompatible. Galbraith himself, in later writings, admits to a modicum of confusion: 'I fear I did not make as explicit as I should the welfare criteria I was employing.' And he goes on to say that although 'increased real income of consumers is the simplest test of improved welfare' we now 'regularly reject' this standard and 'regularly accept measures which raise product prices to ameliorate the grievances or alleviate the tensions of some social group. An opulent society can afford to sacrifice material well-being for social contentment.' It appears that his criterion is not the welfare of consumers but 'the minimization of social tension' (1954, p. 3; 1957, pp. 146–7). This is a surprising tailpiece to find on an economic theory; and almost certainly it is a criterion which creates more problems than it solves.

The most equitable interpretation of Galbraith's book is that he is arguing for equality of bargaining power as a desirable social and economic norm. One can go some considerable distance with him and agree that there is much to be said for certain institutional developments such as a more militant Cooperative movement to provide a check on big business or an intelligent use of counter-vailing power as an instrument of monopoly control.[19] And, of course, no one seriously objects to the statutory powers of trade unions to control the supply of labour and thus offset an other-wise serious bargaining disadvantage. But these are personal and political value judgements: acceptance of them involves no commitment to Galbraith's positive theory.

That is, on the scientific level it must be concluded that the countervailing-power thesis has no solid claim to theoretical status: demonstrably, the empirical basis is lacking and the

19. In fact, the Monopolies Commission has so advised the use of counter-vailing power in certain of its recommendations (see Hunter, 1955). And in the 1956 Restrictive Trade Practices Act provision is specifically made for the exemption of agreements, otherwise restrictive, if they are 'reasonably necessary – to negotiate fair terms' with oligopolistic or monopolistic buyers or suppliers.

internal consistency of the welfare theorem is poor. Indeed, there is serious doubt that countervailing power is primarily of the material of economic theory. On the desirability of pressure groups to offset weak market positions the economist cannot be the main authority; and the assessment of such forces in terms of 'the minimization of social tension' seems to be a task for other disciplines. The economist can be sure of only this: that countervailing power is but occasionally and fortuitously a product of market forces.

References

AMES, J. W. (n.d.), *Cooperative Sweden*.

ANDREWS, P. W. S. and BRUNNER, E. (1955), *The Life of Lord Nuffield*, Blackwell.

BAILEY, J. (1960), *The British Cooperative Movement*, Hutchinson.

CARR-SAUNDERS, A. M., FLORENCE, P. S., and PEERS, R. (1942), *Consumers' Cooperation in Great Britain*, Harper & Row.

DIGBY, M. (1960), *The World Cooperative Movement*, Hutchinson.

GALBRAITH, J. K. (1954), 'Countervailing Power', *Amer. econ. Rev.*, vol. 44, pp. 1–6.

GALBRAITH, J. K. (1957), *American Capitalism*, Hamish Hamilton, rev. edn; 1st edn, 1952; Penguin Books, 1962.

HALL, M., and KNAPP, J. (1955), 'Productivity in retail distribution', *Econ. J.*, vol. 65, no. 257, pp. 72–88.

HEDBERG, A. (1937), *The Swedish Consumer in Cooperation*, Cooperative League of the USA.

HUNTER, A. (1955), 'The Monopolies Commission and economic welfare', *Manchester School of Economic and Social Studies*, vol. 23, no. 1, pp. 22–40.

HUNTER, A. (1956), 'The Monopolies Commission and price fixing', *Econ. J.*, vol. 66, no. 264, pp. 587–602.

JEFFERYS, J. B. (1954), *Retail Trading in Britain 1850–1950*, Cambridge University Press.

LEAK, H., and MAIZELS, A. (1945), 'Structure of British industry', *J. Royal Stat. Soc.*, vol. 108, no. 1–2, pp. 142–99.

MILLER, J. P. (1954), 'Competition and countervailing power', *Amer. econ. Rev.*, vol. 44, pp. 15–25.

MONOPOLIES COMMISSION (1951), *Electric Lamps*, HMSO.

MONOPOLIES COMMISSION (1952a), *Electric Cables*, HMSO.

MONOPOLIES COMMISSION (1952b), *Insulin*, HMSO.

MONOPOLIES COMMISSION (1956a), *Pneumatic Tyres Report*, HMSO.

MONOPOLIES COMMISSION (1956b), *Semi-Manufactures of Copper*, HMSO.

MONOPOLIES COMMISSION (1957a), *Electrical and Allied Machinery and Plant*, HMSO.

MONOPOLIES COMMISSION (1957b), *Electronic Valves and Tubes*, HMSO.

MONOPOLIES COMMISSION (1957c), *Industrial and Medical Gases*, HMSO.

POLITICAL AND ECONOMIC PLANNING (1957), *Engineering Report 2: Motor Vehicles*, Political and Economic Planning.

STIGLER, G. J. (1954), 'The economist plays with blocs', *Amer. econ. Rev.*, vol. 44, pp. 7–14.

TEMPORARY NATIONAL ECONOMIC COMMITTEE MONOGRAPH NO. 21 (1941), United States Government.

WHITE PAPER (1955), *Collective Discrimination*, Cmd. 9504, HMSO.

WILSON, C. (1954), *History of Unilever*, Cassell.

YAMEY, B. S. (1954), *The Economics of Resale Price Maintenance*, Weidenfeld & Nicolson.

Part Six Unequal Partners: Minorities

Power differences arising from the uneven distribution of wealth affect every individual. His station of birth, luck and effort will determine which rank in the power hierarchy he reaches. But in many societies whole groups of people may be deprived of access to power or to the means of power. The discrimination of minorities, apart from being a serious social and moral problem, is an important expression of power influences in economic life. Baran and Sweezy's analysis of the Negro question deals with an outstanding problem of the United States. But it can at the same time be regarded as a case study of minority problems in general.

15 P. A. Baran and P. M. Sweezy

The Socio-Economic Background of the Negro Question

Excerpts from P. A. Baran and P. M. Sweezy, *Monopoly Capital*,
Monthly Review Press, 1966, chapter 9, pp. 256–79.

[. . .]

In the USA Negro emigration from the Old South started before
the end of the nineteenth century but took on really mass proportions only during the war decade. There was a decline in the
rate of flow during the 1930s, but even the heavy unemployment
of that period failed to check the northward movement. The
biggest wave of emigration came with the Second World War and
has continued with but little change ever since.

Almost all of the emigrants from the South settled in the cities
of the North and West. But this was not the only movement of
Negroes. Within the South itself, there has been steady migration
from countryside to city. The upshot is that in the half century
between 1910 and 1960, Negroes have been transformed from a
regional peasantry into a substantial segment of the urban working class. The three to one rural–urban ratio of 1910 has been
almost exactly reversed: today three-quarters of the Negro
population are city dwellers.

It was of course inevitable that Negroes should enter the urban
economy at the very bottom. They were the poorest, most
illiterate, least skilled on arrival. They were doubly burdened by
historic race prejudice and discrimination and by the prejudice
and discrimination that have greeted every group of impoverished
newcomers. The questions we have to ask are: how have they
made out since moving to the cities? Have they been able to
follow in the footsteps of earlier immigrant groups, climbing the
economic ladder and escaping from their original ghettos?

In answering these questions, we must be careful not to mix
up the effects of moving from country to city, a process which
has been continuous for more than half a century, with what has

happened after arrival in the city. The move from countryside to city has on the average unquestionably meant a higher standard of living for Negroes: if it had not, the migration would have ceased long ago. In other words, the bottom of the urban-industrial ladder is higher than the bottom of the Southern agricultural ladder, and when Negroes stepped from the one to the other it was a step up. This is not what primarily interests us, however. It was similarly a step up for impoverished European peasants to leave their homelands and move to the United States: again the proof is that the flow continued until it was cut off by war and legislation. The point is that after they got there, they soon started to climb the new ladder, and fresh immigrant groups took their place at the bottom. What we want to know is whether Negroes have followed the same course, climbing the new ladder after moving to the cities.

A few have, of course, and we shall discuss the role and significance of this minority when we come to the subject of tokenism. But for the great mass of Negroes the answer is, emphatically and unambiguously, no. The widespread opinion to the contrary, to the extent that it has any factual basis, rests on confusing the step from one ladder to the other with a step up the new ladder. This important point was explained to the Clark Committee by Herman P. Miller, Special Assistant to the Director of the Bureau of the Census and one of the country's leading authorities on income distribution:

We heard this morning from Professor Ginzberg that the Negro made a breakthrough in the 1850s. Senator Javits, in his excellent book *Discrimination, USA*, also speaks about the improvement of the economic status of the Negro. Even the Department of Labor refers to the occupational gains that have been made by the Negro in the past twenty years. This is all very true, but I think it can be shown, on the basis of census statistics, that most of the improvement in occupational status that the Negro has made since 1940 has been through his movement out of sharecropping and agricultural labor in the South and into your Northern industrial areas.

When we look at the figures for the Northern and Central states we find that the occupational status of the Negro relative to the white has not improved appreciably since 1940 (United States Senate, 1963b).

With respect to income, the situation is somewhat more complicated, but no more favorable to the theory that Negroes are moving up the ladder. Miller explained it in his statement prepared for the Clark Committee:

Although the relative occupational status of non-whites has not changed appreciably in most states since 1940, the income gap between whites and non-whites did narrow during the Second World War. During the past decade, however, there has been no change in income differentials between the two groups. . . . In 1947, the median wage or salary income for non-white workers was 54 per cent of that received by the whites. In 1962, the ratio was almost identical (55 per cent). . . . In view of the stability of the earnings gap during the postwar period . . . the reduction during the war years cannot be viewed as part of a continuing process, but rather as a phenomenon closely related to war-induced shortages of unskilled labor and government regulations such as those of the War Labor Board designed generally to raise the incomes of lower paid workers, and to an economy operating at full tilt (p. 323).[1]

It is important to understand that the position of Negroes derives not only from the undoubted facts that on the average they have less education and are concentrated in unskilled or semi-skilled occupations. Even when they have the same amount of schooling as whites, their occupational status is lower. Even when they do the same work, they are paid less. And in both respects, the relative disadvantage of the Negro is greater the higher you go in the occupation and income scales.

A non white man who has not gone beyond the eighth grade has very little chance of being anything more than a laborer, a porter or a factory hand. Nearly eight out of every ten non-white men with eight grades of schooling worked as laborers, service workers or operatives at the time of the last census. Among whites with the same amount of education, only five out of ten worked at these low-paid jobs.

The non white high school graduate stands a somewhat better chance of getting a well-paid job; but even his chances are not very good. About six out of every ten non white high school graduates were laborers, service workers, or operatives as compared with only three out of ten whites with the same amount of schooling.

1. Government statistics customarily distinguish between whites and non-whites rather than between whites and Negroes. Since Negroes constitute more than 90 per cent of non-whites, it is legitimate for most purposes to use the two terms interchangeably, as Miller does in his testimony before the Clark Committee.

Non white college graduates seem to be able to find professional employment in relatively large numbers. About three out of every four were professional or managerial workers – nearly the same proportion as white college graduates. But, there is one big difference. Non whites are concentrated in the lower-paid professions. . . .

Non white men earn less than whites with the same number of years of schooling for at least two reasons: (a) they are employed in lower paid jobs; and (b) they are paid less even when they do the same kind of work. The combined impact of these two factors is shown in . . . figures on the lifetime earnings of white and non white men by years of school completed. This table shows that the relative earnings gap between whites and non whites increases with educational attainment. The lifetime earnings of non white elementary school graduates is about 64 per cent of the white total. Among college graduates non whites have only 47 per cent of the white total. The fact of the matter is that the average non white with four years of college can expect to earn less over a lifetime than the white who did not go beyond the eighth grade (pp. 324–5).

Negroes have thus not improved their occupational status relative to whites since 1940, nor their income status since the end of the war. Moreover, in certain other key respects their position has been clearly deteriorating. We refer especially to unemployment and the degree of ghettoization.

Table 1 presents unemployment rates for whites and non-whites at intervals from 1940 to 1962. Here we see a dramatic worsening of the Negro situation. A breakdown of the global unemployment figures reveals certain characteristic disabilities to

Table 1 White and non-white unemployment, 1940–62
(Per cent of labor force)

	Total	White	Non-white	Non-white as per cent of white
1940	13·3	13·0	14·5	112
1950	4·6	4·1	7·9	176
1960	5·4	4·9	8·5	157
1962	5·6	4·9	11·0	225

Source: For 1940, 1950 and 1960, *US Census of Population* (1960) and for 1962, United States Senate (1963a, p. 43).

which Negroes are subject. Some of these were outlined in a statement prepared for the Clark Committee by Under-Secretary of Labor John F. Henning:

The unemployment rate for non whites as a whole is today over twice as high as for whites – in May [1963], 10·3 per cent compared with 5·0 per cent. Among married men with family responsibilities, the difference is even wider, 8 per cent compared with 3 per cent.

The Negro's disadvantage is especially severe when it comes to the better paying, more desirable type of jobs. . . . [A]mong laborers the non white unemployment rate is about one-third greater, and in the skilled occupations it is over twice as great.

Today's unemployment strikes hardest at younger workers. In May this year . . . the rate for non white teenage boys was nearly 25 per cent, but 17 per cent for white boys. For girls the difference was even wider – 33 per cent compared with 18 per cent.

The non white minorities suffer a disproportionate amount of the hard-core or long-term unemployment. Although they constitute only 11 per cent of the work force, they make up 25 per cent of all workers unemployed for six months or more (United States Senate, 1963a).

As to the increasing ghettoization of Negroes in cities all over the country, the evidence is conclusive. After exhaustive investigation, the Commission on Race and Housing reported:

'Segregation barriers in most cities were tighter in 1950 than ten years earlier. . . . The evidence indicates, on the whole, an increasing separation of racial groups as non whites accumulate in the central city areas abandoned by whites and the latter continually move to new suburban subdivisions from which minorities are barred (Commission on Race and Housing, 1958).

And a statistical study based on the Censuses of 1940, 1950 and 1960 by Karl E. and Alma F. Taeuber showed, in the words of a *New York Times* report, that 'with some notable exceptions, racial segregation, far from disappearing, is on the increase in the United States' (Handler 1964). [. . .]

On the basis of the data presented, which could of course be made much more comprehensive and detailed, the conclusion seems inescapable that since moving to the cities, Negroes have been prevented from improving their socio-economic position: they have not been able to follow earlier immigrant groups up the occupational ladder and out of the ghetto.

As always happens in social science, answering one question leads to another. What social forces and institutional mechanisms have forced Negroes to play the part of permanent immigrants, entering the urban economy at the bottom and remaining there decade after decade? (Commission on Race and Housing, 1958, pp. 8–9).

There are, it seems to us, three major sets of factors involved in the answer to this crucially important question. First, a formidable array of private interests benefit, in the most direct and immediate sense, from the continued existence of a segregated subproletariat. Second, the socio-psychological pressures generated by monopoly capitalist society intensify rather than alleviate existing racial prejudices, hence also discrimination and segregation. And third, as monopoly capitalism develops, the demand for unskilled and semi-skilled labor declines both relatively and absolutely, a trend which affects Negroes more than any other group and accentuates their economic and social inferiority. All of these factors mutually interact, tending to push Negroes ever further down in the social structure and locking them into the ghetto.

Consider first the private interests which benefit from the existence of a Negro subproletariat.

1. Employers benefit from divisions in the labor force which enable them to play one group off against another, thus weakening all. Historically, for example, no small amount of Negro migration was in direct response to the recruiting of strikebreakers.

2. Owners of ghetto real estate are able to overcrowd and overcharge.

3. Middle and upper income groups benefit from having at their disposal a large supply of cheap domestic labor.

4. Many small marginal businesses, especially in the service trades, can operate profitably only if cheap labor is available to them.

5. White workers benefit by being protected from Negro competition for the more desirable and higher paying jobs. Hence the customary distinction, especially in the South, between 'white' and 'Negro' jobs, the exclusion of Negroes from apprentice

programs, the refusal of many unions to admit Negroes, and so on.[2] In all these groups – and taken together they constitute a vast majority of the white population – what Marx called 'the most violent, mean, and malignant passions of the human breast, the Furies of private interest', are summoned into action to keep the Negro 'in his place'.

Race prejudice was originally deliberately created and cultivated as a rationalization and justification for the enslavement and exploitation of colored labor. But in time, race prejudice and the discriminatory behavior patterns which go with it came to serve other purposes as well. As capitalism developed, particularly in its monopoly phase, the social structure became more complex and differentiated. Within the basic class framework, which remained in essentials unchanged, there took place a proliferation of social strata and status groups, largely determined by occupation and income. These groupings, as the terms 'stratum' and 'status' imply, relate to each other as higher or lower, with the whole constituting an irregular and unstable hierarchy. In such a social structure, individuals tend to see and define themselves in terms of the 'status hierarchy' and to be motivated by ambitions to move up and fears of moving down.[3] These ambitions and fears are of course exaggerated, intensified, played upon by the corporate sales apparatus which finds in them the principal means of manipulating the 'utility functions' of the consuming public.

The net result of all this is that each status group has a deep-rooted psychological need to compensate for feelings of inferiority and envy toward those above by feelings of superiority and contempt for those below. It thus happens that a special pariah group at the bottom acts as a kind of lightning rod for the frustrations and hostilities of all the higher groups, the more so the nearer they are to the bottom. It may even be said that the very existence of the pariah group is a kind of harmonizer and

2. 'There has grown up a system of Negro jobs and white jobs. And this is the toughest problem facing the Negro southerner in employment.' Dunbar, Executive Director of the Southern Regional Council, in testimony before the Clark Committee (United States Senate, 1963b, p. 457).

3. The crucial importance of the status hierarchy in the shaping of the individual's consciousness goes far to explain the illusion, so widespread in the United States, that there are no classes in this country, or, as the same idea is often expressed, that everyone is a member of the middle class.

stabilizer of the social structure – so long as the pariahs play their role passively and resignedly. Such a society becomes in time so thoroughly saturated with race prejudice that it sinks below the level of consciousness and becomes a part of the 'human nature' of its members.[4] The gratification which whites derive from their socio-economic superiority to Negroes has its counterpart in alarm, anger and even panic at the prospect of Negroes' attaining equality. Status being a relative matter, whites inevitably interpret upward movement by Negroes as downward movement for themselves. This complex of attitudes, product of stratification and status consciousness in monopoly capitalist society, provides an important part of the explanation why whites not only refuse to help Negroes to rise but bitterly resist their efforts to do so. (When we speak of whites and their prejudices and attitudes in this unqualified way, we naturally do not mean all whites. Ever since John Brown, and indeed long before John Brown, there have been whites who have freed themselves of the disease of racial prejudice, have fought along with Negro militants for an end to the rotten system of exploitation and inequality, and have looked forward to the creation of a society in which relations of solidarity and brotherhood will take the place of relations of superiority and inferiority. Moreover, we are confident that the number of such whites will steadily increase in the years ahead. But their number is not great today, and in a survey which aims only at depicting the broadest contours of the current social scene it would be wholly misleading to assign them a decisive role.)

The third set of factors adversely affecting the relative position of Negroes is connected with technological trends and their impact on the demand for different kinds and grades of labor. Appearing before a Congressional committee in 1955, the then Secretary of Labor, James P. Mitchell, testified that unskilled workers as a proportion of the labor force had declined from 36 per cent in 1910 to 20 per cent in 1950 (United States Senate,

4. At this level of development, race prejudice is far from being reachable by public opinion polls and similar devices of 'sociometrics' which remain close to the surface of individual and social phenomena. We have reason for believing that the eradication of race prejudice from whites will be, even in a rational society, a difficult and protracted process.

1955). A later Secretary of Labor, Willard Wirtz, told the Clark Committee in 1963 that the percentage of unskilled was down to 5 per cent by 1962 (United States Senate, 1963a, p. 57). Translated into absolute figures, this means that the number of unskilled workers declined slightly, from somewhat over to somewhat under thirteen million between 1910 and 1950, and then plummeted to fewer than four million only twelve years later. These figures throw a sharp light on the rapid deterioration of the Negro employment situation since the Second World War. What happened is that until roughly a decade and a half ago, with the number of unskilled jobs remaining stable, Negroes were able to hold their own in the total employment picture by replacing white workers who were moving up the occupational ladder. This explains why, as Table 1 shows, the Negro unemployment rate was only a little higher than the white rate at the end of the Great Depression. Since 1950, on the other hand, with unskilled jobs disappearing at a fantastic rate, Negroes not qualified for other kinds of work found themselves increasingly excluded from employment altogether. Hence the rise of the Negro unemployment rate to more than double the white rate by the early 1960s. Negroes, in other words, being the least qualified workers are disproportionately hard hit as unskilled jobs (and, to an increasing extent, semi-skilled jobs) are eliminated by mechanization, automation and cybernation. Since this technological revolution has not yet run its course – indeed many authorities think that it is still in its early stages – the job situation of Negroes is likely to go on deteriorating. To be sure, technological trends are not, as many believe, the *cause* of unemployment: that role is played by specific mechanisms of monopoly capitalism.[5] But within the framework of this society technological trends, because of their differential impact on job opportunities, can rightly be considered a cause, and undoubtedly the most important cause, of the relative growth of Negro unemployment.

5. Under socialism there is no reason why technological progress, no matter how rapid or of what kind, should be associated with unemployment. In a socialist society technological progress may make possible a continuous reduction in the number of years, weeks and hours worked, but it is inconceivable that this reduction should take the completely irrational form of capitalist unemployment.

P. A. Baran and P. M. Sweezy   285

All the forces we have been discussing – vested economic interests, socio-psychological needs, technological trends – are deeply rooted in monopoly capitalism and together are strong enough to account for the fact that Negroes have been unable to rise out of the lower depths of American society. Indeed so pervasive and powerful are these forces that the wonder is only that the position of Negroes has not drastically worsened. That it has not, that in absolute terms their real income and consuming power have risen more or less in step with the rest of the population's, can only be explained by the existence of counteracting forces.

One of these counteracting forces we have already commented upon: the shift out of Southern agriculture and into the urban economy. Some schooling was better than none; even a rat-infested tenement provided more shelter than a broken-down shack on Tobacco Road; being on the relief rolls of a big city meant more income, both money and real, than subsistence farming. And as the nation's per capita income rose, so also did that of the lowest income group, even that of unemployables on permanent relief. As we have seen, it has been this shift from countryside to city which has caused so many observers to believe in the reality of a large-scale Negro breakthrough in the last two decades. Actually, it was an aspect of a structural change in the economy rather than a change in the position of Negroes within the economy.

But in one particular area, that of government employment, Negroes have indeed scored a breakthrough, and this has un-questionably been the decisive factor in preventing a catastrophic decline in their position in the economy as a whole. Between 1940 and 1962, total government employment somewhat more than doubled, while non-white (as already noted, more than 90 per cent Negro) employment in government expanded nearly five times. As a result non-white employment grew from 5·6 per cent of the total to 12·1 per cent. Since non-whites constituted 11·5 per cent of the labor force at mid-1961, it is a safe inference that Negroes are now more than proportionately represented in government employment.[6]

6. If the data were available to compare income received from govern-ment employment by whites and non-whites, the picture would of course be much less favorable for Negroes since they are heavily concentrated in the

Two closely interrelated forces have been responsible for this relative improvement of the position of Negroes in government employment. The first, and beyond doubt the most important, has been the increasing scope and militancy of the Negro liberation movement itself. The second has been the need of the American oligarchy, bent on consolidating a global empire including people of all colors, to avoid as much as possible the stigma of racism. If American Negroes had passively accepted the continuation of their degraded position, history teaches us that the oligarchy would have made no concessions. But once seriously challenged by militant Negro struggle, it was forced by the logic of its domestic and international situation to make concessions, with the twin objectives of pacifying Negroes at home and projecting abroad an image of the United States as a liberal society seeking to overcome an evil inheritance from the past.

The oligarchy, acting through the federal government and in the North and West through state and local governments, has also made other concessions to the Negro struggle. The armed forces have been desegregated, and a large body of civil rights legislation forbidding discrimination in public accommodations, housing, education and employment, has been enacted. Apart from the desegregation of the armed forces, however, these concessions have had little effect. Critics often attribute this failure to bad faith: there was never any intention, it is said, to concede to Negroes any of the real substance of their demand for equality. This is a serious misreading of the situation. No doubt there are many white legislators and administrators to whom such strictures apply with full force, but this is not true of the top economic and political leadership of the oligarchy – the managers of the giant corporations and their partners at the highest governmental levels. These men are governed in their political attitudes and behavior not by personal prejudices but by their conception of class interests. And while they may at times be confused by their own ideology or mistake short-run for long-run interests, it

---

lower-paying categories. But here too there has been improvement. A study made by the Civil Service Commission showed that between June 1962 and June 1963 Negro employment in the federal government increased by 3 per cent and that 'the major percentage gains had been in the better-paying jobs' (*New York Times*, 4 March 1964).

seems clear that with respect to the race problem in the United States they have come, perhaps belatedly but none the less surely, to understand that the very existence of their system is at stake. Either a solution will be found which insures the loyalty, or at least the neutrality, of the Negro people, or else the world revolution will sooner or later acquire a ready-made and potentially powerful Trojan horse within the ramparts of monopoly capitalism's mightiest fortress. When men like Kennedy and Johnson and Warren champion such measures as the Civil Rights Act of 1964, it is clearly superficial to accuse them of perpetrating a cheap political maneuver. They know that they are in trouble, and they are looking for a way out.

Why then such meager results? The answer is simply that the oligarchy does not have the power to shape and control race relations any more than it has the power to plan the development of the economy. In matters which are within the administrative jurisdiction of government, policies can be effectively implemented. Thus it was possible to desegregate the armed forces and greatly to increase the number of Negroes in government employment. But when it comes to housing, education and private employment, all the deeply rooted economic and socio-psychological forces analysed above come into play. It was capitalism, with its enthronement of greed and privilege, which created the race problem and made of it the ugly thing it is today. It is the very same system which resists and thwarts every effort at a solution.

The fact that despite all political efforts, the relative economic and social position of Negroes has changed but little in recent years, and in some respects has deteriorated, makes it a matter of great urgency for the oligarchy to devise strategies which will divide and weaken the Negro protest movement and thus prevent it from developing its full revolutionary potential. These strategies can all be appropriately grouped under the heading of 'tokenism'.

If we are to understand the real nature of tokenism, it is necessary to keep in mind certain developments within the Negro community since the great migration from the Southern countryside got under way. As Negroes moved out of a largely subsistence economy into a money economy and as their average levels of income and education rose, their expenditures for goods and services naturally increased correspondingly. Goods were for the most part supplied by established white business; but segregation, *de jure* in the South and *de facto* in the North, gave rise to a rapidly expanding demand for certain kinds of services which whites would not or could not provide or which Negroes could provide better. Chief among these were the services of teachers, ministers, doctors, dentists, lawyers, barbers and beauty parlors, undertakers, certain kinds of insurance, and a press catering to the special needs of the segregated Negro community. Professionals and owners of enterprises supplying these services form the core of what Franklin Frazier called the black bourgeoisie (1957). Their ranks have been augmented by the growth of Negro employment in the middle and higher levels of the civil service and by the rapid expansion of the number of Negroes in the sports and entertainment worlds. The growth of the black bourgeoisie has been particularly marked since the Second World War. Between 1950 and 1960 the proportion of non-white families with incomes over $10,000 (1959 dollars) increased from 1 per cent to 4·7 per cent, a rate of growth close to three times that among whites. During the same years, the total distribution of income among Negro families became more unequal, while the change among white families was in the opposite direction (Miller, 1963).

The theory behind tokenism, not often expressed but clearly deducible from the practice, is that the black bourgeoisie is the decisive element in the Negro community. It contains the intellectual and political élite, the people with education and leadership ability and experience. It already has a material stake in the existing social order, but its loyalty is doubtful because of the special disabilities imposed upon it solely because of its color. If this loyalty can be made secure, the potential revolutionizing of the Negro protest movement can be forestalled and the world can be given palpable evidence – through the placing of loyal Negroes in prominent positions – that the United States does not pursue a South African-type policy of *apartheid* but on the contrary fights against it and strives for equal opportunity for its Negro citizens. The problem is thus how to secure the loyalty of the black bourgeoisie.

To this end the political drive to assure legal equality for

Negroes must be continued. We know that legal equality does not guarantee real equality: the right to patronize the best hotels and restaurants, for example, means little to the Negro masses. But it is of great importance to the well to do Negro, and the continuation of any kind of disability based solely on color is hateful to all Negroes. The loyalty of the black bourgeoisie can never be guaranteed as long as vestiges of the Jim Crow system persist. For this reason we can confidently predict that, however long and bloody the struggle may be, the South will eventually be made over in the image of the North.

Second, the black bourgeoisie must be provided with greater access to the dominant institutions of the society: corporations, the policy-making levels of government, the universities, the suburbs. Here the oligarchy is showing itself to be alert and adaptable. A *New York Times* survey found that:

Business and industry here, in the face of the civil rights revolution, have been reassessing their employment policies and hiring Negroes for office and other salaried posts that they rarely held before.

Many national concerns with headquarters in New York City have announced new non-discrimination policies or reaffirmed old ones. Personnel officers are taking a new look at their recruiting methods and seeking advice from Negro leaders on how to find and attract the best qualified Negroes.

On a nationwide basis, about eighty of the country's largest companies enrolled under Plans for Progress of the President's Committee on Equal Opportunity have reported substantial increases in the hiring of Negroes for salaried positions. . . .

The latest figures for the eighty companies that filed reports in the last year . . . showed that non-whites got 2241 of the 31,698 salaried jobs that opened up. This represented an increase of 8·9 per cent in the number of jobs held by non-whites in those companies (12 November 1963).

The same thing has been happening in government, as already noted; and in addition to being hired in larger numbers in the better-paying grades, Negroes are increasingly being placed in executive jobs at or near the cabinet level, in federal judgeships and the like. And as Negroes are brought into the economic and political power structure, they also become more acceptable in the middle- and upper-class suburbs – provided of course that their incomes and standard of living are comparable to their neighbors'.

Not many Negroes are affected by these easings of the barriers separating the races at the upper economic and social levels – in fact, it is of the essence of tokenism that not many should be. But this does not deprive the phenomenon of its importance. The mere existence of the possibility of moving up and out can have a profound psychological impact.

Third, the strategy of tokenism requires not only that Negro leadership should come from the black bourgeoisie but that it should be kept dependent on favors and financial support from the white oligarchy. The established civil rights organizations – the National Association for the Advancement of Colored People, the Urban League and the Congress of Racial Equality – were all founded on a biracial basis and get most of their funds from white sources; they therefore present no potential threat. But it is always necessary to pay attention to the emergence of new and potentially independent leaders. Where this occurs, there are two standard tactics for dealing with the newcomers. The first is to coopt them into the service of the oligarchy by flattery, jobs or other material favors. Noel Day, a young Boston Negro leader who ran for Congress in the 1964 election, comments on this tactic:

Although the system is rotten it is nevertheless marvellously complex in the same way as the chambered Nautilus, beautiful in its complexity. The coopting begins at birth; the potential for cooptation is built into the system. It is part of what we are taught is good. We have been taught to feel that the couple of thousand dollars a year more is what is desirable. The Negro and most other minority groups have been taught to desire entrance into the mainstream, they have not been taught to look to themselves and develop any sense of pride or prestige within their group, they have been taught to aspire to become mainstream Americans. In the case of the Negro, to aspire to become white. . . . One way of becoming white is by having a higher salary, or a title or a prestige position. This is not a very simple thing, but it is one of the evil beauties of the system. It has so many built-in checks and controls that come into operation – some of these are vitiating the energy of the freedom movement already. The official rhetoric has changed – in response to the dislocations and pressures we are witnessing an attempt at mass cooptation similar to the mass cooptation of the labor movement. The reaction of American business, for instance, is fantastic. The integration programs of some of the major companies are quick and adept – the fact that the First National Bank of Boston two months ago had about fifty Negro employees and now has over a thousand. Under pressure by CORE, they gave in to CORE's demands within *two weeks. Two months later* one of their top personnel men came into my office and said – now we are really concerned about developing a program for drop outs. What he was saying is that they are so adaptable, so flexible, in maintaining the balance of American business, in substituting reform as an antidote to revolution, that they will even go beyond the demands of the civil rights movement (1964, pp. 44–5).

If cooptation fails, the standard tactic is to attempt to destroy the potentially independent leader by branding him a Communist, a subversive, a trouble-maker and by subjecting him to economic and legal harassments.

The reference in Noel Day's statement to developing a program for drop outs points to a fourth aspect of tokenism: to open up greater opportunities for Negro youths of all classes who because of luck, hard work or special aptitudes are able to overcome the handicap of their background and start moving up the educational ladder. For a 'qualified' Negro in the United States today, there is seemingly no limit to what he may aspire to. A report in the *New York Times* states:

Dr Robert F. Goheen, President of Princeton University, said yesterday that the competition among colleges and universities for able Negro students was 'much more intense' than the traditional competition for football players. . . . Dr Goheen said: 'It certainly is very clear that the number of able colored who have also had adequate educational opportunities is very small. And we find we are all extending our hands to the same relatively few young men and women' (21 October 1963).

Here we can see as under a magnifying glass the mechanics of tokenism. With the country's leading institutions of higher learning falling over themselves to recruit qualified Negro students – and with giant corporations and the federal government both eager to snap them up after graduation – the prospects opened up to the lucky ones are indeed dazzling. But as President Goheen stresses, their number is very small, and it can only remain very small as long as the vast majority of Negroes stay anchored at the bottom of the economic ladder.

The fact that the great mass of Negroes derive no benefits from tokenism does not mean that they are unaffected by it. One of its purposes, and to the extent that it succeeds one of its consequences, is to detach the ablest young men and women from their own people and thus to deprive the liberation movement of its best leadership material. And even those who have no stake in the system and no hope of ever acquiring one may become reconciled to it if they come to believe there is a chance that their children, or perhaps even their children's children, may be able to rise out of their own degraded condition.

It would be a great mistake to underestimate the skill and tenacity of the United States oligarchy when faced with what it regards – and in the case of race relations, rightly regards – as a threat to its existence. And it would be just as serious a mistake to underestimate the effectiveness, actual and potential, of the strategy of tokenism. Yet we believe that in the long run the real condition of the Negro masses will be the decisive factor. If some improvement, however modest and slow, can be registered in the years ahead, a well conceived policy of tokenism may be enough to keep Negroes from developing into monopoly capitalism's 'enemy within the gates'. But if the trends of the recent past continue, if advances are cancelled out by setbacks, if the paradox of widespread poverty and degradation in the midst of potential abundance becomes ever more glaring, then it will be only a matter of time until American Negroes, propelled by the needs of their own humanity and inspired by the struggles and achievements of their brothers in the underdeveloped countries, will generate their own revolutionary self-consciousness.

If this assessment of the situation is correct, it becomes a matter of great importance to know whether the kinds of reforms which are possible within the framework of the existing system – the kinds advocated by the established civil rights organizations and their white supporters – are likely to yield any real benefits to the Negro masses.

It seems clear to us that the answer is negative; that the chief beneficiaries of reforms of this type are the black bourgeoisie; and that, regardless of the intentions of their sponsors, their objective effect is merely to supplement the policy of tokenism. [. . .]

There is really no mystery about why reforms which remain within the confines of the system hold out no prospect of meaningful improvement to the Negro masses. The system has two poles: wealth, privilege, power at one; poverty, deprivation, powerlessness at the other. It has always been that way, but in earlier times whole groups could rise because expansion made room above and there were others ready to take their place at the bottom. Today, Negroes are at the bottom, and there is neither room above nor anyone ready to take their place. Thus only individuals can move up, not the group as such: reforms help the few, not the many. For the many nothing short of a complete change in the system – the abolition of both poles and the substitution of a society in which wealth and power are shared by all – can transform their condition.

References

COMMISSION ON RACE AND HOUSING (1958), *Where Shall We Live?*, Berkeley.

DAY, N. (1964), *Studies on the Left*, Symposium: New Politics.

FRAZIER, E. F. (1957), *Black Bourgeoisie: The Rise of a New Middle Class in the United States*, Collier-Macmillan.

HANDLER, M. S. (1964), 'Segregation rise in United States reported', *New York Times*, 26 November.

MILLER, H. P. (1963), *Trends in the Income of Families and Persons in the United States 1947 to 1960*, Bureau of the Census Technical Paper, no. 8.

US Census of Population (1960), United States Summary: General and Social Characteristics, Washington.

UNITED STATES SENATE (1955), *Automation and Technological Change*, Hearings before the Subcommittee on Economic Stabilization of the Joint Committee on the Economic Report, 84th Congress, 1st Session, pursuant to Section 5 (a) of P.L. 304, 79th Congress, October 14, 15, 17, 18, 24, 25, 26, 27, 28.

UNITED STATES SENATE (1963a), *Nation's Manpower Revolution*, Hearings before the subcommittee on Employment and Manpower of the Committee on Labor and Public Welfare, 88th Congress, 1st session, relating to the training and utilization of the manpower resources of the nation, Pt 1. May 20, 21, 22, 25; Pt 2, June 4, 5, 6, 7.

UNITED STATES SENATE (1963b), *Equal Employment Opportunity*, Hearings before the subcommittee on Employment and Manpower of the Committee on Labor and Public Welfare, 88th Congress, 1st session, July 24, 25, 26, 29, 31, August 2, 20.

Part Seven
Unequal Partners: International Economic Relations

The problem of unequal starting points and unequal distribution of economic and general power has always been prominent in international relations. In spite of this, colonialism and imperialism have obtained surprisingly little attention in economic theory in general, and in international trade theory in particular, though some writers have dealt extensively with these problems.

The uneven power of nations means that weaker and under-developed countries have to submit to conditions and institutions which are mainly designed to serve the interests of important economic groups in the developed country. In many cases these conditions, which hampered the economic development of the colonial areas, were introduced quite deliberately and with all the force of government action. The vicious circle that leads from unequal strength to colonial policy which in turn petrifies and widens the economic discrepancies is well described in Baran's contribution.

But even where direct colonial domination has ceased and deliberate policies of exploitation are less prominent, we still face the problem of power and its uneven distribution. In international economic relations the powerful groups will quite naturally plan institutions which serve their own needs and these institutions will appear to them as 'fair' and 'appropriate'. For, as the well-known political scientist K. W. Deutsch once aptly remarked, 'power is the ability to talk instead of listen. In a sense, it is the ability to afford not to learn.'

Uneven power thus attaches a bias to institutions and regulations. Its effects are particularly important in the relations between developed and underdeveloped countries. Some of them are discussed – for the case of post-war Africa – in the article by Balogh.

Finally, in the Reading by Adler-Karlsson the measures adopted against Cuba after her revolution are presented as an example of using economic policy as a direct weapon in the international politico-economic power struggle.

16 P. A. Baran

Colonialism and Backwardness

Excerpts from P. A. Baran, *The Political Economy of Growth*, Monthly Review Press, 1957, chapter 6, pp. 173–200.

[. . .]

Industrial expansion under capitalism depends largely on its gathering its own momentum. 'Capital rapidly creates for itself an internal market by destroying all rural handicrafts, that is by spinning, weaving, making clothes etc. for all, in fine by transforming into exchange values commodities that were theretofore produced as direct use values – a process that results spontaneously from the severance of the worker (albeit a serf) from land and ownership of his means of production' (Rohentwurf 1953, p. 411).

Not that this dissolution of the pre-capitalist economy, the disintegration of its natural self-sufficiency, has not taken place in most of the now underdeveloped countries. On the contrary in all areas of Western penetration, commercial agriculture to a considerable extent displaced traditional subsistence farming, and manufactured commodities invaded the market of the indigenous craftsman and artisan. Yet although, as Allyn Young put it, 'division of labor depends in large part upon the division of labor' (1928), in the now backward areas this sequence did not unfold 'according to plan'. It took a different course: such division of labor as was bred by the initial division of labor resembled the apportionment of functions between a rider and his horse. Whatever market for manufactured goods emerged in the colonial and dependent countries did not become the 'internal market' of these countries. Thrown wide open by colonization and by unequal treaties, it became an appendage of the 'internal market' of Western capitalism.

While significantly stimulating industrial growth in the West, this turn of events extinguished the igniting spark without which there could be no industrial expansion in the now underdeveloped countries. At a historical juncture when protection of infant industry might have been prescribed even by the sternest protagonist of free trade, the countries most in need of such protection were forced to go through a regime of what might be called industrial infanticide which influenced all of their subsequent development. With their limited demand for manufactured goods amply (and cheaply) supplied from abroad, there was no opportunity for profitable investment in a native industry that would cater to the available domestic market. In the absence of such investment there was, furthermore, no occasion for further investment. For investment is called forth by investment: one investment act gives rise to another, and the second investment act provides the rationale for the third. In fact, it is this clustering of investments, their synchronization, that sets off the chain reaction which is synonymous with the evolution of industrial capitalism. But just as investment tends to become self-propelling, so lack of investment tends to become self-perpetuating.

Without the widening impact of investment, the originally narrow market remained of necessity narrow.[1] Under such circumstances there could be no spreading of small industrial shops that marked elsewhere the transition from the merchant phase of capitalism to its industrial phase. When in the course of time the possibility arose of undertaking some industrial production, whether because of the procurability of the necessary tariffs or of other government concessions, such enterprise was sometimes founded by foreigners (usually in conjunction with domestic interests) who brought to bear their experience and 'know-how' upon the organization of the new venture. Setting out to supply commodities similar in quality and design to those previously brought in from abroad, they erected single large-scale modern plants which were sufficient to meet the existing demand. Although the total amount of capital needed for such a venture was frequently large, the part of it spent in the underdeveloped country was small, with the bulk of the outlays involved taking place abroad on the acquisition of foreign-made machinery, of foreign patents, and the like. The stimulating effect on the eco-

1. This was discovered to their sorrow also by Western capitalists who had anticipated no limits to their ability to export manufactured goods to the thickly populated areas of Western commercial penetration.

nomy as a whole resulting from such investment was accordingly slight. What is more, once an undertaking of that scope had taken place in an industry, both the limitations of demand and the magnitude of the required investment reduced greatly or eliminated the chances of another enterprise being launched in the same field. The amount of capital required to break into the monopoly's privileged sanctuary, the risks attendant upon the inevitable struggle, the leverages that the established concern could use to harass and to exclude an intruder – all tended to decimate the inducement for merchant capital to shift to industrial pursuits. The narrow market became monopolistically controlled, and the monopolistic control became an additional factor preventing the widening of the market.

This is not to say that such industrial development as has taken place in the backward countries did not represent a tremendous advance from the situation in which their industrial markets were entirely controlled by supplies from abroad. These had ruined native handicrafts, and smothered what little industrial development there was in the affected countries without offering the displaced artisans and craftsmen any alternative employment in industry. The corresponding industrial expansion took place in the West. To this the newly founded industrial enterprises represented, as it were, an antidote. They repatriated at least some of the manufacturing part of the original division of labor, undertook at least some industrial investment at home, provided at least some employment and income to native labor. Yet this antidote was inadequate. It not only did not suffice to offset the damage that had been done earlier; the way in which it was administered was such as to give rise to a cancerous growth no less powerful and no less harmful than the evil which in the beginning it partially cured.

The new firms, rapidly attaining exclusive control over their markets and fencing them in by protective tariffs and/or government concessions of all kinds, blocked further industrial growth while their monopolistic price and output policies minimized the expansion of their own enterprises. Completing swiftly the entire journey from a progressive to a regressive role in the economic system, they became at an early stage barriers to economic development rather similar in their effect to the semi-feudal andownership prevailing in underdeveloped countries. Not only not promoting further division of labor and growth of productivity, they actually cause a movement in the opposite direction. Monopolistic industry on one hand extends the merchant phase of capitalism by obstructing the transition of capital and men from the sphere of circulation to the sphere of industrial production. On the other hand, providing neither a market for agricultural produce nor outlets for agricultural surplus labor and not supplying agriculture with cheap manufactured consumer goods and implements, it forces agriculture back towards self-sufficiency, perpetuates the idleness of the structurally unemployed, and fosters further mushrooming of petty traders, cottage industries and the like.

Thus in most underdeveloped countries capitalism had a peculiarly twisted career. Having lived through all the pains and frustrations of childhood, it never experienced the vigor and exuberance of youth, and began displaying at an early age all the grievous features of senility and decadence. To the dead weight of stagnation characteristic of pre-industrial society was added the entire restrictive impact of monopoly capitalism. The economic surplus appropriated in lavish amounts by monopolistic concerns in backward countries is not employed for productive purposes. It is neither plowed back into their own enterprises, nor does it serve to develop others. To the extent that it is not taken abroad by their foreign stockholders, it is used in a manner very much resembling that of the landed aristocracy. It supports luxurious living by its recipients, is spent on construction of urban and rural residences, on servants, excess consumption and the like. The remainder is invested in the acquisition of rent-bearing land, in financing mercantile activities of all kinds, in usury and speculation. Last but not least, significant sums are removed abroad where they are held as hedges against the depreciation of the domestic currency or as nest eggs assuring their owners of suitable retreats in the case of social and political upheavals at home.

This brings us to the role of foreign enterprise in the underdeveloped country's economic system. The totally or partially foreign-owned establishments catering to the *internal* market of the underdeveloped country present no special problem. While some of the economic surplus that they appropriate is spent locally, as on the maintenance of highly paid executives, most of it (including the personal savings of these executives) is transferred abroad. It thus adds to an even lesser extent to capital formation in the underdeveloped countries than what accrues to the domestically owned firms.

More complex – but also more important – is the role played by foreign concerns in an underdeveloped country producing commodities for export. These not only account for the bulk of foreign interests in backward areas, and embody large investments of capital, but are also responsible for a major share of the host countries' and the world's total output of the products in question. To get some notion of their impact on economic development of the underdeveloped countries in which they are located, it will be useful to consider separately the different aspects of their activities: (a) the significance of the *investment* undertaken by the foreign enterprise; (b) the *direct* effect of its *current* operations; and (c) its more *general* influence on the underdeveloped country as a whole.

Beginning with the first, it should be noted that the foreign concerns embarking upon the production of exportable staples (with the exception of oil) have, as a rule, started their activities with relatively little investment of capital. For the control over the necessary natural resources – primarily land for plantations or for mining – was secured either by forcible expropriation of the native populations or by acquiring it at a more or less nominal price from the rulers, feudal lords or tribal chiefs dominating the respective areas. Thus the accrual of capital to the underdeveloped countries that resulted from the initiation of foreign exploitation of their natural resources was negligible. Even later on, when the scope of export-oriented business in the underdeveloped countries markedly increased, the amount of capital actually transferred to them from the advanced countries has been much smaller than commonly supposed. Such expansion as businesses producing for exports were interested in undertaking could be easily financed by the profits derived from their highly remunerative operations. Speaking of the British experience, Sir Arthur Salter observes that 'it was only in an earlier period, which terminated soon after 1870, that the resources for foreign investment came from an excess of current exports over imports. In the whole period from 1870–1913, when total foreign investment increased from about £1000 million to nearly £4000 million the total new investments made were only about 40 per cent of the income from past investments during the same period' (1951, p. 11). The somewhat similar growth of Dutch, French and (later on) American holdings abroad followed substantially the same pattern: it was largely attributable to the plowing back of profits earned by operations in foreign countries.[2] Thus the increase of Western assets in the underdeveloped world is only partly due to capital exports in the strict sense of the term; it is primarily the result of the reinvestment abroad of some of the economic surplus secured abroad.[3] [. . .]

With the benefits to the underdeveloped countries resulting from the investment associated with the establishment or expansion of foreign export-oriented enterprise thus not amounting to much, we may inquire now into the effects of its *current* operations. These consist of producing agricultural commodities or materials such as minerals and oil and shipping them abroad. It is important for us to trace the mode of utilization of the resources thus obtained. We may start with that part of them that is used for remuneration of labor. Determined everywhere by native labor's abysmally low rates of pay, and reflecting in some lines of production a high degree of mechanization with a correspondingly small size of labor force employed, the part of the companies' total revenue that is absorbed by wages is generally small. In Venezuela, petroleum accounts for over 90 per cent of all exports (and for a large part of total national product), but the oil industry employs only some 2 per cent of Venezuela's labor force (Nurkse, 1953, p. 23), and its local-currency expenditures (exclusive of government payments) do not exceed 20 per cent of the

2. With reference to postwar American investments abroad, a recent authoritative government publication states that 'much of these consisted of reinvested foreign branch earnings, rather than new capital raised in the United States' Gray Report (1950, p. 61). And as late as 1954, United States private investments abroad 'increased by nearly $3 billion while the earnings on earlier investments amounted to approximately $2·8 billion' Pizer and Cutler (1955).

3. See also Schiff (1942).

value of exports;[4] some seven-eighths of these expenditures have gone to meet the wages and salaries bill, with the remainder being used for purchases within the country. In Chile 'before the First World War about 8 per cent of the active population was engaged in the mines or associated processing plants, but this proportion has fallen fairly steadily' (United Nations, 1953, p. 39). According to an unpublished study of the International Monetary Fund, the proportion of the value of the industry's total product locally spent is also approximately 20 per cent; the parts of labor and material costs respectively cannot be determined. In Bolivia about 5 per cent of the workers are employed in the tin mines; it has been estimated that during the last half of the 1940s about 25 per cent of total receipts were required to meet wage payments, but this is undoubtedly high, because the low official rate of exchange was used to compare dollar sales figures with Bolivian wage figures (Pollner, 1952). In the Middle East all of 0·34 per cent of the population are engaged in the oil industry (United Nations, 1951, p. 63), while less than 5 per cent of the oil revenues are paid out as wages. In some countries with very small populations and large raw materials developments the proportion of people employed in connection with them is of course larger (for example about 10 per cent in the Northern Rhodesian copper mines), but these cases are exceptional. Even there, moreover, the share of total receipts of the industries that is paid out in wages is approximately the same as in other instances just mentioned.

It would be a mistake, however, to believe that this small part of the total revenue secured through raw materials exploitation serves in its entirety to widen the underdeveloped country's internal market. In the first place some of the labor involved consists of foreigners who fill managerial and semi-managerial positions and whose pay is accordingly high. Although they maintain a high standard of living, they are in a position to set aside sizable shares of their incomes. In fact, one of the main attractions of their jobs is the possibility of accumulating considerable savings in a relatively short time. Needless to say, these

4. Banco Central de Venezuela, *Memoria* (1950), p. 36, quoted in Rollins (1956). I am greatly indebted to Dr Rollins for placing at my disposal the manuscript of this excellent paper from which I have drawn a number of additional references.

savings are either currently sent out of the country or are taken back home eventually when their owners leave their posts.[5] Nor are the amounts which they use for consumption purposes entirely spent on local output. While the housekeeping of foreigners in underdeveloped countries typically involves the employment of numerous native servants, and while obviously many consumer goods are obtained from local sources, a large portion of their spending is directed towards accustomed articles that are supplied from abroad. Thus the total amount that foreign wage receivers spend on locally produced goods and services and that forms an increase of the underdeveloped countries' aggregate demand is normally very small.

In the case of native labor the situation is somewhat different. Doing work requiring little skill, they earn wages that are extremely low, frequently barely sufficient to provide for a narrowly defined subsistence minimum. But even where their pay is higher, allowing for a somewhat better standard of living, it hardly leaves room for saving. Thus the wages received by the native workers can be counted on to be spent on consumption. Yet a certain part of what they purchase is supplied by the employing company itself: in particular, housing. What is more, many workers' camps are so located that it is found to be easier and cheaper to import many of the consumer goods that they buy rather than to procure them from the frequently distant local sources.[6]

In sum, the income derived by the inhabitants of the so-called source countries from the activities of the export-oriented foreign enterprises, consisting primarily of wage payments to a relatively small number of wage earners, is everywhere very small. Since variations in the world demand for the commodities in question

5. The infrequent cases of individuals becoming enamored with the countries in which they are employed and deciding to get 'economically naturalized' can be safely disregarded.

6. This is very noticeable in the case of the Bolivian tin companies; 'for many years the companies maintained stores which were largely stocked from abroad. . .' Rollins (1956). Needless to say, the reason for this is in many cases not so much the lower price of imported goods but the usual motivation underlying the so-called truck system. In the case of the export-oriented firms, the cheapness of shipping *from* the West is an important factor encouraging the importation of goods to be sold in company stores.

affects in the main their price rather than the volume of their output – for technical and economic reasons that need not detain us here – the level of native employment tends to vary but little. And since their wages are also rather sticky, their aggregate receipts *in absolute terms* are on the whole quite stable. They obviously represent a changing *share* of the total value of output depending on the prices at which it is sold. Yet taking good years together with the bad, it would seem that the proportion is somewhere around 15 per cent, with the percentage being as low as 5 in some areas and some years and as high as 25 in others. While even such an addition is undoubtedly most valuable to the poverty-stricken populations of the underdeveloped countries, in appraising its significance to economic development the nature of its recipients should be clearly realized. Accruing for the most part to low-paid workers, it is directed towards acquisition of most elementary wage goods that are produced in agriculture, by local craftsmen, or imported, and therefore cannot possibly form a market encouraging the development of industrial enterprise.[7]

The balance of the aggregate proceeds from the sale of the output of foreign export-oriented enterprise may be grouped under two headings. Its bulk is accounted for by the companies' gross profits (after taxes and royalties) which include depreciation and depletion charges; the remainder consists of payments of taxes, royalties and the like, to the government of the countries in which production takes place. We shall come to the latter presently. As far as the former are concerned, their mode of utilization is subject to considerable variations. As we have seen earlier, for the most part they have been reinvested abroad. This is, however, a statistical balance referring only to global aggregates and to long periods. For individual countries and particular time stretches, the fluctuations of both profit withdrawals and foreign investments have been quite divergent and quite violent. While at times in some countries withdrawals have exceeded investments, at other times and in other places it has been the other way round. While some firms took home all or most of their profits, others engaged in additional foreign investment. World-wide business organizations have frequently transferred their profits from the

7. It gives rise to mercantile profits; these, however, are not what is lacking in underdeveloped countries.

country or countries in which they originated to areas where investment opportunities were superior. Nor can it be said that there has been any community of fate of the underdeveloped countries taken together, and that the profits generated in one underdeveloped country, if not plowed back there, are invested in another underdeveloped country. The opposite has actually been the case: profits derived from operations in underdeveloped countries have gone to a large extent to finance investment in highly developed parts of the world. Thus while there have been vast differences among underdeveloped countries with regard to the amounts of profits plowed back in their economies or withdrawn by foreign investors, the underdeveloped world as a whole has continually shipped a large part of its economic surplus to more advanced countries on account of interest and dividends.[8]

The worst of it is, however, that it is very hard to say what has been the greater evil as far as the economic development of underdeveloped countries is concerned: the removal of their economic surplus by foreign capital or its reinvestment by foreign enterprise. That such has been actually the somber dilemma stems not merely from the pronounced paucity of the direct benefits derived by the underdeveloped countries from foreign investment; it is even more clearly realized if the overall impact of foreign enterprise on the development of underdeveloped countries is given some consideration. [. . .]

It is undoubtedly correct that if the natural resources of the underdeveloped countries were not exploited, there would be no output to provide for the transfers of profits abroad. But it is by no means to be taken for granted that the now underdeveloped countries, given an independent development, would not at some point have initiated the utilization of their natural resources on their own and on terms more advantageous than those received from foreign investors. This could be dismissed if foreign investment and the course taken by the development of the underdeveloped countries were independent of each other. However, as the case of Japan convincingly demonstrates, such independence cannot possibly be assumed. In fact, to assume it amounts to begging the entire issue and prejudging it from the very outset.

8. See Viner in Hoselitz (1952, p. 182).

But there is still another aspect to the problem. With regard to some agricultural products, it might be thought that since they consist of recurring crops, and since an outlet for them can be found only in exports, their production and shipment abroad constitute no sacrifice whatever to the source countries. This is a grievous, albeit commonly accepted, fallacy. Quite apart from the fact that export-oriented corporations have traditionally engaged in the most predatory exploitation of the plantation land under their control, the establishment and expansion of these plantations have brought about the systematic pauperization, indeed in many instances the physical annihilation, of large parts of the native population. The cases are legion, and citing a few will have to suffice: 'The one-crop culture of cane sugar in the Brazilian north-east is a good example. The area once had one of the few really fertile tropical soils. It had a climate favorable to agriculture, and it was originally covered with a forest growth extremely rich in fruit trees. Today, the all-absorbing, self-destructive sugar industry has stripped all the available land and covered it completely with sugar cane; as a result this is one of the starvation areas of the continent. The failure to grow fruits, greens and vegetables, or to raise cattle in the region, has created an extremely difficult food problem in an area where diversified farming could produce an infinite variety of foods.'[9] In most of Latin America, what 'helped in definitively ruining the native populations was the one-track exploitation to which almost every region was dedicated: some were given over to mining, others to coffee planting, some to tobacco and others to cacao. This specialization brought on the deformed economy which is still found in such countries as Salvador, which produces practically nothing but coffee, and Honduras, which exports nothing but bananas.' In Egypt 'a large part of the irrigated land was reserved to produce cash export crops . . . particularly cotton and sugar – which further aggravated the nutritional poverty of the fellah.' In Africa 'the first European innovation which worked to upset

9. De Castro (1952, p. 97). The three following passages quoted in the text are from pages 105, 215, and 221 of this outstanding work. Professor de Castro notes, incidentally, that while soil erosion and exhaustion are a plague of the entire colonial world, experts 'go so far as to assert that, for all practical purposes, there is no such thing as erosion in Japan' (p. 192).

native food customs was the large-scale production of cash crops for exports, such as cacao, coffee, sugar and peanuts. We already know how the plantation system works . . . a good example is that of the British colony of Gambia in West Africa, where the culture of food crops for local consumption has been completely abandoned in order to concentrate on the production of peanuts. As a result of this monoculture . . . the nutritional situation of the colony could hardly be worse.' In what has represented for a long time the internal colony of American capitalism – the Southern states – very similar effects were produced by sugar, and in particular by cotton. 'In the United States, the cotton-growing states make up the nation's lowest income group. The statistical correlation between cotton growing and poverty is startling. Cotton culture has two harmful effects on the soil: (a) depletion of soil fertility . . . (b) the damage done by erosion. . . . All this is realized clearly now, but it was not understood and appreciated in the nineteenth century – the century that measured success in dollars and cents at the expense of lasting assets.'[10]

To avoid misunderstanding, the above is not to be taken as arguing against division of labor, intranational and international specialization, and the resulting increase of productivity. What it clearly demonstrates, however, is that an intranational and international specialization that is so organized that one participant of the team specializes in starvation while the other assumes the white man's burden of collecting the profits can hardly be considered a satisfactory arrangement for attainment of the greatest happiness for the greatest number.

Nor is the 'no sacrifice' proposition much stronger where the output of the export-oriented foreign enterprise is made up not of recurring agricultural crops but of products of extractive industries: minerals, oil and the like. Although in this case the displacement of the native population and the destruction of their traditional bases of existence may have assumed somewhat lesser proportions than in connection with plantation agriculture – it has been not by any means negligible – the long-run effect of this

10. Zimmerman (1951, p. 326). Needless to say, the author discriminates unfairly against the nineteenth century. In the capitalist world of the twentieth, success is still measured by the same yardstick, the difference being only that large-scale enterprise thinks more about its longer-run returns.

type of raw materials exploitation may be no less telling. Indeed, there is no reason to consider the raw materials resources of underdeveloped countries as a free good available in infinite supply. Even if the exhaustion of raw materials for the world as a whole is a bogy that can safely be disregarded, as far as individual countries and specific materials are concerned, the danger is far from minor. Thus to a number of underdeveloped countries what little they receive at the present time for the raw materials with which they are endowed may well turn out to be the mess of potage for which they are forced to sell their birthright to a better future. [. . .]

This brings us to the question concerning foreign export-oriented enterprises' *indirect* effect on the economic development of underdeveloped countries. In a number of areas the establishment and operation of foreign enterprise has necessitated investment in installations not forming an integral part of, but entirely indispensable to, the production and exportation of raw materials. Such facilities are railways and harbors, roads and airports, telephone and telegraph, canals and power stations. Generally speaking, those are good things for any underdeveloped country to get. Even if their construction per se does not contribute much to the widening of the backward areas' internal markets – since most of the investment related to it is apt to be 'investment in kind' consisting of imported equipment – still the projects, once completed, are usually considered to have a beneficial effect by increasing the possibilities for local investment. This effect is referred to as 'external economies' which arise whenever the operation of one enterprise facilitates (cheapens) the establishment or the conduct of another. Thus the construction of a power plant for the purposes of one manufacturing or mining unit may save another manufacturing or mining unit the expense of building a power plant of its own, thus supplying it with cheaper energy than it could otherwise obtain. Similarly the setting up of a sawmill for the requirements of one factory may cheapen the building of another factory in the same area.

It is important to distinguish the amelioration of conditions for economic expansion coming about in this way from what might be called the 'investment-snowball-effect' – the process previously referred to in which investment in one enterprise becomes possible in view of the widening of the market caused by investment in other enterprises. This distinction must be stressed because it tends to be blurred in most writings on economic development, with the resulting confusion leading to serious errors. For while the investment-snowball-effect is nearly synonymous with economic development and necessarily implies the appearance of 'external economies', the emergence of facilities that *could* give rise to external economies need not by any means result in increased investment and in general economic growth.

What this means is that the part that can be played by external economies in promoting investment is the same as the role that can be played in it by the cheapening of any cost factor, for instance, by the lowering of the rate of interest. And just as it has been recognized to be a mistake to expect that on a given level of income and effective demand a mere lowering of the rate of interest will result in an increase of investment, so it is a fallacy to believe that the sheer presence of potential sources of external economies is bound to generate economic expansion. The similarity goes further. As the earlier insistence of economics on the strategic significance of the rate of interest was by no means 'innocent' – implying as it did the desirability of *laissez faire* and of government non-intervention in economic affairs – so likewise the current clamor for providing underdeveloped countries with installations giving rise to external economies (power stations, roads, etc.) is far from being a mere theoretic fad. Its significance becomes transparent as soon as one asks, *to whom* should the facilities that are to be erected furnish the external economies? It is necessary only to take a glance at the statements of official economists and of various big-business dominated organizations to see clearly that such sources of 'external economies' as are to be created in underdeveloped countries are primarily to assist Western enterprise in the exploitation of their natural resources. What is more, the pronounced emphasis on the indispensability of government aid in financing these projects reflects the time-honored notion of business as to what constitutes 'harmonious cooperation' between national administrations and monopolistic corporations: the former should shoulder the costs of establishment and conduct of business with as little as possible financial 'intervention' of the interested firms, while the latter should reap the profits resulting therefrom with as little as possible financial 'intervention' of the public treasury.

Thus while Mr Nelson Rockefeller and his associates stress that 'with critical shortages developing rapidly, a quickened and enlarged production of materials in the underdeveloped countries is of major importance' (International Development Advisory Board, 1951, p. 8), Professor Mason points out that 'such development can rarely take place without the expansion of auxiliary facilities – railroads, roads, port development, electric power and the like – which have a contribution to make to general economic development' (1952). And no bones are made as to who should foot the bill for the necessary investments, and as to what is to enjoy pride of place in judging the urgency of investments in 'auxiliary facilities': those that will promote 'a quickened and enlarged production of materials in the under-developed countries' or those that 'have a contribution to make to [their] general economic development'. The famous Gray Report answers both questions with all possible clarity. After expressing the historically sound view that 'private investment will probably be selective with the bulk of the new funds going into minerals development in a relatively few countries', its authors proceed to explain that 'private investment is the most desirable method of development', that 'the scope for private investment should be widened as far as possible', and 'the need for public investment correspondingly adjusted' (Gray Report, 1950, pp. 52, 61).

The crux of the matter is that the 'auxiliary facilities' in question are for the most part auxiliary to no one but foreign export-oriented business, and that the external economies stemming from them benefit nothing but additional production of raw materials for export. This is due in part to the fact that the installations set up by foreign enterprise or at its behest are naturally so designed and located as to serve its requirements. Whether we consider the railway construction sponsored by foreign enterprise in India, in Africa or in Latin America, the entire layout of which has been such as to facilitate the movement of raw materials towards ports of exit, and the development of harbors, which has been dictated by the needs of raw materials exporters, or whether we think of power plants located so as to supply energy to foreign mining enterprises, and of irrigation schemes designed to service foreign-owned plantations, the picture is everywhere the same. In the words of Dr H. W. Singer, 'the productive facilities for export from underdeveloped countries, which were so largely a result of foreign investment, never became a part of the internal economic structure of those underdeveloped countries themselves, except in the purely geographical and physical sense' (1950). [. . .]

The really important 'indirect influence' of foreign enterprise on the evolution of the underdeveloped countries flows through a multitude of channels, permeates all of their economic, social, political and cultural life, and decisively determines its entire course. There is first of all the emergence of a group of merchants expanding and thriving within the orbit of foreign capital. Whether they act as wholesalers – assembling, sorting and standardizing commodities that they purchase from small producers and sell to representatives of foreign concerns – or as suppliers of local materials to foreign enterprises, or as caterers to various other needs of foreign firms and their staffs, many of them manage to assemble vast fortunes and to move up to the very top of the underdeveloped countries' capitalist class. Deriving their profits from the operations of foreign business, vitally interested in its expansion and prosperity, this comprador element of the native bourgeoisie uses its considerable influence to fortify and to perpetuate the *status quo*.

There are secondly the native industrial monopolists, in most cases interlocked and interwoven with domestic merchant capital and with foreign enterprise, who entirely depend on the maintenance of the existing economic structure, and whose monopolistic status would be swept away by the rise of industrial capitalism. Concerned with preventing the emergence of competitors in their markets, they look with favor upon absorption of capital in the sphere of circulation, and have nothing to fear from foreign export-oriented enterprise. They too are stalwart defenders of the established order.

The interests of these two groups run entirely parallel with those of the feudal landowners powerfully entrenched in the societies of the backward areas. Indeed, these have no reason for complaints about the activities of foreign enterprise in their countries. In fact, these activities yield them considerable profits. Frequently they provide outlets for the produce of landed estates, in many places they raise the value of land, often they offer lucrative employment opportunities to members of the landed gentry.

What results is a political and social coalition of wealthy compradors, powerful monopolists and large landowners dedicated to the defense of the existing feudal-mercantile order. Ruling the realm by no matter what political means – as a monarchy, as a military fascist dictatorship, or as a republic of the Kuomintang variety – this coalition has nothing to hope for from the rise of industrial capitalism which would dislodge it from its positions of privilege and power. Blocking all economic and social progress in its country, this regime has no real political basis in city or village, lives in continual fear of the starving and restive popular masses, and relies for its stability on Praetorian guards of relatively well kept mercenaries.

In most underdeveloped countries social and political developments of the last few decades would have toppled regimes of that sort. That they have been able to stay in business – for business is, indeed, their sole concern – in most of Latin America and in the Near East, in several 'free' countries of South-East Asia and in some similarly 'free' countries of Europe, is due mainly if not exclusively to the aid and support that was given to them 'freely' by Western capital and by Western governments acting on its behalf. For the maintenance of these regimes and the operations of foreign enterprise in the underdeveloped countries have become mutually interdependent. It is the economic strangulation of the colonial and dependent countries by the imperialist powers that stymied the development of indigenous industrial capitalism, thus preventing the overthrow of the feudal-mercantile order and assuring the rule of the comprador administrations. It is the preservation of these subservient governments, stifling economic and social development and suppressing all popular movements for social and national liberation, that makes possible at the present time the continued foreign exploitation of underdeveloped countries and their domination by the imperialist powers. [. . .]

To be sure, neither imperialism itself nor its *modus operandi* and ideological trimmings are today what they were fifty or a hundred years ago. Just as outright looting of the outside world has yielded to organized trade with the underdeveloped countries, in which plunder has been rationalized and routinized by a mechanism of impeccably 'correct' contractual relations, so has the rationality of smoothly functioning commerce grown into the modern, still more advanced, still more rational system of imperialist exploitation. Like all other historically changing phenomena, the contemporary form of imperialism contains and preserves all its earlier modalities, but raises them to a new level. Its central feature is that it is now directed not solely towards the rapid extraction of large sporadic gains from the objects of its domination, it is no longer content with merely assuring a more or less steady flow of those gains over a somewhat extended period. Propelled by well-organized, rationally conducted monopolistic enterprise, it seeks today to rationalize the flow of these receipts so as to be able to count on it in perpetuity. And this points to the main task of imperialism in our time: to prevent, or, if that is impossible, to slow down and to control the economic development of underdeveloped countries.

That such development is profoundly inimical to the interests of foreign corporations producing raw materials for export can be readily seen. There is of course the mortal threat of nationalization of raw materials producing enterprises that is associated with the ascent to power of governments in backward countries that are determined to move their nations off dead center; but, even in the absence of nationalization, economic development in the source countries bodes nothing but evil to Western capital. For whichever aspect of economic development we may consider, it is manifestly detrimental to the prosperity of the raw materials producing corporations.[11] As under conditions of economic growth employment opportunities and productivity expand in other parts of the economy, and the class consciousness and bar-

11. The only possibly favorable effect of income growth in the source countries – the rise of their own demand for raw materials – can be safely neglected. It is nowhere likely to come to much, and certainly not before a very advanced stage of development is reached. Thus in the case in which the internal consumption of the source absorbs the largest observed proportion of its total output, in Venezuela, less than 4 per cent of Venezuelan oil is sold in the domestic market.

gaining power of labor increase, wages tend to rise in the raw materials producing sector. While in some lines of output – on plantations primarily – those increased costs can be offset by the adoption of improved techniques, such mechanization involves capital outlays that are obviously repugnant to the corporations involved. And in mining and petroleum operations even this solution is hardly possible. These in general employ the same methods of production that are in use in the advanced countries, so that the technological gap that could be filled is accordingly very small. With the prices of their products in the world markets representing a fixed datum to the individual companies – at least in the short run – increased labor costs combined with various fringe benefits resulting from growing unionization, as well as rising costs of other local supplies, must lead necessarily to a reduction of profits. If thus the longer-run effects of economic development cannot but be damaging to the raw materials exporting corporations, the immediate concomitants of economic development are apt to be even more disturbing. They will be, as a rule, higher taxes and royalties imposed on the foreign enterprises by the local government seeking revenue to finance its developmental ventures, foreign exchange controls designed to curtail the removals of profits abroad, tariffs rendering the importation of foreign-made equipment more expensive or raising the prices of imported wage goods, and others – all inevitably interfering with the freedom of action of foreign enterprise and encroaching upon its profitability.[12]

Small wonder that under such circumstances Western big business heavily engaged in raw materials exploitation leaves no stone unturned to obstruct the evolution of social and political conditions in underdeveloped countries that might be conducive to their economic development. It uses its tremendous power to prop up the backward areas' comprador administrations, to disrupt and corrupt the social and political movements that oppose them, and to overthrow whatever progressive governments may rise to power and refuse to do the bidding of their imperialist overlords. Where and when its own impressive resources do not suffice to keep matters under control, or where and when the

12. The preceding paragraph is essentially a reformulation of a statement by Rollins in the previously cited paper (1956).

costs of the operations involved can be shifted to their home countries' national governments – or nowadays to international agencies such as the International Bank for Reconstruction and Development – the diplomatic, financial and, if need be, military facilities of the imperialist power are rapidly and efficiently mobilized to help private enterprise in distress to do the required job.[13]

The gearing of policies and opinion in the West to the support of big business in its concerted effort to preserve its positions in the backward countries, and to sabotage their economic development, reflects itself in official pronouncements no less than in economic writings. Thus President Eisenhower defined the aims of American foreign policy as 'doing whatever our Government can properly do to encourage the flow of private investment abroad. This involves, as a serious and explicit purpose of our foreign policy, the encouragement of a hospitable climate for such investment in foreign countries' (1953). This view was echoed by Mr C. B. Randall, the Chairman of the Commission on Foreign Economic Policy, who insists that 'a new and better climate for American investment must be created' – rejoicing at the same time over the fact that 'happily this is being recognized and such countries as Turkey, Greece and Panama have led the way in modernizing their corporate laws and creating the right sort of atmosphere for our investment' (1954, ch. 2).[14] And with what might be called truly 'disarming brutality' the big-business position was expressed by August Maffry, Vice-President of the Irving Trust Company and one of Wall Street's most influential economists. In a special report prepared for the United States Department of State, he

13. It is unfortunately not possible to enlarge here on this tremendously important subject. A comprehensive study of contemporary imperialism is lacking, and the total picture has to be pieced together from scattered information. See the interesting account of imperialist activities centering on oil in O'Connor (1955); the well-documented description of what probably constitutes the outstanding case of imperialist intervention in the postwar period in Keddie (1955); the useful report on United States interventions in Latin America in Smith, Jr (1953) – to name only a few.

14. The list of the countries that rated this special commendation is rather noteworthy. It could be extended to include Franco's Spain, Syngman Rhee's Korea, Chiang Kai-shek's Formosa, Castillo's Guatemala and a few other similarly development-minded parts of the 'free world'.

calls for 'total diplomacy' in the service of the American foreign investment drive. 'The improvement in investment climate in friendly countries by more direct measures should be the objective of a total and sustained diplomatic effort by the United States. ... All agencies of the US Government concerned with foreign economic development should exercise constant vigilance for discriminatory or other actions by foreign governments adversely affecting the interests of American investors and employ all possible diplomatic pressures to forestall or remedy them.' Not too choosy about methods, he further suggests: 'There is still another and a very promising way in which the US Government can assist in achieving better conditions for investment in foreign countries. This is by aiding and abetting by all available means the efforts of private investors to obtain concessions from foreign countries in connection with specific proposed investments. ... Once concessions have been won through combined private and official efforts in a particular case, then the way is open to generalize them for the benefit of all other private investors' (1952, pp. 10–12).

Since 'American private investment abroad is largely concentrated in mining investments, notably in the petroleum field', and since 'it is probably substantially true that in the absence of very special circumstances no American private capital will now venture abroad unless the prospects are good that ... the returns will amortize the investments within five years or so' (Hoselitz, 1952, p. 184), it can be readily visualized what kind of governments in the underdeveloped countries are needed for such investments to be assured of the required hospitality. And it is no more difficult to perceive what type of regime and what variety of social and political forces in the underdeveloped countries have to be furthered by 'total diplomacy' and by the application of 'more direct measures' if the 'right sort of atmosphere' for foreign investment is to be created in the raw materials-rich parts of the backward world.

References

CASTRO, J. DE (1952), *The Geography of Hunger*, Little, Brown.
EISENHOWER, D. (1953), State of the Union Message.
GRAY REPORT (1950), *Report to the President on Foreign Economic Policies*.

HOSELITZ, B. F. (ed.) (1952), *The Progress of Underdeveloped Areas*, University of Chicago Press.

INTERNATIONAL DEVELOPMENT ADVISORY BOARD (1951), *Report to the President on Partners in Progress*.

KEDDIE, N. (1955), 'The Impact of the West on Iranian Social History', University of California at Berkeley.

MAFFREY, A. (1952), 'Program for increasing private investment in foreign countries', New York.

MARX, K. (1953), *Rohertwurfs der Grundrisse der Kritik der Politischen Ökonomie*, Berlin.

MASON, E. S. (1952), 'Raw materials, rearmament and economic development', *Q.J. Econ.*, vol. 66, no. 3, pp. 327–41.

NURKSE, R. (1953), *Problems of Capital Formation in Underdeveloped Countries*, Oxford University Press.

O'CONNOR, H. (1955), *The Empire of Oil*, Monthly Review.

PIZER, S. and CUTLER, F. (1955), 'International investments and earnings', *Survey of Current Bus.*, vol. 35, no. 8, pp. 10–20.

POLLNER, M. D. (1952), 'Problems of national income estimation in Bolivia', New York University.

RANDALL, C. B. (1954), *A Foreign Economic Policy for the United States*, University of Chicago Press.

ROLLINS, C. E. (1956), 'Mineral development and economic growth', *Social Research*, vol. 23, no. 4, pp. 253–80.

SALTER, A. (1951), *Foreign Investment*, Princeton University Press.

SCHIFF, E. (1942), 'Direct investment, terms of trade, and balance of payments', *Q.J. Econ.*, vol. 56, no. 2, pp. 307–20.

SINGER, H. W. (1950), 'The distribution of gains between investing and borrowing countries', *Amer. Econ. Rev.*, vol. 40, no. 2, pp. 473–85.

SMITH, O. E. JR. (1953), *Yankee Diplomacy*, Southern Methodist University Press.

UNITED NATIONS (1951), *Review of Economic Conditions in the Middle East*.

UNITED NATIONS (1953), *Development of Mineral Resources in Asia and the Far East*.

YOUNG, A. (1928), 'Increasing returns and economic progress', *Econ. J.*, vol. 38, no. 152, pp. 527–42.

ZIMMERMAN, E. W. (1951), *World Resources and Industries*, Harper & Row.

17 T. Balogh

The Mechanism of Neo-Imperialism

T. Balogh, 'The mechanism of neo-imperialism', *Bulletin of the Oxford University Institute of Statistics*, vol. 24, 1962, pp. 331–46.

Most African territories since their liberation from colonial rule have made accelerated progress. This has happened despite the loss of experienced administrators and technical experts in all fields through the rapid Africanization of all public services, though in some territories, especially those formerly under French rule, the process has not been as fast as in other territories. The development must be also seen against a background of a systematically damaging impact on the terms of trade of African territories of the development of the world economy in the 1950s. The return to the exclusive use of monetary controls, the trend towards convertibility and non-discrimination, have undoubtedly retarded growth in important markets of Africa and thus contributed to the depressing effect of monetary policy itself on primary goods prices. While these goods have to be sold in world markets, and therefore are subject to monetary pressures, the price of most of Africa's imports – manufactures – has been administered and showed a continuous upward trend.

The record thus seems remarkable and encouraging. In the present paper the view will be put forward that this acceleration of growth is to some extent exceptional and cannot be relied on to continue. It has been the result of the disappearance of the limitations imposed by the monetary and commercial institutions, arrangements and policies on the economic evolution of Africa during the colonial period. These were dominated by the relations of African territories with their erstwhile metropolitan countries. A historical analysis of the origins and rationale of these relationships is therefore necessary to establish the future requirements of a deliberate acceleration of development.

I believe it can be shown that the automatism which evolved

represents by itself a severe limitation on the possibility for the full development of the weaker partner in the 'colonial pact', even if there is no conscious policy which aims at the exploitation for the benefit of the metropolitan area.[1] Beyond this the philosophy of monetary and fiscal soundness itself represents a further handicap to the weaker area. If this analysis is correct two conclusions follow, both unpalatable to current conventional wisdom. The first is that the present upsurge in the ex-colonial areas provides no guarantee of a stable and steady progress in future if special efforts are not made to substitute positive stimuli for the negative ending of colonial limitation. The second is that neo-imperialism does not depend on open political domination. The economic relations of the US to South America are in no way different from those of Britain to her African colonies. The International Monetary Fund fulfils the role of the colonial administration of enforcing the rules of the game which bring about the necessary consequences.

The theme is fraught with emotional implications. On the one hand strenuous efforts are made to underline the exploitation aspects of the colonial subjection. On the other side the increasing importance of aid, in terms both of technical knowledge and of resources, is stressed, especially contributions to the budgets of African countries, the provision of preferential arrangements in commodity sales, provision of capital.

The rise of preferential systems before the war

Practically all countries of Africa, both those whose independence dates back a long time and those which have only lately achieved it, belong, or belonged until recently, to monetary and banking systems and commercial areas centred in a highly developed metropolitan country and its institutions (Balogh, 1954, 1959a, 1959b). All the modern economic organs in Africa grew up in response to the needs of their creators, these metropolitan countries, whose main interest in Africa lay in the supply of food and raw materials from the tropical zone.[2]

1. I have tried to analyse some of these aspects in a paper written for the Economic Commission for Latin America (1961).
2. Though the immediate reason for their establishing territorial bases in Africa in the nineteenth century was, in many cases, their effort to curb slave trading.

There was, until very recently, no autochthonous demand in these areas for modern monetary or economic institutions, colonial governments were not encouraged to undertake financial operations in the territory for which they were responsible, the large foreign companies operating there had easy access to the capital markets of the metropolis for any financial needs beyond their retained profits. There was thus nothing to deflect the evolution of the monetary and banking institutions of the periphery from responding almost exclusively to the requirements of the centre.

These requirements could best be satisfied by safeguarding the absolute stability of the colonial monetary unit in terms of the metropolitan currency and by encouraging the establishment of banking institutions which would at all times be safe.

Monetary stability

The former aim was achieved by the simple expedient of providing for a 100 per cent cover for the colonial currency. It was immaterial whether the institution in charge was a private bank (as in French Africa) or a currency board (as in British Africa), so long as the assets held against the note issue were metropolitan. In this way any increase in the currency circulation in the dependent area resulted in a *de facto* loan by it to the metropolis; on the other hand this arrangement provided an absolute guarantee for the sufficiency of reserves. In a way it reduced the risk of extreme crises. It would incidentally also have prevented conscious policies for economic stabilization and consciously accelerated development in the dependency, if such policies had (or could have) been conceived in this framework before the war.[3]

Banking services

The second requirement, the provision of reliable banking services was obtained automatically by encouraging the establishment of large (specialized) banking institutions in the metropolis to handle the commerce of the colonial area. These banks became powerful when banking had become stabilized in the metropolitan

3. It did actually impose limitations to the extension of 'Keynesian' policies in the short period after the war before independence was won.

area and their policies had become impeccably sound and solid. Their freedom of operation, especially the choice of their investments, was not limited by any regulation such as a *minimum reserve* having to be kept *in the colonial or peripheral territory*. There was no other agency for handling the slowly emerging domestic savings of these territories at a time when few, if any, liquid assets of the required quality were available in those areas.

It was then a matter of natural 'evolution' that the colonial banking system to a considerable extent had to find uses for its deposits in the metropolis. Under the canons of sound banking, however, they had to confine their lending to 'self-liquidating' purposes. In practice this meant the finance of the foreign trade of the colonial area, of exports of colonial primary produce and imports of metropolitan manufactures. A large part of total resources was thus necessarily kept in metropolitan 'reserves' i.e. in liquid sterling or franc assets. Thus a further and increasing flow of (in effect short-term) lending at low rates of interest originated from the periphery (which was so terribly short of capital) to the centre.[4] In some dependent areas (such as the British) where savings banks and postal saving institutions were legally bound to invest in the government securities of the metropolis, there was an additional loss of savings to the dependency.

The export of liquid savings to the metropolitan area and the consequent reliance of the dependency on the metropolis for long-term capital for development secured for the banking system of the latter a useful income, while its control over the financial and economic policy of the dependency (already assured by the hold of the metropolitan administration over the colonial government) was further reinforced and the participation of the ruling financial interests in its administration obtained. All long-term expenditure for which long-term loans were needed – and the reluctance to increase taxation, and in especial to introduce direct taxation, in practice reduced the possibility of covering capital expenditure out of current budgetary resources – was thus made

4. They were used especially before the First World War to finance short term credits (acceptances). After 1920 they served increasingly as the basis of British long-term lending first to finance European reconstruction after the First World War, and after the Second to prosperous developing areas (South Africa, Australia etc.). It proved to be an embarrassing change.

subject to financial veto.[5] This made any change in policy difficult, for the 'credit-worthiness' of colonial governments became dependent on their strictly abiding by the limitations imposed upon them. If the metropolis offered special facilities for colonial borrowing (e.g. the concession by Britain of trustee status to colonial securities) this grant did not by any means fully offset the gains secured to the banking system and the capital market by the special relationship.

The provision of cheap facilities for the finance of foreign trade while domestic activity was unable to obtain capital at comparable terms further distorted the productive structure of the colonial area. It accentuated the unfavourable integration of its economy, in which a subsistence agriculture, tribal or feudal, coexisted with a developed market economy. The differential ease with which the international movement of goods could obtain finance at world rates of interest further enhanced the supremacy of the merchandizing, mining and plantation operations of large foreign firms, because long-term capital needed for the diversification of the economy and the rise of domestic industry was either not available at all or only on extortionate conditions (Balogh, 1961).

Automatic commercial preference

Thus the divergence in the tropics between private profitability and real social advantage was widened, and the tropical countries' dependence on primary exports was automatically perpetuated. Diversification would have increased productivity and real in-income. But it was, in the circumstances, practicable only given *positive* economic intervention, and such positive economic intervention for the conscious acceleration of development of the colonial area was not contemplated so long as the territories were not independent. The role of the state was conceived as limited to assuring law and order.

This so-called *pacte colonial*, the exchange of colonial primary produce against metropolitan manufactures and services was thus in the nineteenth century (in contrast to the eighteenth century) not generally based on explicit restrictive or preferential legislation in favour of the metropolis (the monopoly of French shipping to

5. The history of the establishment of a Central Bank in Ceylon is a good illustration of this veto.

Algeria and Madagascar represented one of the few exceptions). Over a large part of Africa, for example, the Congo basin and Morocco, international treaties or agreements enforced free trade, or at least non-discrimination. The free play of the price mechanism (as in the case of the 'independent' countries of Latin America and the Caribbean) was quite sufficient to restrict the less developed countries to a status of permanent economic inferiority. The implicit preference of the colonial administrations for the metropolitan products did the rest. Their orders on public and private account – and these represented a large portion of the total money demand of the colonial area – in the main flowed toward the metropolis.

As time went on and international industrial competition became more acute these rather informal relationships were increasingly reinforced by preference conceded explicitly in formal legal arrangements. The British Imperial Preference and the French Customs Union, even before the war, brought about a closer integration in those areas in which international treaties did not prescribe free trade or non-discrimination. They were to be reinforced by quantitative restrictions and exchange control. All these arrangements on the whole, secured greater advantages to the metropolitan areas than to the periphery, because the preference granted to the primary produce of the latter was, without quantitative regulation, often ineffectual.[6] The currency disturbances of the inter-war period, during which the dependencies had no option but to share the monetary fate of the dominant country – which meant that the risk of exchange fluctuation was eliminated in the relation of the centre to the periphery – acted as a further bond of some importance. The metropolis continued to secure a large, often overwhelming, share in both the exports and imports of the colonies.

The impact of war economies: the rise of exchange areas

The war brought fundamental changes, not merely in the economic relations of the metropolis to the dependencies, but also in the attitude of the colonial administrations to economic problems.

6. The export capacity of the areas entitled to Imperial Preference was in excess of metropolitan import requirements except in the case of a few products, e.g. oil-seeds and tobacco.

This change strengthened the economic relationship between the metropolis and the periphery while the responsibility of the metropolis for fostering political and economic development became more and more recognized. The fact that the emergent political leaders of the dependencies obtained an increasingly influential voice in the administration of the African territories explains to a large extent, though perhaps not wholly, the recognition of the view that the conscious fostering of economic and social development represents one of the most important, if not the most important, functions of the state.

At the same time, the net effect of the change cannot unequivocally be said to have favoured the rapid growth of the dependencies. Even the profound change in the relationship between the prices of primary produce and manufactures which took place during the war and persisted well into the post-war period was insufficient to break the vicious circle of poverty. It is the contrast between the change in government attitude and the improvement of the resources at the disposal of the African territories and the relatively unsatisfactory degree of progress that asks for an explanation. It is provided by the contrary effects of the interconnection with the metropolitan area on the progress of the dependency.

Already before the war the unrest due to the low prices for colonial primary produce caused by the Great Depression resulted in the appointment of several official committees to inquire into the problem of the marketing of export produce.[7] Their reports question for the first time the adequacy and efficacy of a 'free' market in these commodities. They question the assumption that bargains between weak peasants lacking knowledge and capital, and the indigenous merchants or the agents of the great metropolitan corporations who purchased the produce of the colonies could be said to be between equal partners. They foreshadow the development of government agencies which, by conscious policy, would secure that balance between the two sides which was supposed to be brought about by the free interplay of market forces in perfect markets.[8]

7. e.g. The Cocoa Marketing Inquiry.

8. The critics of marketing boards in their argumentation implicitly and illicitly assume that the peasant obtained a 'perfectly competitive price in the free system'. This is nonsense.

The outbreak of the war which disrupted trade in tropical produce merely occasioned a change which would have come about without it. On the one hand, the market for colonial produce was guaranteed by the metropolitan countries. This undoubtedly conferred a great advantage on the colonial area, if only or mainly in the sense that claims on the metropolis were accumulated which could at some point in the future be made effective. It also served to maintain equity in the distribution of incomes within the colonies which would have been gravely disturbed by a collapse of export prices. At the same time it might be and has been argued that this guarantee prevented a partial reorientation of colonial production towards food and other products needed in the home market. It is questionable, however, whether the cost of such readjustment would have been tolerable, or, in the long run, even in the interests of the colonies.

The war brought about another important change on the plane of commercial policy. This was the strong reinforcement of the rudimentary preferential arrangements, the grant of privileged treatment of colonial and metropolitan products respectively in each other's market, by the imposition of *direct controls over imports and over foreign payments*, i.e. payments outside the confines of the group. The *de facto* advantage of a stable currency became consciously and powerfully reinforced by explicit regulation. The loose automatic associations between London and the British dependencies, and Paris and the French ones, were transformed into the powerful groupings of the Sterling Area and the Franc Zone. The reciprocal possibility of obtaining finance between the metropolis and the dependencies created a unique framework for mutual profitable economic development. During this stage of the monetary and commercial development a series of special connections grew up, which made their interdependence far closer and more purposefully contrived than it had been at any time since the middle of the nineteenth century.

The economic significance of these special relationships is difficult to discern. They must not be evaluated singly because they are to a large extent interdependent and their effect on welfare must be judged as a whole. Efforts on either side to show the effectiveness of policy in lessening inequality and promoting development, by pointing to specific measures, e.g. the guarantee of purchases of colonial produce well above world price levels, are obviously beside the point. Nor must grants for particular projects, however admirable, by the metropolis to the periphery be accepted automatically at their face value. It would have to be shown first that a grant was effectively transferred, i.e. not offset by the automatic working of the monetary mechanism through increasing the liquid reserves of the colony at the centre. Even if effective transfers took place, the indirect effects of this expenditure might result in a net burden to the periphery. The advantage gained by groups of individuals or firms in the periphery or in the centre might well be more than offset by the disadvantages of others. The net effect either of subsidies or of special privileges might be negatived by the basic mechanism of the system.

The advantages and disadvantages moreover might be in causal relation to one another – in other words, either party might be unable or unwilling to grant advantages or suffer disadvantages without some compensation. For instance, it would seem beside the point to argue in favour of 'untied', convertible, grants when the balance of payments position of the donor countries was such as to make a cut in the grant inevitable if convertibility were insisted upon. The cut might more than offset gains due to the possibility of using 'convertible' money in a third and cheaper market. A detailed evaluation, from the view point of welfare, of the special relationship between the metropolitan areas and their dependencies which have by now emerged into full independence is therefore needed if an adequate policy for the social and economic development of the areas is to be worked out and a suitable international commercial framework is to be established.

To this task we now turn.

The impact of preference and aid

The preferential treatment accorded to goods and services in intra-group trade may take the form of commercial preferences – commodity purchase agreements, tariff preferences, administrative (quota) preferences – or of a discriminatory application of monetary controls. Of the various types of commercial preferences the first was the most important to the dependent or erstwhile dependent areas and the second to the metropolitan areas. The monetary arrangements seem to have worked largely in the interest of the metropolitan areas (or rather certain groups in those countries) and had the result of diminishing the contribution provided for the periphery in terms of resources and technical knowledge. It should be added, however, that in certain cases the net advantage to the metropolitan area would arise not so much through price relationships as through the fact that the periphery was for one reason or another unable to make full use of the purchasing power which resulted from its sales to the metropolitan area (and *a fortiori*, to third 'hard currency' areas, the proceeds of which accrued to the 'common' pool of reserves) or which was put at its disposal in other ways.

Commodity agreements

Commodity agreements provide for the purchase of unlimited or of specified quantities of the African territories' produce. The former type was general during the war. As wartime scarcities lessened and the terms of trade moved against the primary producing areas limitation on quantity became the rule.

1. In the British territories the war-time system was continued in the immediate post-war period of shortages. After 1950 – and indeed already under the Labour Government – they were first attenuated and their duration shortened and then – partly because of producers' protests during the Korean boom at being forced to deliver their produce at low prices – purchase at current market price was agreed to. This would have worked against the primary producers after 1953. But in any case after 1951 most bulk purchase was discontinued. Among the exceptions the Imperial Sugar Agreement, the most notable, did not affect Africa substantially.

The post-war bulk purchase agreements seem to have generally worked to the disadvantage of the African colonies inasmuch that in a period of a rising trend of prices long-term purchases in practice proved to be made below current prices on the world markets (ECE, 1949). Two things need to be said in this context, however. The first is that the relation of prices to the so-called 'world price' is by itself insufficient as a criterion for determining welfare effects of such agreements; world prices are not independent of the existence of the agreement itself. One of the effects of the agreement might be a benefit far beyond the direct advantage or disadvantage experienced on the sale to the metropolitan country.[9] Nor must the security of market given by bulk purchases be disregarded.

What might be said to have been really objectionable in British policy from a welfare point of view was the decision to abandon bulk purchase at the precise moment when the world trend of primary prices (and terms of trade with manufacturers) turned and when the countries of Africa would have benefited by, and had a strong case for, the continuation of purchases.

2. In the *French* territories (and to some extent in Somalia) the provision of preferential markets through quota regulation of the metropolitan market and price guarantees still plays a very important part in the marketing of coffee and groundnuts, and also of cocoa, groundnut oil, palm kernels and palm oil. Their impact is to increase the income of the periphery or rather production of the commodities in question relative to the production capacity of the world as a whole. It should be noted, however (and this qualification is habitually omitted in most treatments of this question) that this relative 'distortion' of the productive structure might in fact not be so significant because the innate potentialities of the periphery might be much greater than the actual production, e.g. because of ignorance or inertia and that 'artificially' high prices might just achieve what would be achieved automatically by the influence of a better working price mechanism on more knowledgeable producers. This is important because this consideration suggests that it is conceivable that the discontinuance of the provision of preferential markets (because

9. This is a significant consideration for the future, e.g. when considering the effects of bulk purchase by the Soviet Union on the world price of surpluses and commodities. If Soviet purchases push up free world prices sufficiently for African countries to obtain the same income from sales of smaller quantities to other countries they will represent a net benefit. Thus the fact that the Russians may have bought the commodities at less than the world price ruling *after* the agreement cannot be said to prove that they have exploited the African areas.

It is one of the mysteries of Soviet policy that the Russians did not respond eagerly to the solicitations of Nkrumah to support the cocoa price by purchasing rather limited amounts of cocoa against industrial output. There seems to be a large unsatisfied demand for chocolate in the Soviet Union and they could have worsened the terms of trade of the West to the benefit of Africa and at relatively little cost to themselves.

it is not unconnected with the achievement of technical progress) will *not* have a net discouraging effect on production. It is quite likely that such technical progress will be stimulated by the ending or modification of the favourable commodity agreements, especially as this coincides with greater activity by FEDOM [10] and other 'European' funds and the international agencies to channel technical knowledge to Africa (Balogh, 1962a).

Duties and quantitative controls

The impact of reciprocal *preferential tariffs* (where they existed) seems to have been more effective in securing advantages for the metropolitan country than for the periphery. This follows partly from the fact that the tariffs in force for food and raw materials in the metropolitan area (even in France) were rather moderate and partly (especially in the case of the British territories) because in the case of a number of commodities the metropolitan countries were unable to absorb the whole of the export surplus of the periphery. As the exports were homogeneous this meant that the preference became inoperative. The preference granted on manufactures was substantial in a number of areas and it was also effective.

So far as *quantitative regulations are concerned*, their impact worked more evenly in the British zone until the acceptance by Britain of the GATT principles of non-discrimination reduced the advantages of the periphery. In the French territories the primary producers continued to enjoy advantages from the discriminatory restriction of imports from outside areas coupled with price guarantees. Their effect on welfare was offset and perhaps more than offset by the discriminatory import controls in the African territories on non-French manufactures. As we shall see [11] the problem resolves itself mainly to one of income redistribution between the various classes in both the metropolitan and peripheral areas.

Monetary and exchange policy

Discriminatory exchange control reinforced the effect on the pattern of commerce of quantitative import regulations. The ease with which payment could be made and finance secured obviously

10. The European Fund for the Development of Africa.
11. See pp. 334–7.

contributed to the strengthening of intra-group trade even where price relationships were not as favourable as they would have been with other parties. More important than this immediate effect on trade was the impact of exchange restrictions in the financial sphere.

Capital movements: Historically the essence of the functioning of currency areas has been the unlimited freedom of capital movements. This is not necessarily a condition of a functioning of currency areas. Both Australia and India have instituted strict controls on capital, even for transfers within the currency area in which they belong. It certainly has been a feature, until recently, of the relations of both the Franc Zone and the Sterling Area.[12]

It is obvious that a discriminatory ease of capital transfers from the metropolitan area to the periphery would encourage investment there even if this were not as advantageous, or profitable, as investment elsewhere. The assurance of being able to repatriate purchasing power would be an additional incentive. This may well be reinforced by the advantages secured to these investments by the commercial preferences system discussed above. It should be noted, however, that by and large the establishment of new large scale productive units was encouraged more *in the centre*[13] than in the periphery and that it would be impossible to assert that the latter did not suffer a relative disadvantage in consequence.

In recent years with the accelerated movement towards independence it seems likely that the freedom of capital movement on private account predominantly favoured the centre rather than the periphery. The capital flow was dictated not so much by normal profit incentives as by precautionary motives, i.e. capital was repatriated to the metropolis. This certainly seems to have been the case in the Franc Zone, but it probably played some part in the Sterling Area too.[14] The resultant weakening of the periphery is obvious. It must not, however, be judged without

12. Great protests were encountered by the Governments of Ghana and British Guiana when they introduced control on capital flight.

13. Or in other highly developed parts of the currency area. In the case of the Sterling Area it was South Africa and Australia which mainly benefited.

14. Some of the unexplained credit items of the British balance of payments might well be connected with this capital repatriation.

reference to another feature of the functioning of these economic groupings, the grant of aid in terms of loans or outright contributions from the centre to the periphery.[15]

The monetary and fiscal policy of the colonial areas continued to be dominated by Victorian canons. The plans prepared – especially in the British territories[16] – were little more than a haphazard collection of departmental investment projects unconnected with one another and decided upon without any analysis of their general economic effects. The reserves which were accumulating were kept in separate accounts in the metropolitan centre and thus could not be pooled for an imaginative use for general development. Balanced budgets and conservative finance, the use of long term capital only for long term investment remained the watchword of the administrations. Even when Central Banks were established, against rugged opposition of the metropolis, their powers remained sharply limited. No conscious anti-cyclical policies were conceived of for these areas even after the victory of Keynesian techniques in the metropolis. To some extent this was due to the complete failure to recruit a new type of personnel to devise and execute policy.

Exchange rates

The rates of exchange fixed for the African countries and especially those in the Franc Zone had important effects on the relations of Africans to the metropolitan areas.

So far as the *British Territories* are concerned the problem was dominated and modified by the policy of the marketing boards, which paid less than the world market price to the farmers, thus limiting the incomes in the African territories and until after independence steadily accumulating rather large nest eggs, whose real value has been steadily declining.[17] The fact that the British-

15. See p. 335.

16. Planning became respectable at a much earlier date in France as a result of the activity of the *Commissariat du Plan*. Young economists and planners were made available to colonial administrations much sooner and in considerable numbers. The British administrations did not encourage such extravagance.

17. The Ghana Government complained that the *sterling* value of the assets purchased also declined by fifteen million pounds. The loss in real terms must have been far greater, perhaps as high as sixty million pounds.

African currencies were devalued together with sterling in 1939 and again in 1949 though their balances of payments were showing surpluses may have further slightly worsened the terms of trade of the African countries in comparison to their competitors in, say, Latin America. The policy pursued would have been indefensible had it not happened just before the violent reversal, in 1951, of the post-war improvement in the prices of primary products relative to those of manufactures. Thus the effects of devaluation were completely swamped by the collapse of primary prices. Indeed, the African territories under British control may have benefited by the fact that their currency was at a relatively low level at that critical date, while their price-level was not influenced by the boom owing to its relatively short duration.

In the case of the *French Territories*, the value of the colonial currency was lifted during the post-war monetary vicissitudes of France to a level double that of the metropolitan franc. This decision together with the structure of commercial relations within the franc area resulted in a violent upward thrust of domestic prices in terms of dollars as the price level in the African territory was never revised, when shortages became less acute, and the colonial franc appreciated. The quantitative control imposed on imports from outside and the preferential relationships which French manufacturers enjoyed within the area, prevented the correction of the anomaly and secured exceptional profits to the metropolitan exporters. The producers of those primary products which had preferential markets in France were also shielded from the consequences of the revaluation of the colonial currency on their sale-prices. These included the great tribal–feudal–religious chiefs and the metropolitan corporations interested in plantations and ranches. In a number of areas, e.g. Senegal, those who suffered comprised the least privileged part of the population. The policy of high prices (and salaries) also favoured all those whose income and savings accrued in colonial francs but who wanted to spend them in France. Inasmuch as a considerable portion of the money (in contrast to subsistence) incomes in the French area were earned by individuals and firms from France, the high value of the currency had the tendency of enhancing the potential claims against these territories on capital account.

Too much, however, must not be made of this, because most of the money incomes provided in the colonies were strongly influenced either by commodity agreements or by direct subsidies granted by France. To that extent the arrangements meant merely that the French consumer of certain colonial produce and the French taxpayer were burdened with the cost of relatively higher payments to French firms trading in Africa and French citizens in the service of the African territories.

Taxes, subsidies and welfare contributions

1. Until as late as the last war, it was a general rule in imperial arrangements, that the colonies had to 'fend for themselves'. This expression was obviously interpreted by the colonial powers in a rather flexible manner. In the majority of cases the colonial taxation systems precluded the territory from benefiting from a direct contribution from incomes accruing in the territory to the nationals and firms of the metropolitan area, and this income represented a rather considerable portion of the total monetized and taxable income of the country. Even indirect levies and excise did not discriminate to any extent between essential and non-essential goods and thus accentuated the regressive character of colonial taxation which, as a whole, was biased in favour of the nationals of the metropolitan and other highly developed areas. This was thought to be needed to attract foreign capital. The conventional view is undoubtedly correct that the activities of foreign, or rather, metropolitan, firms represented an overwhelming proportion of total capital investment in the area, and their activity undoubtedly contributed most to such progress in the areas as was made. Whether they would have curtailed their activity if a different taxation policy had been pursued is a different question. The answer is difficult, for a different taxation policy would also have increased the pace of the development of technical knowledge and markets, and increased the attractiveness of investment.

The conclusion that the metropolis exploited the colony cannot be substantiated on the basis alone of the fact that they were able to earn large profits which were not taxed to any extent. It might perhaps be fairer to say that the share of profits and salaries going to the metropolis was substantial and that the latter reaped a greater part of the benefits of the development which it initiated and which would not otherwise have taken place. In the framework of taxation as it was and with a large supply of labour the forces of the 'free' market alone would have strongly favoured the productive factor in shortest supply, i.e. capital. These forces were massively supported by the fact that the 'free' market implied a strong *monopoly* economic power buttressed by political influence on the part of the expatriate individuals and firms. The resultant distribution of income was far more unfavourable to Africans than the corresponding one in Europe.

2. The attitude of the metropolitan powers to their dependent territories underwent substantial changes *after the war*. In the British territories the Colonial Development and Welfare Act made available grants for capital expenditure on education and other social services, e.g. health and also for substructure investment. In the French territories FIDES, CCFOM (now CCCE and PAC) and lately the European Fund for Social Development, FEDOM, made grants on an impressive scale. In addition the French Government defrayed the cost of the metropolitan military and a large proportion of the civil personnel stationed in former French territories, but in certain instances granted direct contributions to the regular budgets of the new countries.

It has been claimed[18] that these grants represent a complete break with the past, an application to the relation of the metropolis to the dependent territories (soon to be granted independence) of the principles of the welfare state.[19] It would be wrong to discount altogether the importance of the change, but its welfare impact can be exaggerated.

In the first place the grant of these subsidies codetermined the policies of the African countries concerned and deflected them from the courses upon which the countries themselves might have decided. To some extent, therefore, they might be thought to be objectionable from the point of view of the self-determination of

18. e.g. Colonial Office White Paper on the U K contribution to Development, Cmnd. 1308 of 1961.

19. It might be argued of course that the sudden willingness of the Conservative parties to grant independence ('to preside over the liquidation of Empire') is not unconnected with this new relationship. In fact France refused, at first, to make grants, or give technical collaboration to those countries which did not accept a special ' new' political relationship. There was willingness to purchase 'greatness' by continuing grants to the rest.

the territory concerned. This rather constitutional argument is reinforced by the fact that the foreign grants almost always result in increased expenditure which has to be financed from domestic resources. This is clear in the case of capital grants which imply commitments (as in the case of the British-financed universities) for current and maintenance expenditure outside the scope of the 'welfare' fund. This expenditure might be burdensome and/or for purposes for which otherwise resources would not have been found. In many instances the returns were not commensurate even to the net burden to the country.[20] Moreover such grants may have general repercussions on the budget and on the distribution of income which might be considered out of keeping with the general situation of the territory.[21]

In the second place, the welfare effects of subsidies or contributions by the metropolitan countries will be strongly influenced if not determined by the geographical distribution of the final expenditure which is undertaken on the basis of these grants. As we have argued above, the very existence of dependent relationships did result in a powerful influence favouring purchases from the metropolitan area, even though they may not have been the most favourable from the economic point of view of the dependency. This preferential system has been perpetuated, if not strengthened, by the impact of the system of subsidies. The grants would have been used in the metropolitan country even if currency regulations and other restrictive measures had not meant a very substantial commercial preference between the metropolitan area and the periphery. In addition capital investment embodied in metropolitan manufactures necessitates purchases for replacement and extension and makes metropolitan goods familiar. Thus, in gauging the net contribution to the

20. This has only too often happened in the case of Technical Assistance.
21. One blatant example which springs to mind is the foundation of the Oxford and Cambridge type of university colleges in the British territories. These not merely burdened the emergent independent states with heavy expenditure, but, we have argued in a different section had an unfortunate impact on the social balance and in all probability also influenced and increased the discrepancy between the average income of the population as a whole and of those employed in the Government and other institutions founded by the Metropolitan area, with unfavourable long run implications on the investment capacity of the country. See my article (1962b).

recipient countries' welfare of the payments made, the relative terms of trade would also have to be taken into account. These were not favourable to the African countries.

In addition to the assistance or contributions made by the former metropolitan countries, technical and resource contributions were made by the United States of America on a bilateral basis. These were not large but are increasing rapidly. Soviet contributions to African countries south of the Sahara have been restricted to Guinea, Ethiopia and Ghana. They take the usual form of long-term loans at low rates of interest for capital development purposes, combined in some cases with bulk purchase arrangements. It should be noted, however, that in the case of Africa, large-scale purchases outside the world market have as yet not been undertaken by Russia, despite the favourable conditions which the fall in primary prices has presented in recent years.

International institutions were less active in the 1950s in Africa than in other continents. The relative insignificance of their contribution is explicable by the fact that few countries in Africa were independent before the 1950s and the metropolitan countries did not favour their activity in dependent areas. With expanding independence a very rapid increase in the activity of the international institutions has come about. Thus in calculating the net magnitude of the contribution of the metropolitan to the welfare of the African countries account would have to be taken of the aid which these countries could have obtained from outside sources, from which they were barred while in a dependent status. These must have been very substantial.[22]

Conclusion

In summing up this lengthy discussion of the close interrelationship of the now independent African countries with the erstwhile metropolitan countries, two things need to be noted.

22. In the case of the British Territories it can be argued (*ex-post* at any rate) that those contributions would have been rather higher than the aid effectively obtained from Britain: American aid is already a multiple of the British aid in the past and their aid to a large extent was offset by the increase in the assets of the colonies. It is doubtful however, whether, in the absence of the spread of the Cold War to Africa, this would have happened. But British claims must be sharply discounted.

The first is the development of their terms of trade, influenced as these were by the special relationships existing and the balance of payments and, more especially, the changes in their reserves held in the metropolitan centre. The impression one obtains is that the *British* territories on the whole have not been able to use the favourable opportunities presented in the immediate postwar period of rising prices fully, though in certain instances – sugar (which is of no importance for the British territories in Africa) is a conspicuous case – purchases from British territories took place at a relatively higher level. In the case of the main export commodities of Africa, however, the bulk purchase agreements undertaken by Britain in the immediate past were relatively (if to some extent fortuitously) unfavourable to the African dependencies. The African territories, moreover, did not benefit from bulk purchase agreements in general after the price trend changed in 1952. The French-speaking territories, on the contrary, continued to benefit by such agreements. The impression is unmistakable, however, that the quantitative controls did encourage purchases in the metropolitan area even though the metropolitan area prices were far less favourable to those countries than world prices.

The second criterion is the development of the balance of their payments. In this respect, the British territories continuously increased their reserves in the metropolitan country. This meant that the subsidies and loans granted to the dependent areas could not be effectively transferred (even though the areas incurred liability for interest payments in the case of loans). On the other hand, the combined effect of upward trend in prices and the decline in gilt-edged securities, in which the sterling reserves were partly invested, has severely reduced the real value of the reserves thus acquired. This has necessarily meant a heavy loss to the territories concerned.

So far as the French-speaking territories are concerned, a large portion of the public transfers (in some cases nine-tenths) have been offset by private transfers towards the metropolis of which the visible balance of payments only represents a fraction. At times the invisible operations, mainly capital transfers from the colonies towards the metropolis, amounted to double the invisible current balance. Nevertheless, as is shown on the official statistics, the French colonies were at times unable to use the public transfers fully and accumulated unused balances at the Banque de France despite the fact that capital flight from the colonies was very considerable. The effective transfers of capital for use in the colonial area has thus been even smaller.

If account is taken of the opportunities of obtaining capital and aid from sources outside the metropolitan countries the view that the African territories benefited by this special relationship to the metropolis must be sharply discounted. Even in the post-war period the net aid reaching them was more than offset by the concessions or special trading relations granted or obtained for metropolitan firms or individuals. The failure of the administrations dominated by the metropolis to use taxation and direct controls to speed development consciously further increased the loss of the dependencies. This perhaps explains that it was possible and how it was possible, to accelerate economic progress in a number of areas as soon as independence was gained despite the loss of experienced administrators and the emergence of depressing political complications.

The implications of this analysis are disturbing. The mechanism of what one might call welfare or neo-imperialism seems to have artificially restricted the development of colonial areas by preventing viable infant industries from being established. The present surge of activity might just be the consequence of making up this *artificial backwardness*. Once the obvious manufactured import-substitution has come to an end Africa might be in danger of a Latin American or Middle Eastern frustration. Unless the vast primitive agricultural sector can be energized into a response, the upward surge will not become cumulative, but as in Latin America and the Middle East will peter out. There will remain a vast and increasingly dissatisfied ill-employed class in the primitive subsistence sector confronted with a small privileged class in the cities, unable to provide either supplies or markets for the latter. Only if the rural response were adequate, if productivity and income increased and justified a cumulative increase in industry could a self-sustaining upward spiral be confidently expected. This has not happened yet, and some of the development plans, with their neglect of agriculture and rural technical education seem to be disquietingly inept for the exacting task in hand (Balogh, 1962b).

References

BALOGH, T. (1954), 'Those sterling balances', *Venture*, vol. 5, no. 12, pp. 6–8.

BALOGH, T. (1959a), 'A note on the monetary controversy in Malaya', *Malayan econ. Rev.*, vol. 4, no. 2, pp. 21–6.

BALOGH, T. (1959b), 'Britain and the dependent commonwealth', *New Fabian Colonial Essays*, Dent.

BALOGH, T. (1961), 'Economic policy and the price mechanism', *Econ. Bull. Latin America*. vol. 6, no. 1, pp. 41–53.

BALOGH, T. (1962a), 'Africa and the Common Market', *J. Common Market Stud.*, vol. 1, no. 1, pp. 79–112.

BALOGH, T. (1962b), 'Educational policy for Africa', *Centennial Rev. of Michigan State Univ.*

ECE (1949), *Economic Survey of Europe in 1948*, Geneva.

18 G. Adler-Karlsson

Economic Warfare: The Case of Cuba

G. Adler-Karlsson, *Western Economic Warfare 1947–1967*, Almqvist &
Wiksell, 1968, chapter 17, pp. 208–14, 247–8.

Pre-1959 US–Cuban economic relations

During most of this century Cuba has been very closely tied to
the United States economy by one agreement or another or by
unilateral American actions.[1] Long before the Cuban–American
crisis the Cuban economy was heavily dependent on the United
States both in its domestic economy, its foreign trade and its
investments (Smith, 1960; United States Department of Commerce, 1956; Cuba, 1960).

This dependence can be illustrated by a few figures on Cuban
foreign trade and on American investments in the last years of
the Batista government.

In 1958 the geographical composition of Cuba's foreign trade
was the following:

	Exports	Imports
United States	492	543
Latin America	10	80
Sterling area	48	37
Other Western Europe	57	73
Other	127	44
Total	734	777 million dollars

Source: Seers, 1964, p. 19; United Nations, 1963, p. 273.

The commodity composition of the exports clearly reveals the
importance of sugar:

1. The Reciprocity Treaty of 1930; the Hanley Shoot Tariff Act, 1930;
the Reciprocal Trade Agreement, 1934; the Jones-Costigan Act, 1934.

	Million dollars
Sugar	594
Tobacco	50
Minerals	44
Other	46
Total	734

The American investments in Cuba in 1958 amounted to one billion dollars and were diversified in the following manner:

	Million dollars
Agriculture	265
Petroleum and mining	270
Manufacturing	80
Services	386
Total	1001

Source: Seers, 1964, p. 16.

These investments gave high profits, estimated to 9 per cent by official American statistics and to 23 per cent by the Castro government (Goldenberg; *Die Wirtschafft*, 8 April 1965). The outflow of profits and interests during 1952–58 has been estimated to correspond to 2 per cent of the Cuban GNP (Goldenberg, 1965).

40 per cent of the sugar plantations were under American domination (*Dagens Nyheter*, 2 January, 1959; *Le Monde*, 14 February 1959). The unemployment rate in 1956–57 was 16 per cent, to which should be added a considerable disguised unemployment (Seers, 1964, p. 12).

These figures indicate that whatever economic reforms were undertaken in Cuba, they would by necessity have affected private American economic interests. Economic development efforts, which would necessitate some controls over foreign trade, would particularly have hit American interests, even if they had been completely general, without any discrimination between nations. This is an example of the real dependence which smaller countries may find themselves in, in spite of all formal legal sovereignty.

The economic measures

General measures

On 1 January 1959 Castro took over the Cuban government, which was recognized by the United States on 7 January. Castro's goal was to turn Cuba into an advanced industrial economy as fast as possible. A number of long-term targets for employment, wages, sugar and industrial production were proclaimed.

The first concrete measure was to tighten exchange controls. Under the new regulation imports of a long list of goods, such as refrigerators, TV sets, automobiles, furniture and other non-essentials, required a currency permit. It was at the same time stressed by the head of the National Bank that 'no restrictions will be applied to the Government's aim to encourage the continuation of (foreign) investments' (*New York Times*, 12 February 1959).

As naturally followed from the regional trade structure, this exchange control mainly affected the export from the United States. While Cuban exports to the United States in 1959 remained on the 1958 level, approximately 470 million dollars, Castro succeeded in achieving a better balance in his payment position by decreasing the imports from the United States from 543 to 435 million dollars in 1959.

It is of importance to notice that the American sugar quota from the very beginning influenced Castro's thinking. Already in February 1959 he said in a television speech that 'USA continually threatens Cuba with a reduction of the sugar quota. Anything occurring in Cuba that displeases the United States Congress immediately brings a threat to stop buying sugar from Cuba, or reducing the quota' (*New York Times*, 21 February 1959; Department of State Bulletin, 1959b). It seems likely that this statement may have reflected conversations with American diplomats about the exchange controls. The sugar quota in the United States, which was of prime importance for the economy of Cuba, could be unilaterally changed at any time by the United States.

In May 1959 Castro announced his Agrarian Reform Program. Property holdings in excess of 1000 acres were to be nationalized. The owners were to be compensated with 4·5 per cent, twenty-year government bonds (Watt, 1963, p. 377). American and Cuban sugar mill owners immediately presented a memorandum to the US State Department in which they said that the Agrarian Reform Law would lead to a catastrophe, and that the American sugar quota should be used not as a reprisal but as a defence. In trying to calm the fears about the future sugar production, Castro in June 1959 offered the United States a chance to buy eight million tons of sugar in 1961, or almost three times more than the actual Cuban quota (*New York Times*, 29 May and 5 June 1959). This offer was turned down by the American side (Department of State Bulletin, 1959a).

A number of other incidents led up to the final break. In the end of 1959 a number of bombs were dropped on Cuba by private planes from Florida. Washington declared that it was unable to control the activities of these private aircraft (*Economist*, 2 July 1960; Watt, 1963, p. 376). In February 1960 Cuba and the Soviet Union made a barter deal of oil and sugar. On 15 March, President Eisenhower asked Congress to give him stand-by authority to cut US purchases of Cuban sugar, if necessary. He said that there was no justification for taking it as a reprisal, whatsoever (*US News and World Report*, 28 March 1960, p. 66). In the early summer Cuba seized the oil refineries of Texaco and Standard Oil because of their refusal to refine Russian crude oil (*Economist*, 2 July 1960, p. 17; Suarez, 1963; Department of State Bulletin, 1960c, p. 716). On 27 May the United States ended the remaining aid to Cuba.

On 6 July 1960 the US Congress passed a bill giving the President power to lower the Cuban sugar quota, and President Eisenhower immediately did so in a way which virtually eliminated Cuban sugar export to the United States for the second half of the year. The official motivation was that Cuba had committed so much of its future sugar production to the communist bloc that the United States could no longer rely on the Cuban supplies (Department of State Bulletin, 1960a, p. 962; Public Law 86–592, 1960; *Economist* 9 July 1960; Department of State Bulletin, 1960b). Instead of hurting the new Cuban government, it may be claimed that through American reduction of the sugar quota, 'Castro's internal position was strengthened immeasurably' (Suarez, 1963).

A month later Castro retaliated by nationalizing American

property valued at half a billion dollars or more than five times as much as the loss due to the decision by President Eisenhower. (Smith, 1963).

Embargo measures

Finally, on 19 October 1960 the United States imposed an embargo on all exports to Cuba. An embargo on arms had been started already in March, and American pressures had been exerted to prevent arms sales to Cuba (Department of State, 1960c, pp. 715–16; *US News and World Report*, 31 October 1960, pp. 60–62; Watt, 1963, pp. 385–91; *The Times*, 17 October 1959; *New York Times*, 29 October, 1 November 1959). The economic embargo was not officially motivated as a political pressure. The State Department instead said the embargo was 'reluctantly' imposed in order to 'defend the legitimate economic interests of the people of this country against discriminatory, aggressive and injurious economic policies of the Castro regime' (Department of State Bulletin, 1960c, p. 716; *US News and World Report*, 31 October 1960, p. 91).

Later, however, the US embargo on trade with Cuba has been frankly recognized as an exercise in economic warfare. In the words of Secretary Rusk, the Administration has four objectives with this embargo: '(a) to reduce Castro's will and ability to export subversion and violence to other American States; (b) to make plain to the people of Cuba that Castro's regime cannot serve their interests; (c) to demonstrate to the peoples of the American Republics that communism has no future in the Western Hemisphere; and (d) to increase the cost to the Soviet of maintaining a communist outpost in the Western Hemisphere' (McKitterick, 1966).

We cannot here go into all the ensuing events, the US–Cuban diplomatic rupture in January 1961, the extensive economic agreements with the Soviet Union in December 1960, the CIA invasion of April 1961, the missile crises of October 1962, etc. These events were, or course, the important events of the deteriorating Cuban–American relations. The economic embargo actions imposed by the United States in between these events were more in the nature of demonstrations and their effects were small. The major trade discriminations were the following:

1. An extension by President Kennedy in December 1961 of the prohibition to import Cuban sugar.

2. An embargo on all imports from Cuba in February 1962 which did not change the situation much as the import in 1961 had dwindled down to some fifteen million dollars.

3. An outright naval blockade of Cuba between 22 October and 20 November 1962 in the context of the missile crisis.[2]

4. A blacklisting of ships going to Cuba, with consequent denials to enter US ports.

5. Restrictions on financial dealings with Cuba, imposed in July 1963.

(*Dagens Nyheter*, 24 October, 5 December 1961; *Economist*, 10 February 1962, 20, 21 October 1962, 22 February 1964; *The Times*, 9 July 1964.)

Response in Western Europe to US embargo actions

At the end of 1963, without asking for it, the American Administration was given a new weapon by Congress. Included in the Foreign Aid Act of 1963 was a clause requiring the President to cut off aid to recipients who did not take 'appropriate steps' to curtail shipments to Cuba – unless the President found it in the national interest to waive the penalty. After two months it was decided by the United States, under the authority of the new clause in the Foreign Aid Act, that military aid should be terminated to Britain, France and Yugoslavia, and that military and economic aid to Spain and Morocco should be held up until those two countries explained what they were doing to halt commerce with Cuba (*New York Times*, 23 February 1964; *US News and World Report*, 2 March 1964).

Britain was not badly hurt by this rebuke for trading with Cuba, as the aid which was cut off was worth only $7000. Since the war she had received $8·7 billion in military and economic aid from the United States (*Economist*, 22 February 1964).

What was the British crime? In January 1964 the Leyland

2. During this crisis Castro demanded that, amongst other things, all US economic restrictions must be removed before the crisis could be ended (Utrikespolitiska Institutets Kalendarium, 1962, p. 566).

Motor Company sold 450 passenger buses for $11·2 million to Cuba under the option of selling an additional 500 buses to Havana (*US News and World Report*, 6 July 1964).[3] This met with strong opposition in the United States, as they stressed the political aspect of trading with the communist and quasi-communist countries. It is even reported that the United States offered the European nations more participation in nuclear control in exchange for ending trade with Cuba! (*New Statesman*, 15 May 1964). The British, however, had a purely commercial view and could not consider buses a strategic good, especially as this kind of trade had been carried on with the communist nations for years (*Economist*, 11 January 1964). Also, the official permission granted to American exporters to sell surplus wheat to the Soviet Union had developed a fundamental weakness in the Administration's effort to induce allied and neutral nations to join the United States in an economic boycott of Cuba (*New York Times*, 24 February 1964, *Economist*, 22 February 1964). As the Head of the Leyland Company said: 'If America has surplus on wheat, we have surplus on buses' (*New York Times*, 23 February 1964). The American answer was that food was a 'non-strategic' commodity, but buses and airplanes, which had also been considered for sale, were not; they were indispensable to the build-up of the Cuban economy and the military system (*New York Times*, 24 February 1964). The same applied to France's export of locomotives and Spain's of fishing-vessels.

The basic British argument was not so much that an increase in trade with Cuba might help to soften communist political attitudes, which was what the British said about trade with Russia. In Cuba's case, they said, the total cutting off of trade was unlikely to achieve what the Americans wanted to achieve, and forfeited the advantages of keeping in touch. Thus, it was an argument about the probable ineffectiveness of an embargo (Gordon Walker, 1964).

Another effect of the US pressure was to decrease American good will in England. A spokesman for the Labour Party, Patrick Gordon Walker, stated clearly that, 'We dislike United

3. An official State Department note said that Leyland had sold 400 buses, and that Cuba had an option to buy 1000 buses (Information Service, 4 February 1964).

States' pressure to prevent our legitimate trade with Cuba' (1964).

In the case of France, it had been selling locomotives to Cuba, which in the American Administration's view was considered more undesirable than the British sale of buses (*Financial Times*, 22 January 1964). But the US did not expect so much cooperation from the French as from the British, who, it was thought, should know better (*Economist*, 9 May 1964). The trickle of aid to France was also stopped altogether.

Spain and Morocco were more daring in their relations with Cuba, as they got substantial aid from the United States. Spain had been negotiating a large sugar contract with Cuba against the sale of what had been reported to be a hundred Spanish fishing-vessels (*Economist*, 11 January 1964). But by stopping aid the United States might be dealing a severe blow to its own policies, as they had great military interests in Spain. Ways had to be found to avoid this, but a review of aid to these countries was also necessary. A compromise had to be reached (*Economist*, 26 September 1964).

Canada had continued to sell large quantities of various products, mostly wheat, to Cuba. Also in a contract with Canada the Soviet Union included 245,000 tons of wheat and 150,000 tons of flour (equivalent to 205,000 tons of wheat) specifically for shipment to Cuba. The Soviet Union was financing these shipments (Committee on Foreign Relations, 1964).

The countries mentioned wanted to trade with Cuba for various commercial reasons, but there were quite a few countries which had another principal reason for continuing to deal with Cuba. These were the shipping nations of the world which strongly opposed the American restriction, e.g. for ships being refused entry to an American harbour after having been in a Cuban port or being exposed to special controls when passing the Panama Canal. They stressed the 'freedom of the seas' principle, but their shipping trade was so crucial that, to a large extent, they had to obey the American restrictions, though under protest. Violations were registered by an American ship which was cruising day and night outside Havana, and the ships arriving were blacklisted. Of course, mainly ships from Eastern Europe called at the harbour, but there were also, for example, Norwegian and Greek ships

(*Dagens Nyheter*, 18 September 1964; *The Times*, 12 January 1963; *New York Times*, 17 October 1962; *New York Herald Tribune*, 17 January 1964).

In the case of fourteen countries who traded with Cuba in 1963, the American President used the waiver not to cut the aid on the ground that 'appropriate steps' to curtail Cuban trade were being taken – though the criteria for this judgement were not explained (*New York Times*, 23 February 1964).

American attempts to influence the Latin American countries

In the relations between Latin America and the United States the Cuban issue was a hot one. Even at an early stage, the leaders of most Latin American countries felt rather uneasy to have a neighbour with a communist tendency and they felt they had not become more secure after the Cuban Revolution. But while many leaders probably would have been glad to see Castro go, there were few who could safely say so. They also had to be cautious in approving of the United States actions to press Cuba. When the American sugar quota reductions were imposed, the Latin American press was well aware that the main Latin American complaints against the United States had been about the import regulations and price fluctuations that complicated the sale of all of the twenty Latin American countries' sale of primary products. Economic retaliation revived ugly memories (*Economist*, 9 July 1960).

Inter-American relations had been settled in various conferences and congresses of the loose Pan-American Union since 1889–90, and in 1948 the Organization of American States (OAS), was founded through the charter of Bogotá. In this charter non-intervention in the internal affairs of other members was inscribed, but this was relative, as another article of the charter allowed collective measures for the maintenance of peace and security. The charter also prohibited economic sanctions to be levied among the twenty-one member states. The foundation of the OAS was laid down in the treaty of Rio de Janeiro in 1947, where the states bound themselves to regard an attack against one as an attack against all. Joint measures for the protection of peace could be taken when an American state was menaced from outside, even without direct, military assault. This apparently referred to the menace of communist infiltration. In the Resolution of Caracas of 1954 the states agreed to consult if the government of any American state should come under the domination of international communism (Goldenberg, 1965).

In August 1960, in a conference of the Foreign Ministers of the OAS, an anti-communist declaration, the so-called San José doctrine, was adopted which without mentioning the name of Cuba, strongly hinted that Castro was threatening the security and solidarity of the Western hemisphere. Washington had thus lifted the American–Cuban quarrel to a dispute over a threat to the security of the Western hemisphere, although this declaration did not solve anything. The declaration condemns the intervention, 'even when conditional', of any extra-continental power; declares that the acceptance of any such offer is a threat to peace; rejects any attempt by Russia or China to exploit politically, economically or socially any American state; and calls upon all American states to submit to 'the discipline of the inter-American system' (*Economist*, 3 September 1960).

The two main fears the US had about Cuba were that Cuba would be a permanent stronghold for communism in the Western hemisphere and that Cuba would be the origin and source for continued communist subversion in other Latin American countries. 'Fidelismo' was not confined to Cuba and Cuban subversion, but was a spreading movement with seeds planted in every Latin American republic (*Economist*, 6 October 1962).

The Alliance for Progress was instituted at Punta del Este, Uruguay in August 1961. The fundamental economic and social thought of this programme originated from Latin American economists, and also from Fidel Castro who in 1959, in an OAS committee, asked the United States to give thirty billion dollars within ten years to the development of Latin America. But the Alliance in its final form became an instrument for American policy, which partly aimed at conquering Castroism, preventing its expansion to other countries and preventing revolutions after the Cuban pattern in other countries. This could be achieved in two ways: direct intervention in Cuba and the realization of deep social reforms in Latin America (Goldenberg 1965).

In January 1962, the Foreign Ministers of the OAS voted to

expel Cuba from the OAS and the Inter-American Defense Board. Six of the nations abstained from the vote, however, and these six constituted 70 per cent of the population of Latin America. Earlier most of the Latin American countries had opposed an American proposal to call for automatic sanctions against Cuba if it did not break its ties with the communist countries. The formal expulsion of Cuba from OAS was effected on 14 February 1962 (Smith, 1963, p. 338).

During 1963 the United States did not press the OAS nations too hard to impose an economic embargo on Cuba, because of the intense opposition of the most influential governments in the hemisphere, notably those of Brazil, Chile and Mexico (*The Times*, 8 July 1963). However, on 26 July 1964 the OAS, with fifteen votes against four (Mexico, Chile, Uruguay and Bolivia), decided to use diplomatic and economic sanctions against Castro's Cuba. According to the decision, the American states undertook: (a) not to maintain diplomatic or consular relations with the present regime of Cuba, (b) to cut off all trade with Cuba, with the exceptions of foodstuffs and medicine, and (c) to discontinue all sea transports to Cuba (United States Information Service, 1964). At the same time the OAS appealed to all non-communist states outside the Western hemisphere – with an obvious address to Britain and France – to sustain the blocking measures. This OAS decision had in practice no revolutionary consequences, but it was welcomed by the United States as an evidence of a collective defence will (United States Information Service, 1964).

It seems as if Chile, Uruguay and Bolivia quietly cooperated with the United States, but that Mexico posed some serious problems. One observer has claimed that this was 'the most serious crisis in the recent history of inter-American relations', and that 'Mexico's attitude was a challenge to the very basis of the OAS' (Azicri, 1964; *Economist*, 29 August 1964). Other reports, however, give quite another picture. 'For example, the Mexicans, the most reluctant of all to take a vigorous anti-Castro position in public, are actually cooperating with us in ways which may be, strictly speaking, illegal under their constitution,' states one American observer (Quigg, 1964).

The trade restraining policy has continued. On 22 to 24 Sepember 1967, the Twelfth Meeting of Consultation of the Ministers of Foreign Affairs of the OAS was held in Washington. At this meeting Secretary Dean Rusk made a plea for further trade restrictions by all nations against Cuba, and a resolution was taken demanding that non-member states of OAS restrict their trade and financial operations with Cuba (Department of State, 1967, pp. 690-98).

The efficiency of the embargo

In Cuba the embargo policy has shown itself to be an inefficient policy. It has been a punishment, a demonstration that the United States did not want to have any relations with Cuba, and a continuation of a policy which by other nations has been recognized as being ineffective even before the Cuban-American crises started.

As in the case of China, the embargo may have had serious effects on the internal economy, possibly serious enough to cause an uprising against Castro, had it been total. But, as in the case of China, it was not total because the Communist countries came to Cuba's aid. The American endeavours to strain communist shipping facilities by blacklisting were counteracted in the East by chartering Western ships for transport between European and Russian communist ports, thereby releasing the communist-owned cargoes that were normally travelling these routes, e.g. between Leningrad and Vladivostok, for trade with Cuba.

The embargo was also inefficient because, as with China after 1957, the United States could not even get its closest Western allies to agree to follow its embargo policy against Cuba. The termination of aid to some European nations in 1964 was never taken seriously, and the British exports to Cuba more than tripled from 1963 to 1964 (*New York Times*, 13 January 1965).

The embargo also created a number of illegal trading activities from US traders, who could continue to sell to Cuba via Mexico (*US News and World Report*, 2 October 1961).

It is only possible to speculate about the reasons for the American embargo behaviour, assuming that the American authorities must have known beforehand that neither Eastern nor Western European trade with Cuba would be much affected by the American embargo actions.

One hypothetical rationalization for the American behaviour

vis-à-vis Cuba may be that the country is smaller, and being an island, much more isolated. Thus the effects may have been estimated to be greater than in the other contexts. But, as *New Statesman* said in an editorial: 'It passes belief that a Western embargo on trade with Cuba can bring that small island economy to its knees' (15 May 1964).

A second explanation may be that the Americans wanted to demonstrate to the other Latin American republics that any flirtation with what the United States considered to be communism would be punished by economic measures that would force these republics into full dependence on the Soviet Union. And that dependence may be even less enjoyable than that on the United States (United States Information Service, 1964).

A third hypothetical explanation may be that the failure of the embargo policies against Eastern Europe and China has never been officially admitted by the American policy-makers, and that they may just have continued the same old policy of ineffectual demonstrations, without much consideration for the possible effects. This is the explanation used by Senator Fulbright, who deemed that the US trade actions 'can have no real effect other than to create an illusory image of "toughness" for the benefit of our own people' and that 'the boycott policy is a failure as an instrument for bringing about the fall of the Castro regime' (1965; Millis, 1965).

We can play around with hypotheses of that type. But at the moment it does not seem to be possible to pinpoint any explanation as being the main, or the only one.

References

AZICRI, M. (1964), 'The OAS and the Communist challenge', *Communist Affairs*, vol. 2, no. 4, pp. 8–11.

COMMITTEE ON FOREIGN RELATIONS (1964), Hearings before the Committee on Foreign Relations, United States Senate, 88th Congress, 2nd session, Pt 1, 23 March 1964.

CUBA (1960), *Cuba's Reply to the Note of the United States of America*.

DEPARTMENT OF STATE (1959a), *Bulletin*, no. 1044, 29 June.

DEPARTMENT OF STATE (1959b), *Bulletin*, no. 1070, 28 December.

DEPARTMENT OF STATE (1960a), *Bulletin*, no. 1094, 13 June.

DEPARTMENT OF STATE (1960b), *Bulletin*, no. 1100, 25 July.

DEPARTMENT OF STATE (1960c), *Bulletin*, no. 1115, 7 November.

DEPARTMENT OF STATE (1967), *Bulletin*, 16 October.

FULBRIGHT, J. W. (1965), *Old Myths and New Realities*, Cape.

GOLDENBERG, B. (1965), *The Cuban Revolution and Latin America*, Praeger.

GORDON WALKER, P. C. (1964), 'The Labour Party's defences and foreign policy', *Foreign Affairs*, vol. 42, no. 3, pp. 391–8.

MCKITTERICK, N. (1966), *East–West Trade: The Background of US Policy*, Twentieth-Century Fund.

MILLIS, W. (1965), *An End to Arms*, Atheneum.

PUBLIC LAW 86–592 (1960), *An Act to amend the Sugar Act of 1948, as amended*, 6 July, H.R.12311.

QUIGG, P. W. (1964), 'Latin America: a broad-brush appraisal', *Foreign Affairs*, vol. 42, no. 3, pp. 399–412.

SEERS, D. (ed.) (1964), *Cuba: The Economic and Social Revolution*, University of North Carolina Press.

SMITH, R. F. (1960), *The United States and Cuba: Business and Diplomacy 1917–1960*, College and University Press.

SMITH, R. F. (1963), *What Happened in Cuba?* Twayne.

SUAREZ, A. (1963), 'Castro between Moscow and Peking', *Problems of Communism*, vol. 5.

UNITED NATIONS (1963), Economic Survey of Latin America.

UNITED STATES DEPARTMENT OF COMMERCE (1956), *Investment in Cuba: Basic Information for United States Businessmen*.

UNITED STATES INFORMATION SERVICE (1964), *News Bulletin*, 14 February and 27 July 1964.

WATT, D. C. (1963), *Documents on International Affairs 1959*, Oxford University Press.

Further Reading

Normally it is not too difficult to compile a list of books and articles which offer the reader further insights into the theme under discussion. In the present case such a procedure is more problematic. This volume is not concerned with some traditional or well-defined field of economic theory, but rather with the all-pervasive element of power which turns up in all sorts of economic relations. The consideration of power in economics is not a subject with clear-cut frontiers but rather an approach which should (but usually does not, as has been argued in the Introduction) show up in economic writings dealing with very different topics.

Under these conditions it is not easy to recommend specific titles for further reading. A restriction to studies which deal directly with the relationship between power and economics would yield a very limited harvest. (As one of the very few items pointing in this direction we may mention Sylvia K. and Benjamin M. Selekman, *Power and Morality in a Business Society*, McGraw Hill, 1956.) On the other hand, any attempt to present items, which at one point or other have some bearing on the power problem, would necessarily lead to a rather diffuse and haphazard selection. The best one can do in view of these circumstances is probably to direct the attention of the reader to some *authors* (and some of their writings) who have been outstanding in their grasp of the power–economic interrelationships. An acquaintance with their work should greatly increase the 'feel' for the type of problems which have been treated in this book.

To begin with one should certainly mention Marx and the Marxist school. Marx's endeavour had always been to study the social process as a whole and his intensive interest in economic 'laws' only served the aim to reveal the social and power relations connected with them. All great Marxist classics offer this wide canvas on which the interdependence of social and economic power relations becomes visible. In addition to the writings of Marx and Engels themselves – e.g. K. Marx and F. Engels, *The*

Communist Manifesto, F. Engels, *The Origin of the Family, Private Property and the State* (Kerr, 1902) and, of course, Marx's monumental three-volume work *Capital* (Kerr, 1933 and numerous other editions) – one should mention R. Hilferding, *Finance Capital* (Vienna, 1904), R. Luxemburg, *The Accumulation of Capital* (Monthly Review Press, 1964) and N. Lenin, *Imperialism, the Highest Stage of Capitalism* (Lawrence & Wishart, n.d.). Among more modern authors writing in the Marxist tradition we might refer to P. M. Sweezy and P. Baran, both represented in this volume, and to M. Dobb (*Political Economy and Capitalism*, Routledge & Kegan Paul, 1937; *Studies in the Development of Capitalism*, Routledge & Kegan Paul, 1946).

Also outside the Marxist group we find a number of authors who were not content to view the economic process as an isolated market mechanism to be studied without reference to the social and power problems connected with it. Though in many cases influenced by Marx these writers often start from different methodological and ideological premises. What they have in common is the attempt towards a more integrated analysis of social, political and economic processes. Some of these authors originate from the economists' camp, others come from the sociological side.

In the first group we might mention T. Veblen (*The Theory of the Leisure Class*, New American Library, 1953; *The Theory of Business Enterprise*, Scribner, 1904; *The Vested Interests and the Common Man*, Kelley, 1964), J. A. Hobson (*Imperialism*, Allen & Unwin, 1948), and J. A. Schumpeter (*Capitalism, Socialism and Democracy*, Harper & Row, 1942). Power aspects also play a part in some recent economic interpretations of capitalist development, such as J. Strachey's *Contemporary Capitalism* (Gollancz, 1956), J. K. Galbraith's *American Capitalism* (Houghton-Mifflin, 1952) and *The New Industrial State* (represented in this volume), and A. Shonfield's *Modern Capitalism* (Oxford University Press, 1965). Among the sociologists, who have paid special attention to economic aspects of power relations, one could refer to Max Weber in earlier days (particularly his *Wirtschaft und Gesellschaft*, Tübingen, 1922) and to C. Wright Mills in more recent times (*The Power Elite*, Oxford University Press Inc., 1956).

So far the stress has been on authors who have tried to cover the socio-economic process as a whole, and have not over-looked the power aspect involved in it. In some specialized branches of economics power problems are more obvious and have received somewhat greater attention. The locus of power in the modern corporation with its division between managers and owners has been the subject of many controversies. The classical contribution was A. A. Berle and G. C. Means, *The Modern Corporation and Private Property* (Macmillan Co., 1932). Later contributions are – among many others – A. A. Berle, *Power without Property* (Harcourt, Brace & World, 1959) and G. C. Means, *The Corporate Revolution in America* (Crowell-Collier, 1962).

Similarly, the danger of neglecting the inequality of economic and political power positions became obvious in the discussion of international economic relations, particularly where countries of unequal economic strength are concerned. An important early pioneer study in this field was A. O. Hirschman's *National Power and the Structure of Foreign Trade* (University of California Press, 1945). G. Myrdal has been at pains to stress the inadequacy of a 'pure' economic approach to development problems as is shown, for instance, in his *Economic Theory and Underdeveloped Regions* (Duckworth, London 1957; in America: *Rich Lands and Poor*, Harper & Row, 1957) and in his monumental *Asian Drama* (Twentieth-Century Fund, and Penguin Books, 1968).

Finally – as has been mentioned in the Introduction – there exists an extensive literature on monopoly and trade-union questions which has traditionally been concerned with power problems. References to these special fields can be found in the readings lists of the Volumes mentioned in footnote 10 on page 16.

Acknowledgements

Permission to reproduce the Readings in this volume is acknowledged to the following sources:

1 Kyklos Verlag
2 University of Chicago Press and E. Ronald Walker
3 *Social Research*
4 *Behavioral Science* and J. Harsanyi
5 Harvard University Press
6 Macmillan & Co. Ltd
7 Oxford University Press and M. D. Reagan
8 Columbia University Press
9 Columbia University Press
10 Houghton Mifflin Company
11 McGraw Hill Book Company
12 *The Manchester School*, T. Lupton and C. S. Wilson
13 De Erven F. Bohn N.V.
14 Royal Economic Society and A. Hunter
15 Monthly Review Press and P. M. Sweezy
16 Monthly Review Press
17 Basil Blackwell and T. Balogh
18 G. Adler-Karlsson

Author Index

Subject Index

Penguin Modern Economics Readings

Other titles available in this series:

Public Enterprise
Edited by R. Turvey

Public Finance
Edited by R. W. Houghton

Regional Analysis
Edited by L. Needleman

Transport
Edited by Denys Munby